W9-BRC-708

GREGG SHORTHAND FOR COLLEGES

VOLUME ONE

SHORTHAND WRITTEN
BY CHARLES RADER

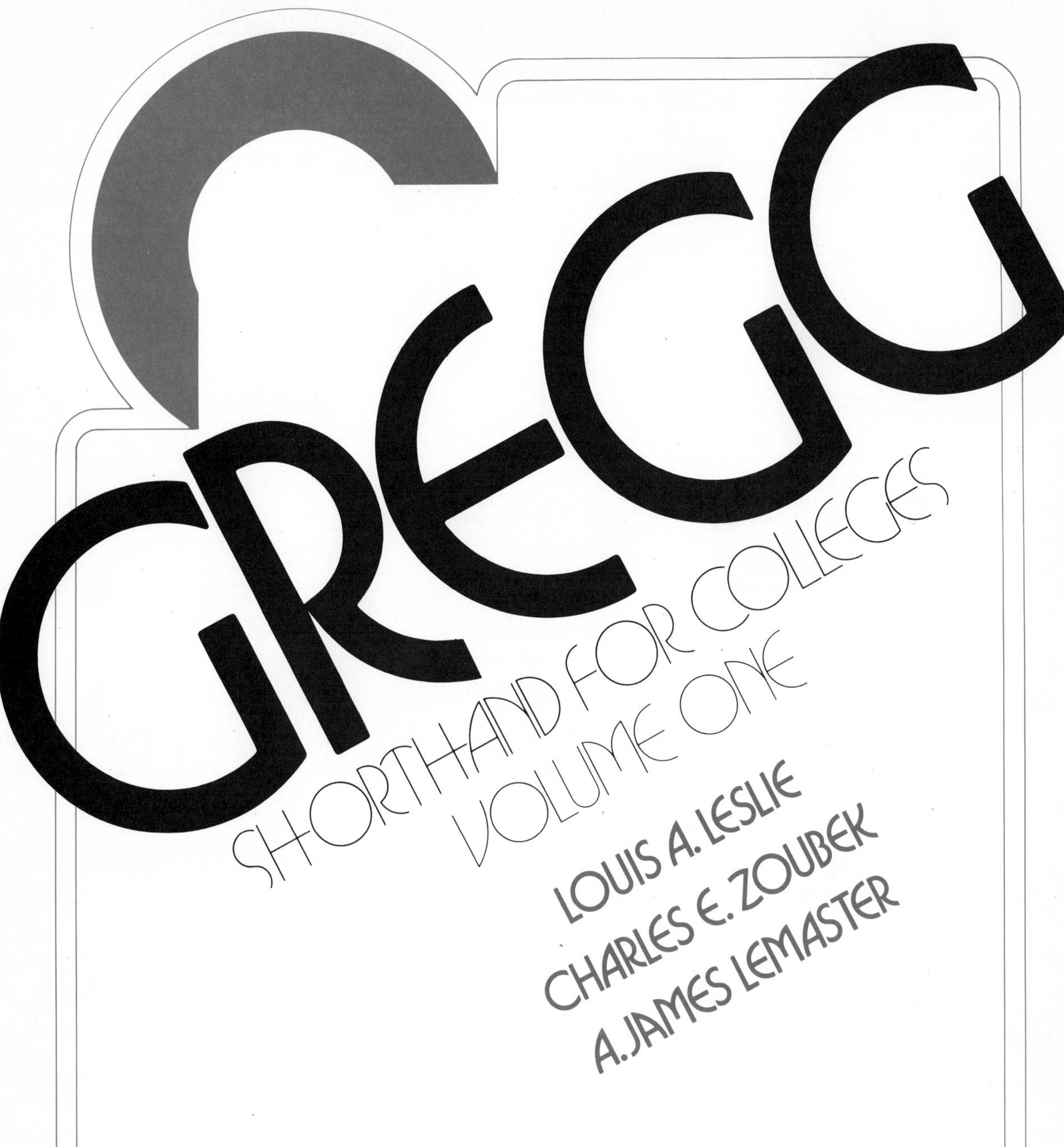

Gregg Division
McGraw-Hill Book Company
New York / Atlanta / Dallas / St. Louis / San Francisco / Auckland
Bogotá / Düsseldorf / Johannesburg / London / Madrid
Mexico / Montreal / New Delhi / Panama / Paris / São Paulo
Singapore / Sydney / Tokyo / Toronto

This text was prepared by members of the Gregg Shorthand staff:

Editorial: Barbara J. Hann, Diana M. Johnson, Albert H. Rihner

Production: Jerome P. Edelman, Mary C. Buchanan, Michael S. Valentine, Linda Sklar

Art & Design Coordinator: Tracy A. Glasner

Designer: A Good Thing Inc.

Cover photo: Peter Roth *(taken at Automation House, Inc., New York City)*

Interior photos: Martin Bough/Studios Inc.

Library of Congress Cataloging in Publication Data

Leslie, Louis A date

Gregg shorthand for colleges, series 90.

Includes index.

1. Shorthand—Gregg. I. Zoubek, Charles E., date joint author. II. Lemaster, A. James, joint author. III. Title.

Z56.2.G7L48 1980 653′.427 79-12060
ISBN 0-07-037749-9 (v. 1)
ISBN 0-07-037754-5 (v. 2)

Gregg Shorthand for Colleges,
Volume One, Series 90

4 5 6 7 8 9 0 DODO 8 8 7 6 5 4 3 2 1

Preface

Gregg Shorthand, the universal system

Gregg Shorthand was first published on May 28, 1888, and has been learned and used successfully by millions of writers throughout the entire world. Gregg Shorthand was written in English but has been successfully adapted to numerous other languages, including Spanish and French. The terms *shorthand* and *Gregg* are synonymous to most people. Gregg Shorthand is the universal system of shorthand; it is used by more shorthand writers than any other system in the world.

Gregg Shorthand is used by secretaries as a tool that enables them to obtain and hold interesting and rewarding positions. It is used by business and professional people who are relieved of the burden of writing longhand in making notes, preparing important papers, and drafting reports.

The success of any system of shorthand rests on the merits of its alphabet. The Gregg alphabet is the most logical, consistent, and efficient shorthand alphabet devised in more than 2,000 years of shorthand history. The fact that this alphabet, virtually without change, has been the basis of Gregg Shorthand for more than 90 years is a tribute to the genius of its inventor, John Robert Gregg.

Gregg Shorthand for Colleges, Volume One, Series 90

The Series 90 revision of Gregg Shorthand was first published in the ninetieth anniversary year of the Gregg system. This revision involves a small number of system changes which have been deemed desirable to make learning and writing Gregg Shorthand even easier and more consistent. A major change has been made in the order of presentation of the theory principles. This change was made to provide better, more logical business letters even in the very early lessons in the text. Teachers will find the system changes to be logical and the teaching and learning suggestions helpful.

To meet the needs of business schools, colleges, junior colleges, community colleges, universities and other post-high school institutions, *Gregg Shorthand, Series 90,* has been made available in a college edition. This edition provides shorthand instructional materials that are different from those used in high schools, materials that are more challenging and that are geared to the interests of the more mature college student.

Objectives

The major objectives of this text are:

1 To teach the students to read and write Gregg Shorthand rapidly and accurately in the shortest possible time.

2 To develop and improve the students' grasp—concurrently with the teaching of shorthand—of the nonshorthand elements of transcription, which include vocabulary development, spelling, punctuation, grammar, and typing style.

Organization

Gregg Shorthand for Colleges, Volume One, Series 90, is divided into three parts—Principles, Reinforcement, and Shorthand and Transcription Skill Building. These parts are subdivided into 10 chapters and 70 lessons.

Part 1: Principles—Chapters 1–8 Each chapter contains six lessons. The first five lessons of each chapter contain new theory principles, and the sixth lesson is a review. The last group of new principles is presented in Lesson 47.

Part 2: Reinforcement—Chapter 9 Chapter 9 contains eight lessons, each of which reviews intensively the principles presented in one of the eight chapters in Part 1. For example, Lesson 49 reviews Chapter 1 intensively. There are no theory principles in Lesson 49 that have not been introduced in Lessons 1–5. Therefore, Lesson 49 may be used for supplemental practice after either Lesson 5 or Lesson 6. Lesson 50 reviews Chapter 2, and so on.

Part 3: Shorthand and Transcription Skill Building—Chapter 10 This chapter consists of fourteen lessons, each of which is designed to strengthen the students' grasp of a major principle of Gregg Shorthand. In addition, each lesson continues to develop the students' vocabulary and to improve their ability to spell, to punctuate, and to apply rules of grammar.

Format

Gregg Shorthand for Colleges, Volume One, Series 90, is published in the same two-column format that proved popular in the last edition. This format makes it possible to present the shorthand practice material in columns that are approximately the width of the columns of the students' shorthand notebooks. The short lines make reading easier because the eye does not have to travel very far from the end of one line of shorthand to the beginning of the next. The format also makes it possible to highlight the words from the Reading and Writing Practice that are identified for spelling attention. The words are placed in the margins near the corresponding shorthand outline.

Building transcription skills

Gregg Shorthand for Colleges, Volume One, Series 90, continues to place great stress on the nonshorthand elements of transcription, which are taught concurrently with shorthand. It retains all the helpful transcription exercises of the former edition. These include:

Business Vocabulary Builders Beginning with Chapter 3, each lesson contains a Business Vocabulary Builder consisting of several business words or expressions for which meanings are provided. The words and expressions are selected from the Reading and Writing Practice.

Spelling—Marginal Reminders Beginning with Chapter 4, words singled out from the Reading and Writing Practice for special spelling attention appear in the margins of the shorthand. Usually each word appears on the same line as its shorthand outline. These words appear in a second color in the shorthand.

Spelling—Families An effective device for improving spelling is the study of words in related groups, or spelling families. In the Series 90 edition, the students study six spelling families.

Similar-Words Drills These drills teach the students the difference in meaning between similar words that secretaries often confuse—*it's, its; addition, edition; there, their, they're;* and so on.

Punctuation Beginning with Lesson 31, nine frequent usages of the comma are introduced. Only one comma usage is introduced in any given lesson. The commas are circled and appear in the shorthand; the reason for the use of the comma is shown above the circle.

Common Prefixes An understanding of the meaning of common English prefixes is an effective device for developing the students' understanding of words. In *Gregg Shorthand for Colleges, Volume One, Series 90,* the students study five common English prefixes.

Grammar Checkups In a number of lessons, drills are provided on rules of grammar that students often apply incorrectly.

Transcription Quizzes Beginning with Lesson 57, each lesson contains a Transcription Quiz consisting of a letter in which the students have to supply the internal punctuation. This quiz provides them with a daily test of how well they have mastered the punctuation rules presented in earlier lessons.

Reading and writing practice

In *Gregg Shorthand for Colleges, Volume One, Series 90,* most of the material is new. That which has been retained from former editions has been thoroughly updated.

A brief-form letter is included in every lesson of Part 1 (except the review lessons), beginning with Lesson 5. The reading level of the text is 7-8.

Other features

Shorthand spelling helps When a new letter in the shorthand alphabet or a theory principle is presented, the shorthand spelling is given.

Chapter openings Each chapter is introduced by a well-illustrated spread that paints a picture of the life and duties of a secretary and encourages the students in their efforts to acquire the necessary skills.

Student helps To be sure that the students get the greatest benefit from each phase of their shorthand study, they are given step-by-step suggestions on how to handle each phase when it is first introduced.

Reading scoreboards At various points in the text, the students are given an opportunity to determine their reading speed by means of a scoreboard. The scoreboard enables the students to calculate the number of words a minute they are reading. By comparing their reading speed from scoreboard to scoreboard, they see an indication of their shorthand reading growth.

Recall charts A recall chart is provided in the last lesson of each chapter in Part 1. The chart contains illustrations of theory principles taught in the chapter. It also contains many illustrations of theory principles the students have studied up to that chapter.

Checklists To keep the students constantly reminded of the importance of good practice procedures, occasional Checklists are provided. These Checklists deal with writing shorthand, reading shorthand, homework, proportion, and so on.

Appendix The Appendix contains a number of additional teaching aids. These include:

1 A brief-form chart giving all brief forms in Gregg Shorthand, Series 90, in the order of their presentation.

2 A list of common geographical expressions.

3 A chart showing Gregg outlines for common metric expressions.

Computer control

All of the connected matter in *Gregg Shorthand for Colleges, Volume One, Series 90,* has been checked by a carefully written computer program to ensure adequate, proper, and sequential coverage of the theory principles and brief forms. The computer program helped the authors of the book to ensure that the points were properly covered in the lessons in which they were presented as well as in a number of lessons following their initial presentation.

• • •

Gregg Shorthand for Colleges, Volume One, Series 90, is published with pride and with the confidence that it will help teachers of Gregg Shorthand do an even more effective job of training rapid and accurate shorthand writers and transcribers.

The Publishers

Contents

SHORTHAND PRACTICE PROCEDURES

The rate at which your shorthand skill develops will depend largely on two factors: (1) The amount of time you devote to practice. (2) The efficiency with which you practice.

The person who practices efficiently will derive more benefit from an hour's practice than another who may spend several hours on practice but follows no plan.

By following the procedures suggested here, you should derive the maximum benefit from your investment in practice time.

Reading word lists

Each principle of Gregg Shorthand that you study is accompanied by a list of illustrations in shorthand and in type. Practice each list in this way:

1 With the type key to the shorthand exposed, pronounce and spell aloud—if possible—each word and shorthand outline in the list, thus: *say, s-a; see, s-e.* Reading aloud will help to impress the shorthand outlines in your mind. Read all the shorthand words in the list in this way—with the type exposed—until you feel you can read the shorthand outlines *without* referring to the key.

2 With a card, cover up the type key to the first colum of the list. Then read aloud from the shorthand, thus: *s-a, say; s-e, see.*

3 If the spelling of a shorthand outline does not immediately give you the meaning, move your card aside and refer to the type key. Do not spend more than a few seconds trying to decipher an outline.

4 Follow this procedure with the remaining columns of words in the list.

5 After you have read all the words in the list from the shorthand, read the entire list once or twice again.

NOTE: In reading brief forms and phrases, which first occur in Lesson 3, you need not spell the shorthand outlines.

Reading sentences, letters, and articles

Each lesson contains a Reading Practice (Lessons 1–6) or a Reading and Writing Practice (Lessons 7–70).

Sentences, letters, or articles are written in shorthand. Reading this material will help to impress the shorthand principles in your mind and enable you to develop a large shorthand vocabulary.

Two procedures for reading shorthand are outlined here—the first for those students who have been supplied with the *Student's Transcript of Gregg Shorthand for Colleges, Volume One, Series 90;* the second for those students who will work without the *Student's Transcript.*

Procedure 1: With Student's Transcript

1 Place your *Student's Transcript* to the right of your textbook and open it to the transcript of the Reading Practice or Reading and Writing Practice you are about to read.

2 Place your left index finger under the shorthand outline that you are about to read and your right index finger under the corresponding word in the *Student's Transcript.*

3 Read the shorthand outlines aloud until you come to an outline that you cannot read. Spell the outline. If the spelling does not immediately give you the mean-

Refer to your Transcript whenever you cannot read an outline. Keep your left index finger anchored on the shorthand; the right index finger, on the corresponding place in the Transcript.

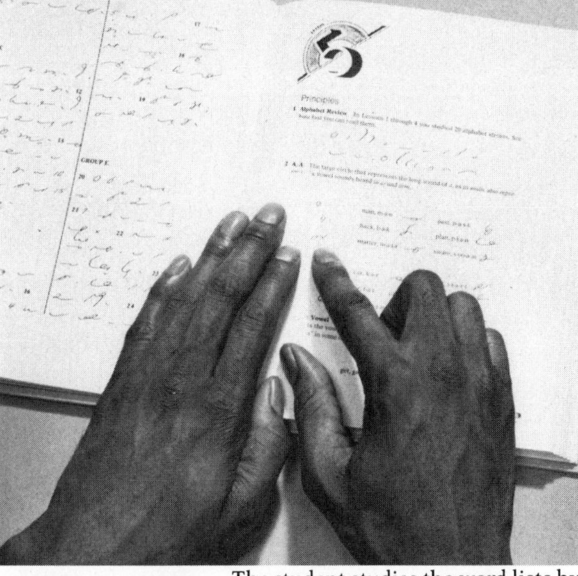

The student studies the word lists by placing a card over the type key and reading the shorthand words aloud.

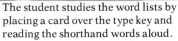

The student reads the Reading and Writing Practice, writing on the card any outlines that cannot be read after spelling them.

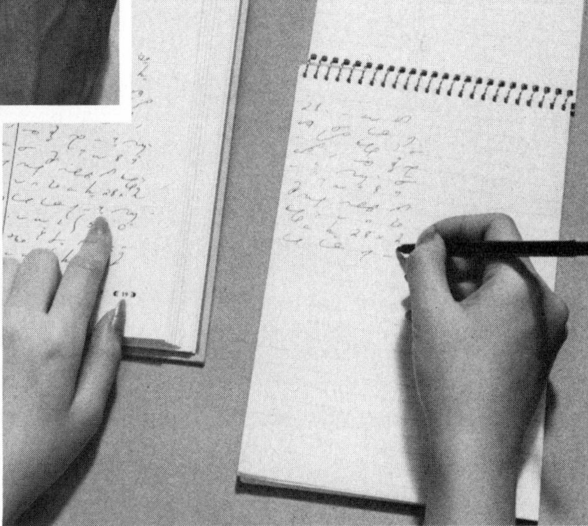

When copying, the student reads a convenient group of words aloud and then writes that group in the notebook. Notice how the student keeps the place in the shorthand.

ing, anchor your left index finger on the outline and look in the transcript, where your right index finger is resting near the point at which you are reading.

4 Determine the meaning of the outline you cannot read and place your right index finger on it.

5 Return to the shorthand from which you are reading—your left index finger has kept your place for you—and continue reading.

6 If time permits, read the material aloud a second time, again spelling any outline you cannot read and referring to the transcript when the spelling does not immediately give you the meaning.

By following this procedure, you will not lose any time finding your place in the shorthand and in the transcript when you cannot read an outline.

Procedure 2: Without Student's Transcript

1 Before you start your work on a Reading Practice or Reading and Writing Practice, have a sheet of paper and a pen handy.

2 Read the shorthand outlines aloud.

3 When you come to an outline that you cannot read, spell it. If the spelling does not immediately give you the meaning of the outline, write the outline on your sheet of paper (or circle it in your book if it is your personal property) and continue reading. Do not spend more than a few seconds trying to decipher the outline.

4 After you have gone through all the material in this way, repeat the procedure if time permits. On the second reading you may be able to read some of the outlines that escaped you the first time. When that happens, cross those outlines off your sheet.

5 Finally—and very important—at the earliest opportunity ask your teacher or a classmate the meaning of the outlines you could not read.

During the early stages of your shorthand study, your reading rate may not be very rapid, but this is only natural as you are, in a sense, learning to read a new language. If you read each lesson faithfully, following the procedures just suggested, your shorthand reading rate will increase almost from day to day.

Writing the reading and writing practice

After you have read the Reading and Writing Practice of a lesson, you should make a shorthand copy of it. Before you do any writing, however, you should give some thought to the tools of your trade—your notebook and your writing instrument.

Your notebook – The best notebook for shorthand writing is one that measures 6 x 9 inches and has a vertical rule down the middle of each sheet. If the notebook has a spiral binding, so much the better, as the spiral binding enables you to keep the pages flat at all times.

Your writing instrument – Use a good ball-point pen for your shorthand writing. Why use a pen for shorthand writing rather than a pencil? It requires less effort to write with a pen; consequently, you can write for long periods of time without fatigue. In addition, when you write with a pencil, the point soon becomes blunt, and the blunter it gets, the more effort you have to expend as you write. Pen-written notes remain readable almost indefinitely; pencil notes soon become blurred and hard to read.

Having selected your writing tools, you should follow these steps in working with each Reading and Writing Practice:

1 Read the material you are going to copy, following the suggestions given under the heading "Reading Sentences, Letters, and Articles" on page 10. Always read the Reading and Writing Practice before you copy it.

2 Read a convenient group of words from the printed shorthand and then write that group. If possible, say each outline aloud as you write it. Keep your place in the shorthand with your left index finger if you are right-handed; with your right index finger if you are left-handed.

Quite naturally, your early writing efforts may not be very rapid, nor will your shorthand outlines look as pretty as those in the book. With regular practice, however, you will soon become so proud of your shorthand notes that you won't want to write any more longhand!

PRINCIPLES

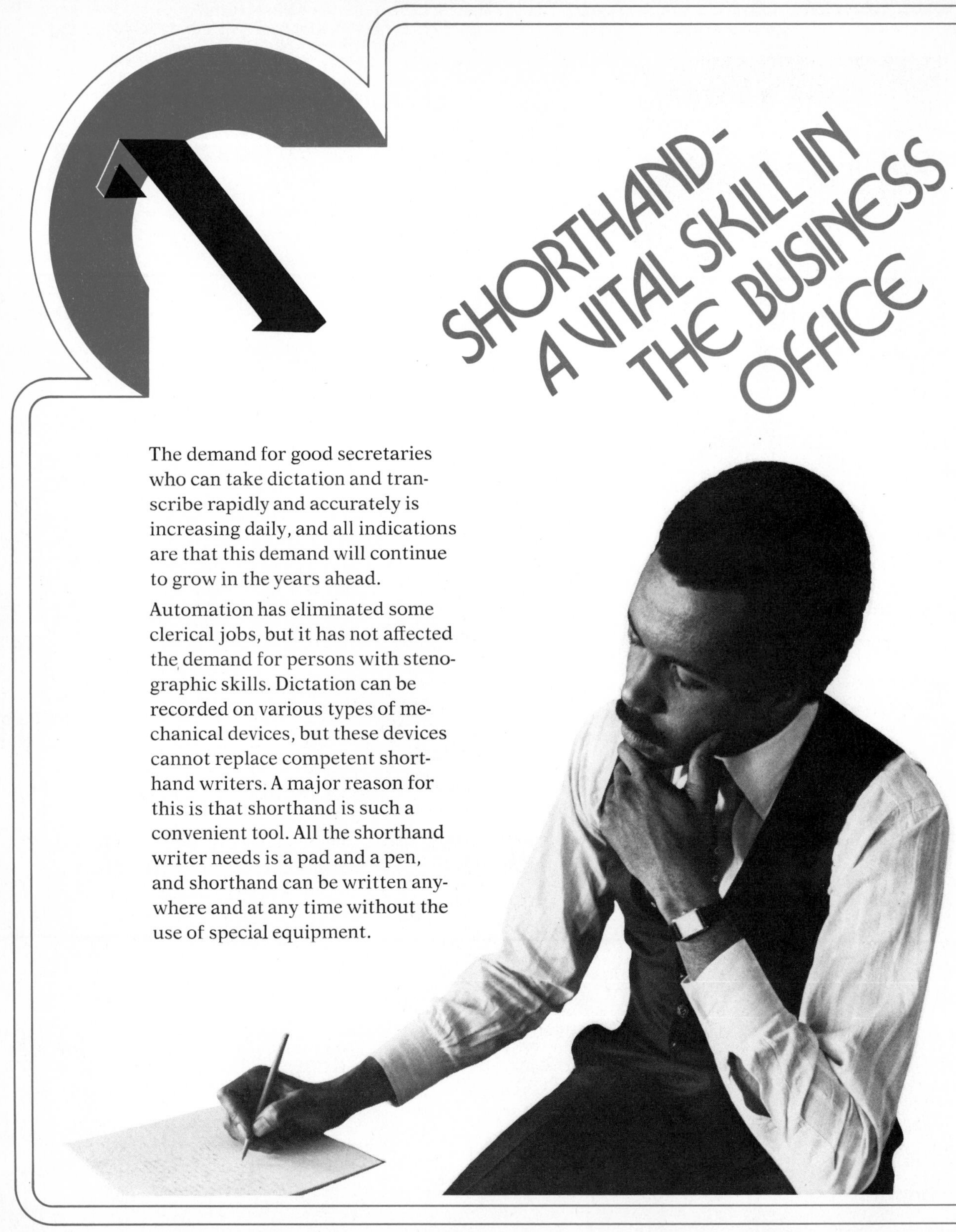

SHORTHAND—A VITAL SKILL IN THE BUSINESS OFFICE

The demand for good secretaries who can take dictation and transcribe rapidly and accurately is increasing daily, and all indications are that this demand will continue to grow in the years ahead.

Automation has eliminated some clerical jobs, but it has not affected the demand for persons with stenographic skills. Dictation can be recorded on various types of mechanical devices, but these devices cannot replace competent shorthand writers. A major reason for this is that shorthand is such a convenient tool. All the shorthand writer needs is a pad and a pen, and shorthand can be written anywhere and at any time without the use of special equipment.

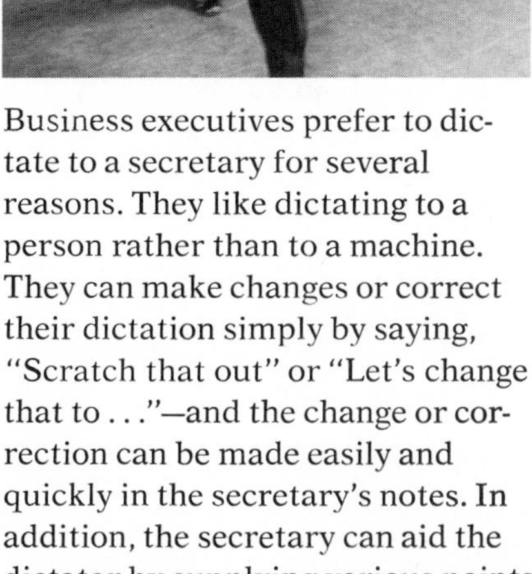

Business executives prefer to dictate to a secretary for several reasons. They like dictating to a person rather than to a machine. They can make changes or correct their dictation simply by saying, "Scratch that out" or "Let's change that to . . ."—and the change or correction can be made easily and quickly in the secretary's notes. In addition, the secretary can aid the dictator by supplying various points of information as needed during the dictation period.

Obviously, shorthand is a vital skill for the secretary; it is also valuable as a personal-use tool. Shorthand can be used for taking notes during lectures and discussions in college classes.

You have made a wise decision to study Gregg Shorthand; once you have learned it, you will have a lifelong skill. Shorthand will help you to obtain an interesting and profitable position. When you have completed the course, Gregg Shorthand will help you throughout your entire business life.

GREGG SHORTHAND IS EASY TO LEARN

Before you enrolled in your shorthand class, you may have asked yourself this question: "Can I really learn Gregg Shorthand?" Of course you can, just as millions of others have. If you learned to write longhand—and of course you did—you can learn to write Gregg Shorthand. The strokes you write in longhand—curves, hooks, circles, straight lines—are the same strokes you will write in Gregg Shorthand.

Actually, you will find that Gregg Shorthand is easier to learn than longhand. Do you find this statement hard to believe? Well, the following illustration should convince you of its truth.

Do you know how many different ways you can write the longhand letter *f*? Here are six of them—and there are more!

In addition, in many words the sound of *f* is expressed by combinations of other letters of the English alphabet—*ph*, as in *phase*; *gh*, as in *rough*.

In Gregg Shorthand there is one way—and only one way—to express the sound of *f*, as you will learn later in this lesson.

With Gregg Shorthand you can reach any speed goal you set for yourself. All it takes is faithful, intelligent practice.

Principles

GROUP A

1 **S-Z** Perhaps the most frequently used consonant in the English language is *s*, partly because of the great many plurals that end with *s*. The shorthand *s* is a tiny downward curve that resembles the longhand comma in shape.

s

Because in the English language *s* often has the sound of *z*, as in *saves*, the same tiny stroke is used to express *z*.

2 A A very important sound in the English language is *a*. In Gregg Shorthand *a* is simply the longhand *a* with the final connecting stroke omitted.

A

The circle may be written in either direction.

3 Silent Letters In English there are many words containing letters that are not pronounced. In Gregg Shorthand these silent letters are omitted; only the sounds that you actually hear are written. Example: the word *say* would be written *s-a*; the *y* would not be written because it is not pronounced. The word *face* would be represented by the shorthand characters *f-a-s*; the *e* would be omitted because it is not pronounced, and the *c* would be represented by the shorthand *s* because it is pronounced *s*. By omitting silent letters, we save a great deal of writing time.

In the following words what letters would not be written because they are not pronounced?

snow	dough	aid	save
main	day	right	knee

4 S-A Word With the strokes for *s* and *a* you can form the shorthand outline for the word *say*.

say, s-a

5 F, V The next two shorthand strokes you will learn are *f* and *v*.

F The shorthand stroke for *f* is a downward curve the same shape as *s*, but it is somewhat longer—approximately half the height of the space between the lines of your shorthand notebook.

V The shorthand stroke for *v* is also a downward curve the same shape as *s* and *f*, but it is very large—approximately the full height of the space between the lines of your shorthand notebook.

◉ *Observe the difference in the sizes of* s, f, *and* v.

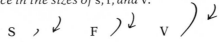

S F V

F

safe, s-a-f　face, f-a-s　safes, s-a-f-s

◉ *Observe that the* c *in* face *is represented by the shorthand* s *because it has the sound of* s.

V

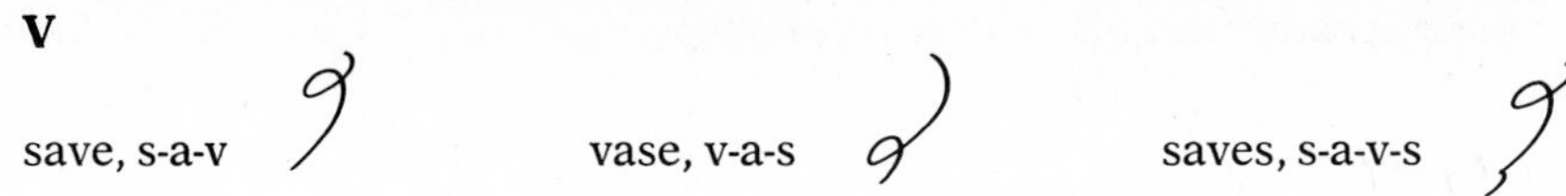

◉ *Observe that the final* s *in* saves *has the* z *sound, which is represented by the* s *stroke.*

6 **E** Another very important vowel in the English language is *e*. In shorthand, *e* is represented by a tiny circle. It is simply the longhand *e* with the two connecting strokes omitted. The circle may be written in either direction.

E

◉ *Observe the difference between the sizes of* a *and* e.

A E

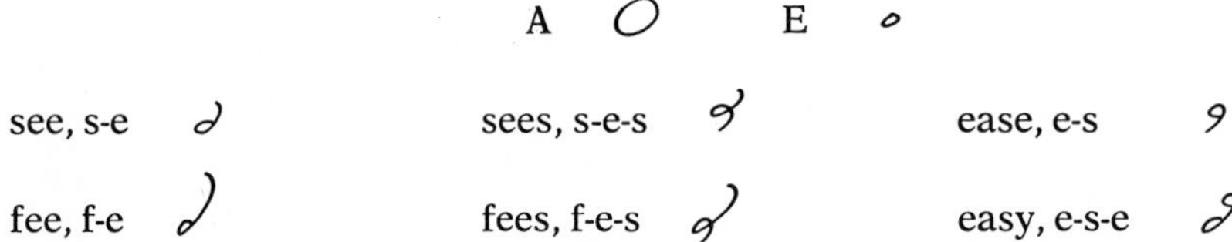

◉ *Observe that the* y *in* easy *is pronounced* e; *therefore, it is represented by the* e *circle.*

Suggestion: At this point you will find it helpful to read the procedures outlined for practicing lists of words on page 10. If you follow those procedures, you will derive the greatest benefit from the time you invest in practice.

GROUP B

7 **N, M** The shorthand stroke for *n* is a very short forward straight line. The shorthand stroke for *m* is a longer forward straight line.

N M

N

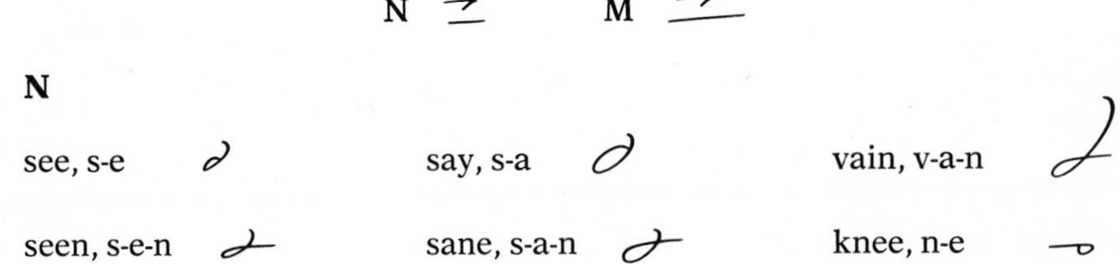

◉ *Observe that the* k *and the final* e *in* knee *are not written because they are not pronounced.*

M

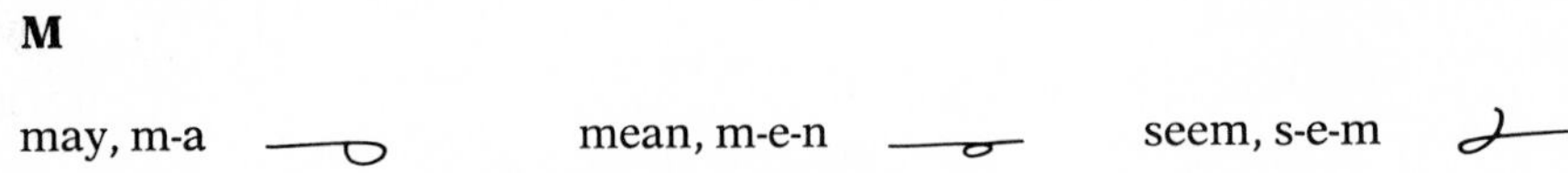

main, m-a-n   aim, a-m   same, s-a-m

8 **T, D** The shorthand stroke for *t* is a short upward straight line. The shorthand stroke for *d* is a longer upward straight line.

T   D

T

eat, e-t	meet, m-e-t	stay, s-t-a
neat, n-e-t	tea, t-e	safety, s-a-f-t-e

D

aid, a-d	feed, f-e-d	stayed, s-t-a-d
made, m-a-d	day, d-a	deed, d-e-d
need, n-e-d	date, d-a-t	saved, s-a-v-d

9 **Punctuation and Capitalization**

period	paragraph >	parentheses
question mark ×	dash	hyphen =

The regular longhand forms are used for all other punctuation marks.

Capitalization is indicated by two upward dashes placed underneath the word to be capitalized.

Dave   Fay   Mae

Reading Practice

With the nine strokes you have studied in this lesson, you can already read shorthand sentences with the help of an occasional longhand word.

Read the following sentences in this way:

☐ 1 Spell each shorthand outline aloud as you read it, thus: *N-a-t, Nate; m-a, may; s-t-a, stay.*

☐ 2 If you cannot determine the meaning of a shorthand outline after you have spelled it, refer to the key that follows this reading practice.

☐ 3 Reread the entire reading practice if time permits.

GROUP A

GROUP C

GROUP B

GROUP D

[97]

GROUP A

1 Nate may stay for tea. **2** Dave made the Navy team in May. **3** I need a vase. **4** Nate ate the meat. **5** Amy sees Dean Meade on May 15.

GROUP B

6 Fay is mean and vain. **7** Fay stayed all day with me. **8** Amy made a date with Dave. **9** Fay Day may meet me on East Main Street. **10** The deed is in Dave's safe.

GROUP C

11 Dean made $10 on May 18. **12** Dave's fee is $18. **13** Nate stayed at 15 East Main all day. **14** The Meade team faced Navy on May 10. **15** Dave made a safety.

GROUP D

16 Amy made me eat the meal. **17** Fay saved a seat for me. **18** The dean is easy to see. **19** May heard Fay say, "Feed me." **20** Dean Meade will see Dave on May 18.

Principles

1 **Alphabet Review** Here are the nine shorthand strokes you studied in Lesson 1. How rapidly can you read them?

2 **O, R, L** In this paragraph you will study three extremely useful strokes—*o, r, l.*

O The shorthand stroke for *o* is a small deep hook.

R The shorthand stroke for *r* is a short forward curve.

L The shorthand stroke for *l* is a longer forward curve about three times as long as the stroke for *r*.

◉ *Observe how these three strokes are derived from their longhand forms.*

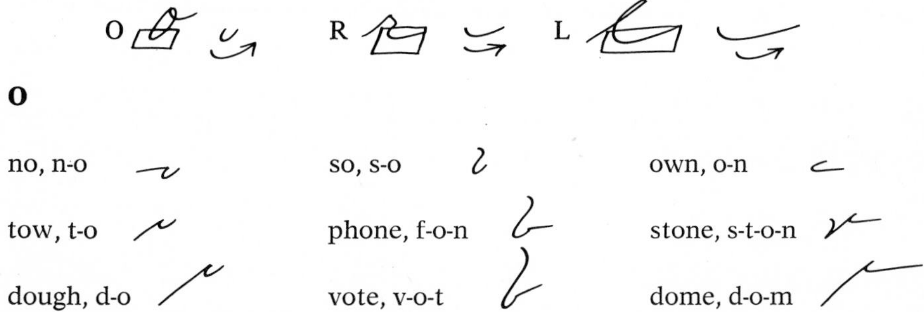

O

no, n-o	so, s-o	own, o-n
tow, t-o	phone, f-o-n	stone, s-t-o-n
dough, d-o	vote, v-o-t	dome, d-o-m

◉ *Observe that in the words in the third column, the* o *is placed on its side before* n *and* m. *This enables us to obtain smoother, more easily written outlines than we would obtain if we wrote the* o *upright in these and similar words.*

R

ear, e-r	raid, r-a-d	fear, f-e-r
near, n-e-r	trade, t-r-a-d	fair, f-a-r

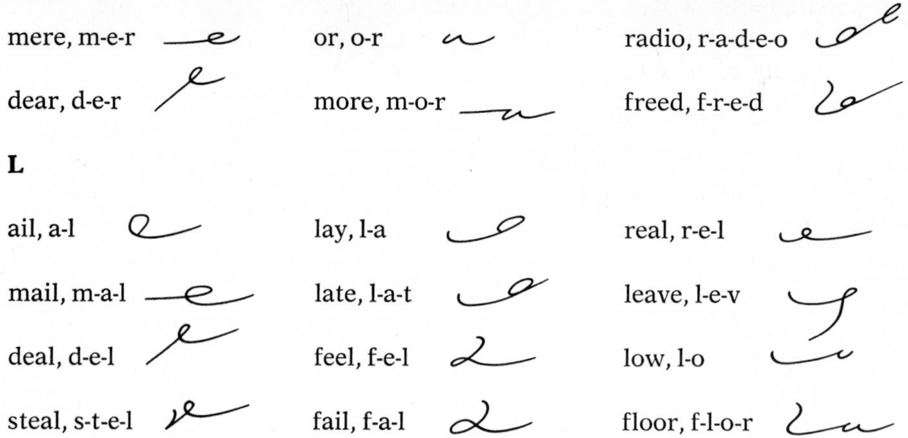

mere, m-e-r	or, o-r	radio, r-a-d-e-o
dear, d-e-r	more, m-o-r	freed, f-r-e-d

L

ail, a-l	lay, l-a	real, r-e-l
mail, m-a-l	late, l-a-t	leave, l-e-v
deal, d-e-l	feel, f-e-l	low, l-o
steal, s-t-e-l	fail, f-a-l	floor, f-l-o-r

◉ *Observe that* f-r, *as in* freed, *and* f-l, *as in* floor, *are written with one sweep of the pen, with no stop between the* f *and the* r *or* l.

freed   floor

3 **H, -ing** The letter *h* is a dot placed above the following vowel. With few exceptions, *h* occurs at the beginning of a word.

Ing, which almost always occurs at the end of a word, is also represented by a dot.

H

he, h-e	home, h-o-m	whole, h-o-l

-ing

hearing, h-e-r-ing	heating, h-e-t-ing	mailing, m-a-l-ing

4 **Long Ī** The shorthand stroke for the long sound of *i*, as in *my*, is a large broken circle.

I

my, m-ī	sight, s-ī-t	high, h-ī
might, m-ī-t	side, s-ī-d	try, t-r-ī
sign, s-ī-n	line, l-ī-n	tire, t-ī-r

5 Omission of Minor Vowels Many words in the English language contain vowels that are sounded only slightly or are slurred. For example, the word *even* is really pronounced *e-vn; meter* is pronounced *met-r.* (The dictionary calls these minor vowels "schwas.") These vowels are omitted in shorthand when their omission does not detract from facility of writing or from legibility.

evening, e-v-n-ing	writer, r-ī-t-r	season, s-e-s-n
meter, m-e-t-r	vital, v-ī-t-l	total, t-o-t-l
dealer, d-e-l-r	final, f-ī-n-l	heater, h-e-t-r

Reading Practice

With the aid of a few words in longhand, you can read the following sentences. Spell each shorthand word aloud as you read it; refer to the key when you cannot read a word.

GROUP A

1 at

2

3 is

4 at 7;

5 buy a

GROUP B

6 last

7 a $5

8 is

9 on

10 is 80.

GROUP C

11 to in a

12 in on

GROUP D

GROUP E

[144]

GROUP A

1 Ray Stone may phone me at my home. **2** Lee may fail writing. **3** My whole right side is sore. **4** My train leaves at seven; Dale Reeve's train leaves later. **5** Steven may buy a mail meter.

GROUP B

6 Lee Reed stayed home last evening. **7** He made me a $5 loan. **8** My reading rate is low. Is Dave's reading rate high? **9** Ray may rely on me. **10** My final rating is 80.

GROUP C

11 I hear he might fly to Rome in a day or so. **12** I need more light in my retail store on Vail Drive. **13** Ray is leaving home; Lee is remaining here. **14** My writing style is fair. **15** Dale wrote a fine story. **16** He drove the whole night. **17** The freight train is late.

GROUP D

18 Is it snowing or raining or hailing? **19** Is my train late? **20** He notified me he may fly home later. **21** I may sign my lease. **22** Dale may fly home later.

GROUP E

23 Dave is feeling fine. **24** Fay dyed her hair; Mary might dye her hair too. **25** He notified me my radio was stolen.

Principles

1 Alphabet Review You have already studied 14 alphabet strokes. How fast can you identify them?

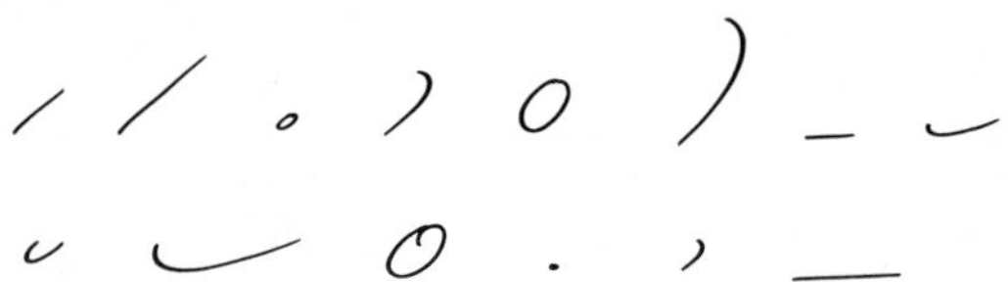

2 Brief Forms There are some words in the English language that occur again and again when we speak or write. As an aid to rapid writing, special abbreviations, called brief forms, are provided for some of these common words.

This process of abbreviation is common in longhand. For example, we abbreviate *Street* to *St.*; *Mister* to *Mr.*; *Saturday* to *Sat.*

Because the words for which brief forms have been provided occur so frequently, be sure you learn them well.

I	have	it, at
am	will, well	in,* not
Mr.	a, an	are, our, hour

**In-* is also used as a word beginning in words like:

indeed, in-d-e-d   inside, in-s-ī-d   invite, in-v-ī-t

◉ *Did you observe that some shorthand outlines have two or more meanings such as the shorthand forms for* are, our, hour; will, well? *You will have no problem selecting the correct meaning of a brief form when it appears in a sentence. The sense, or context, will give you the answer.*

3 Phrasing The use of brief forms for common words enables you to save time. Another device for saving writing time is called "phrasing," or the writing of two or more shorthand outlines together. Here are a number of phrases built with the brief forms you have studied.

I have	I will have	I am
I have not	he will	in our
I will	he will not	it will

4 **Left S-Z** Earlier you learned one stroke for *s* and *z*. Another stroke for *s* and *z* is also used in order to provide an easy joining in any combination of strokes—a backward comma, which is also written downward. For convenience, it is called the "left s."

At this point you need not try to decide which *s* stroke to use in any given word; this will become clear to you as your study of Gregg Shorthand progresses.

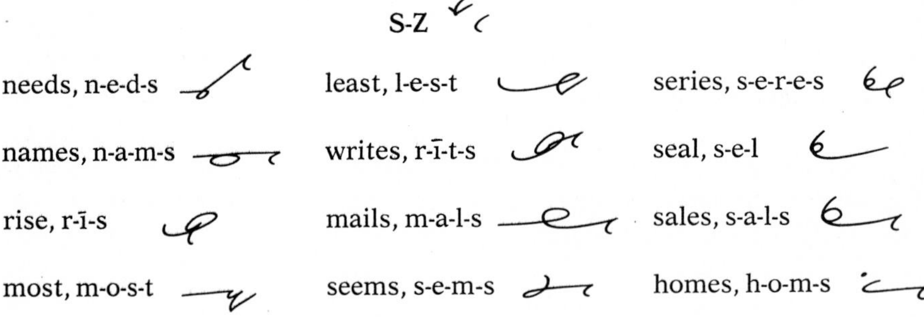

S-Z
needs, n-e-d-s
least, l-e-s-t
series, s-e-r-e-s
names, n-a-m-s
writes, r-ī-t-s
seal, s-e-l
rise, r-ī-s
mails, m-a-l-s
sales, s-a-l-s
most, m-o-s-t
seems, s-e-m-s
homes, h-o-m-s

5 **P, B** The shorthand stroke for *p* is a downward curve the same shape as the left *s* except that it is larger—approximately half the height of the space between the lines in your shorthand notebook.

The shorthand stroke for *b* is also a downward curve the same shape as the left *s* and *p* except that it is *much* larger—approximately the full height of the space between the lines in your shorthand notebook.

◉ *Observe the difference in the sizes of the* s, p, *and* b.

S P B

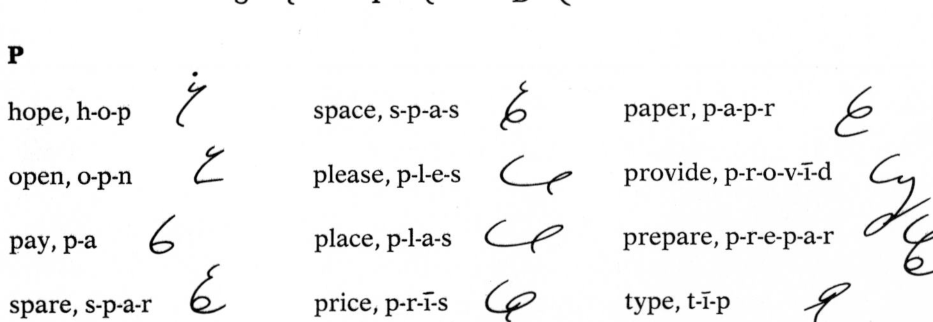

P
hope, h-o-p
space, s-p-a-s
paper, p-a-p-r
open, o-p-n
please, p-l-e-s
provide, p-r-o-v-ī-d
pay, p-a
place, p-l-a-s
prepare, p-r-e-p-a-r
spare, s-p-a-r
price, p-r-ī-s
type, t-ī-p

B

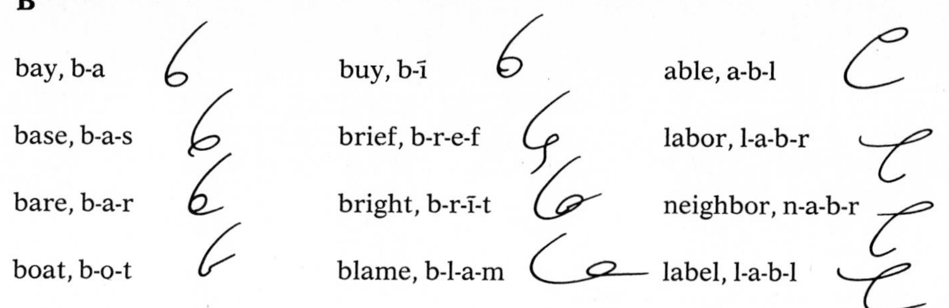

◉ *Observe that the combinations* p-r, *as in* price; p-l, *as in* please; b-r, *as in* bright; *and* b-l *as in* blame, *are written with one sweep of the pen without a pause between the* p *or* b *and the* r *or* l.

price please bright blame

Reading Practice

You can already read sentences written entirely in shorthand.

Suggestion: Before you start your work on this Reading Practice, take a few minutes to read the practice procedures for reading shorthand on page 10 .

GROUP A

1

2

3

4

5

6

7

[55]

GROUP B

8

9

10

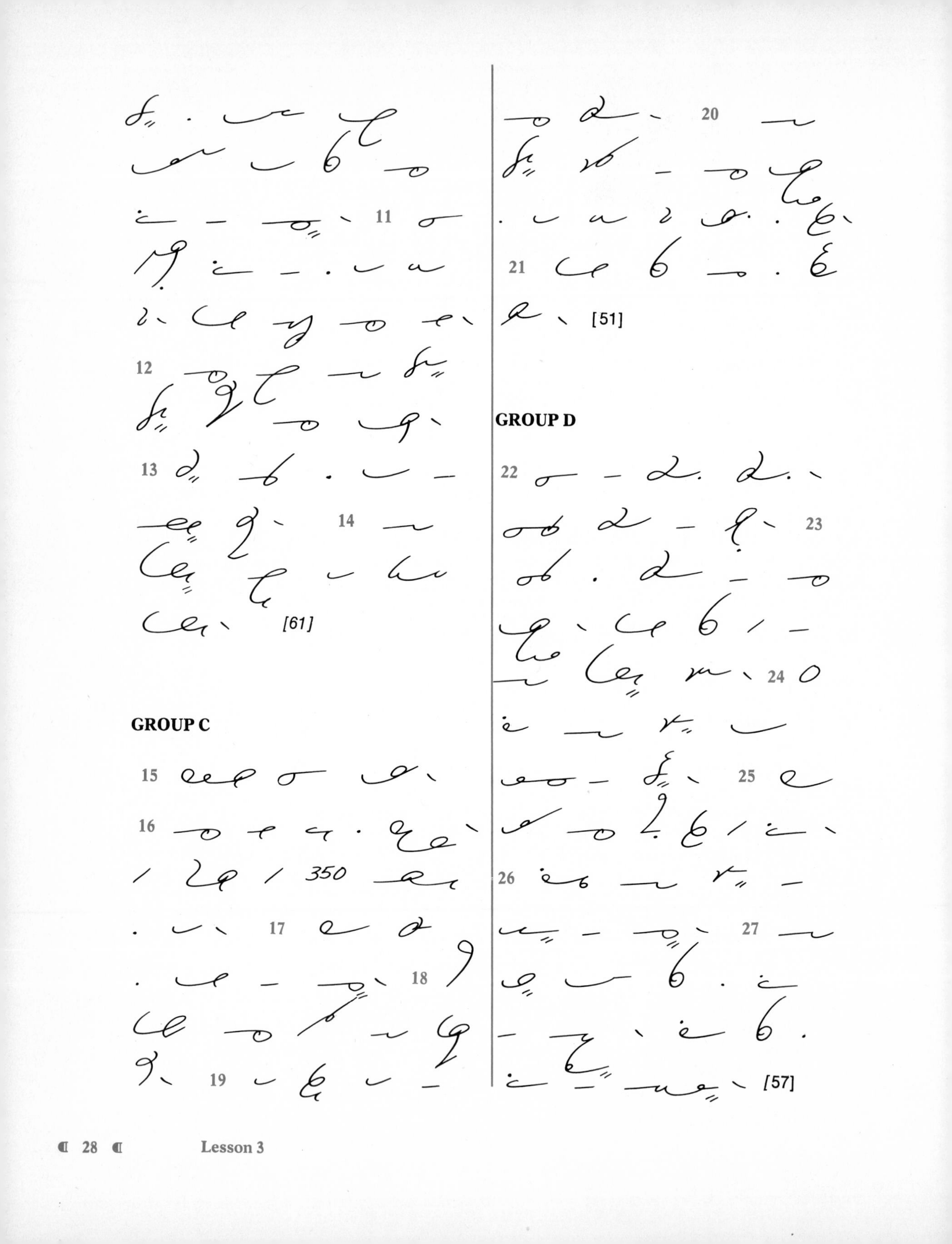

11

12

13

14

[61]

GROUP C

15

16

350

17

18

19

20

21

[51]

GROUP D

22

23

24

25

26

27

[57]

Principles

1 Alphabet Review You have already studied 17 strokes in the Gregg Shorthand alphabet. How fast can you read them?

2 OO The shorthand stroke for the sound of *oo*, as in *to*, is a tiny upward hook.

OO

to (two, too), t-oo	suit, s-oo-t	produce, p-r-o-d-oo-s
do (due), d-oo	room, r-oo-m	new (knew), n-oo
who, h-oo	poor, p-oo-r	noon, n-oo-n
food, f-oo-d	true, t-r-oo	move, m-oo-v

◉ *Observe that the* oo *is placed on its side when it follows* n *or* m, *as in* new, noon, move. *By placing the hook on its side in these combinations rather than writing it upright, we obtain smooth joinings.*

3 W, Sw At the beginning of words *w*, as in *we*, is represented by the *oo* hook; *sw*, as in *sweet*, by *s-oo*.

we, oo-e	wade, oo-a-d	sweet, s-oo-e-t
way, oo-a	wear, oo-a-r	sway, s-oo-a
wait, oo-a-t	wife, oo-ī-f	swear, s-oo-a-r

4 Wh *Wh,* as in *why* and *while,* is also represented by the *oo* hook.

why, oo-ī	white, oo-ī-t	whale, oo-a-l
while, oo-ī-l	wheel, oo-e-l	wheat, oo-e-t

5 Useful Phrases Here are a number of useful phrases that use the *oo* hook.

we are	we may	who will not
we will	who are	I do
we have	who will	I do not

6 K, G The shorthand stroke for *k* is a short forward curve.

The shorthand stroke for the hard sound of *g,* as in *game,* is a much longer forward curve. It is called *gay.*

◉ *Observe the difference in the size and shape of* oo, k, *and* gay.

OO K Gay

K

take, t-a-k	week (weak), oo-e-k	clear, k-l-e-r
cake, k-a-k	cool, k-oo-l	increase, in-k-r-e-s
make, m-a-k	case, k-a-s	claim, k-l-a-m
came, k-a-m	scale, s-k-a-l	clean, k-l-e-n

Gay

gain, gay-a-n	go, gay-o	gale, gay-a-l
game, gay-a-m	goal, gay-o-l	glue, gay-l-oo
gate, gay-a-t	great, gay-r-a-t	legal, l-e-gay-l
gave, gay-a-v	grade, gay-r-a-d	gleam, gay-l-e-m

◉ *Observe that* k-r, *as in* increase, *and* gay-l, *as in* legal, *are written with a smooth wavelike motion.*

increase legal

But k-l, *as in* claim, *and* gay-r, *as in* great, *are written with a hump between the* k *and the* l *and the* gay *and the* r.

claim great

Reading Practice

The sentences that follow contain many illustrations of the new shorthand strokes you studied in this lesson. They also contain many illustrations of the strokes, brief forms, and phrases you studied in Lessons 1 through 3.

Read the sentences aloud, spelling each shorthand outline you cannot immediately read.

GROUP A

1

2

3

4

5

[61]

GROUP B

6

7

8

9

10

[38]

GROUP C

11

12

13

14

[43]

GROUP D

15

16

17

18

19

[40]

GROUP E

20

21

22

23

24

[38]

Principles

1 Alphabet Review In Lessons 1 through 4 you studied 20 shorthand strokes. See how fast you can read them.

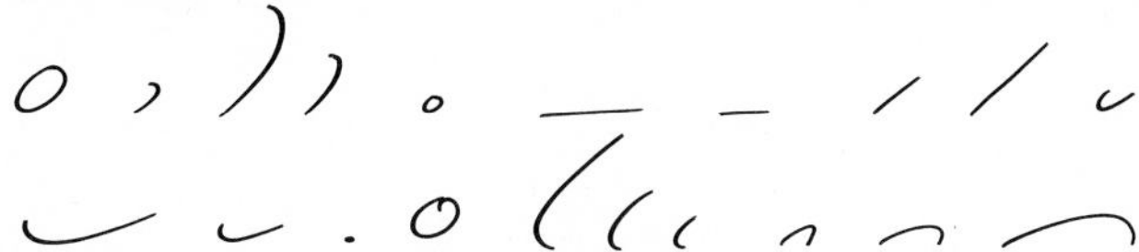

2 A, Ä The large circle that represents the long sound of *a*, as in *main*, also represents the vowel sounds heard in *as* and *arm*.

A

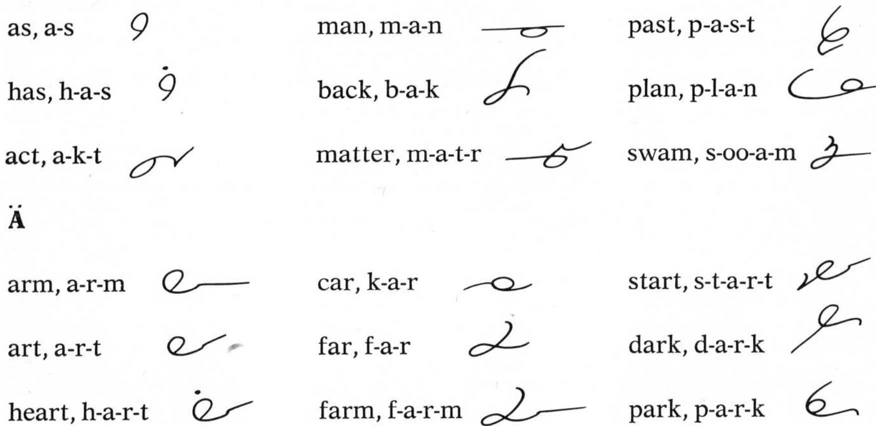

3 E, I, Obscure Vowel The tiny circle that represents the sound of *e*, as in *heat*, also represents the vowel sounds heard in *let*, *him*, and the obscure vowel sound (called "schwa" in some dictionaries) in *her*, *hurt*.

E

let, l-e-t   get, gay-e-t   said, s-e-d

letter, l-e-t-r | head, h-e-d | sell, s-e-l

address, a-d-r-e-s | help, h-e-l-p | tell, t-e-l

best, b-e-s-t | less, l-e-s | test, t-e-s-t

I

him, h-e-m | did, d-e-d | if, e-f

bill, b-e-l | fill, f-e-l | list, l-e-s-t

big, b-e-gay | give, gay-e-v | simple, s-e-m-p-l

Obscure Vowel

her, h-e-r | clerk, k-l-e-r-k | answer, a-n-s-e-r

hurt, h-e-r-t | serve, s-e-r-v | insert, in-s-e-r-t

earn, e-r-n | learn, l-e-r-n | infer, in-f-e-r

4 **Th** Two tiny curves, written upward, are provided for the sounds of *th*. These curves are called "ith."

At this time you need not try to decide which *th* stroke to use in a word; this will become clear to you as your study of Gregg Shorthand progresses.

Over Ith   Under Ith

Over Ith

these, ith-e-s | theater, ith-e-t-r | teeth, t-e-ith

then, ith-e-n | thick, ith-e-k | faith, f-a-ith

theme, ith-e-m | thief, ith-e-f | truth, t-r-oo-ith

Under Ith

though, ith-o | both, b-o-ith | health, h-e-l-ith

those, ith-o-s | birth, b-r-ith | thorough, ith-e-r-o

three, ith-r-e | earth, e-r-ith | through, ith-r-oo

5 **Brief Forms** Here is another group of brief forms for frequently used words. You will be wise to learn them well.

the	you, your	is, his
that	can	Mrs.
with	of	but

6 **Common Phrases** Here are some useful phrases employing these brief forms.

in the	with you	it is
in that	I can	in his
you are	I cannot	with his

◉ *Observe that in the phrases in the third column, the left* s *is used for* is *and* his.

Reading Practice

You have made such rapid progress that you can already read business letters written entirely in shorthand.

7 **Brief-Form Letter** The following letter contains one or more illustrations of the brief forms in this lesson and in Lesson 3.

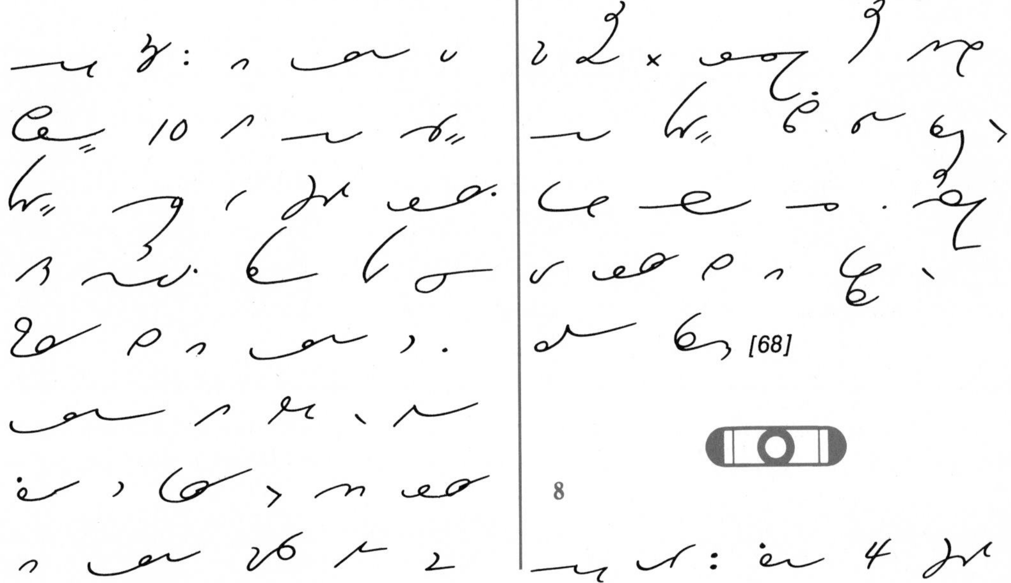

450

[94]

9

[72]

10

[63]

11

555-1612

[90]

12

[73]

RECALL

Lesson 6 is a "breather"; it contains no new shorthand principles for you to learn. In this lesson you will find an Alphabet Review, a simple explanation of the principles that govern the joining of the strokes you have studied thus far, a Recall Chart, and a Reading Practice.

1 **Alphabet Review** Here are the 22 shorthand strokes you studied in Lessons 1 through 5. Can you read them in 20 seconds or less?

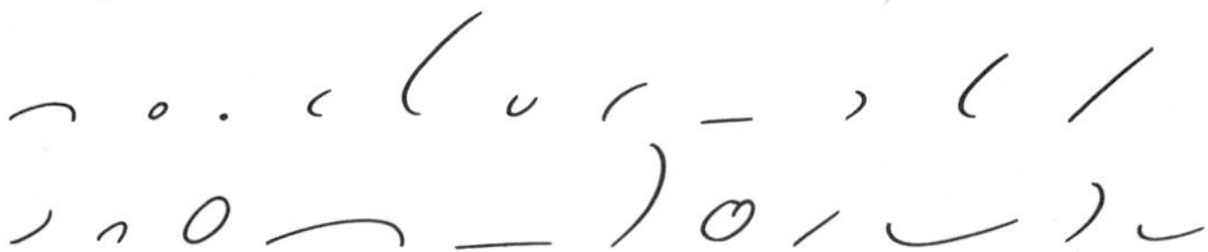

Principles of Joining

As a matter of interest, you might like to know the principles under which the words you have already learned are written. Notice the groups into which the joinings naturally fall.

2 Circles are written inside curves and outside angles.

appeal, a-p-e-l late, l-a-t same, s-a-m

give, gay-e-v relief, r-e-l-e-f needless, n-e-d-l-e-s

3 Circles are written clockwise (in this direction) on a straight stroke or between two straight strokes in the same direction.

may, m-a date, d-a-t aim, a-m

man, m-a-n stayed, s-t-a-d name, n-a-m

4 Between two curves written in opposite directions, the circle is written on the back of the first curve.

care, k-a-r   gear, gay-e-r   vapor, v-a-p-r

rack, r-a-k   lake, l-a-k   pave, p-a-v

5 The *o* hook is written on its side before *n, m* unless a downward stroke comes before the hook.

own, o-n   stone, s-t-o-n   loan, l-o-n

but

phone, f-o-n   bone, b-o-n   zone, s-o-n

6 The *oo* hook is written on its side after *n, m*.

news, n-oo-s   noon, n-oo-n   moved, m-oo-v-d

7 The under *ith* is used when it is joined to *o, r, l*; in other cases, the over *ith* is used.

though, ith-o   through, ith-r-oo   health, h-e-l-ith

but

these, ith-e-s   thick, ith-e-k   then, ith-e-n

8 **Recall Chart** The following chart reviews the shorthand devices you studied in Lessons 1 through 5.

Spell each word aloud thus: *ith-o, though*. You need not spell the brief forms and phrases as you read them.

The chart contains 84 words and phrases. Can you read the entire chart in 9 minutes or less?

WORDS

1

2

3

4

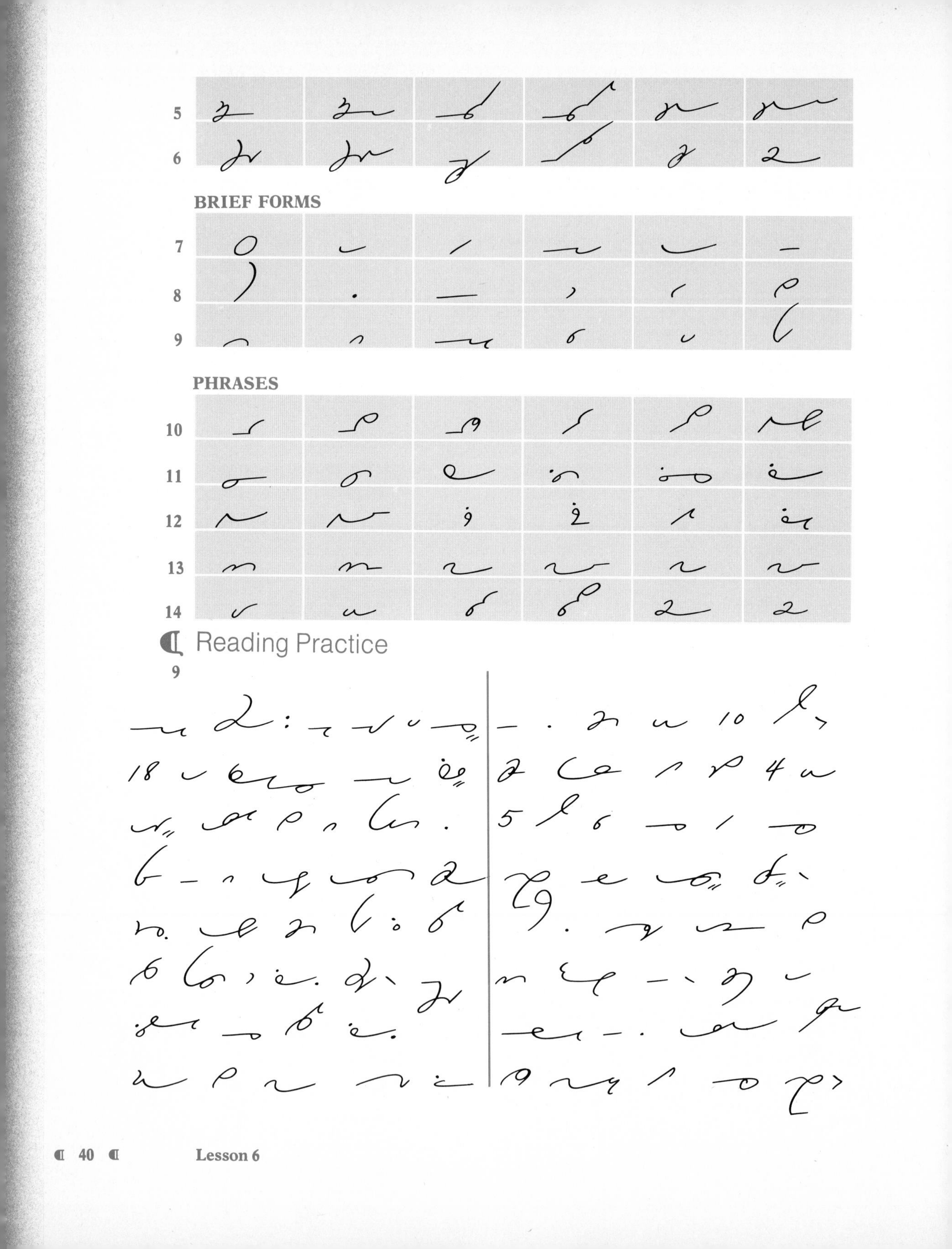

5

6

BRIEF FORMS

7

8

9

PHRASES

10

11

12

13

14

Reading Practice

9

[89]

10

[79]

11

(206) 555-8172

[90]

2 SHORTHAND—A USEFUL SKILL IN ANY CAREER

In addition to the desire of secretarial students to obtain good stenographic positions after graduation, college students study shorthand for another reason: Shorthand opens the door to other types of jobs.

Many students look upon shorthand as a door-opener and as insurance. There are many competitive fields, such as the arts and publishing, in which there are many more applicants than there are available positions. Being able to list shorthand under the "Other Skills" section on your application or résumé gives you a plus in the eyes of prospective employers because you have something extra to offer them.

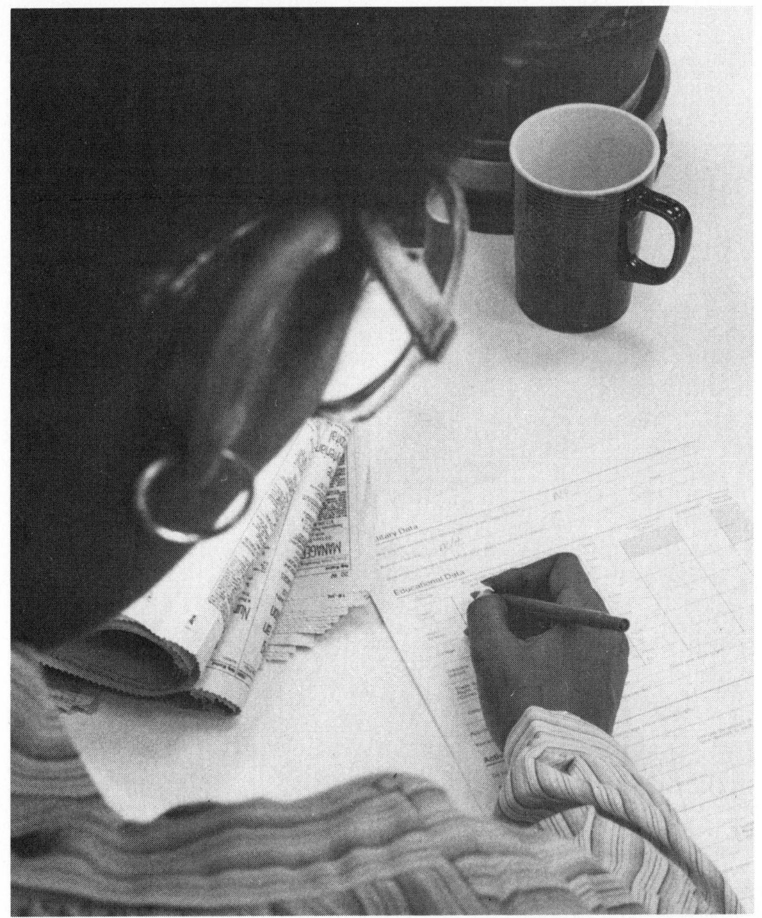

Even though you may not start work with the job title you desire, starting in a secretarial job in your chosen field at least helps you get your "foot in the door." This has proved to be true, especially for liberal arts majors.

In addition to this advantage, shorthand is a skill that can be useful to you when you do get the specific job you want. Reporters, for example, can quickly note their observations at important events and are sure to get an accurate record during an interview or press conference. High-level executives in any business can quickly and easily jot down important points brought out at business meetings and conferences, and they can save time by writing their own "dictation" while traveling so that their secretaries just have to transcribe the notes.

Whatever *your* major is, you can be sure that shorthand is a compatible, beneficial, and useful skill to have.

Principles

1 **Sh, Ch, J** These three sounds are represented by downward straight lines.

Sh The shorthand stroke for *sh* (called "ish") is a very short downward straight stroke.

Ch The shorthand stroke for *ch* (called "chay") is a somewhat longer straight downward stroke approximately one-half the height of the space between the lines in your shorthand notebook.

J The shorthand stroke for the sound of *j*, as in *age* and *jury*, is a long downward straight stroke almost the full height of the space between the lines in your shorthand notebook.

◉ *Observe carefully the difference in the sizes of these strokes.*

Ish Chay J

Ish

she, ish-e	share, ish-a-r	ship, ish-e-p
shown, ish-o-n	issue e-ish-oo	insure, in-ish-oo-r

Chay

check, chay-e-k	chair, chay-a-r	search, s-e-r-chay
choose, chay-oo-s	teach, t-e-chay	church, chay-e-r-chay

J

age, a-j	change, chay-a-n-j	jury, j-oo-r-e
wages, oo-a-j-s	large, l-a-r-j	jewels, j-oo-l-s

2 **O, Aw** The small deep hook that represents the sound of *o*, as in *no*, also represents the vowel sounds heard in *hot* and *all*.

O

hot, h-o-t	office, o-f-e-s	sorry, s-o-r-e

copy, k-o-p-e

job, j-o-b

policy, p-o-l-s-e

stock, s-t-o-k

stop, s-t-o-p

watch, oo-o-chay

Aw

all, o-l

small, s-m-o-l

cause, k-o-s

bought, b-o-t

thought, ith-o-t

daughter, d-o-t-r

author, o-ith-r

install, in-s-t-o-l

wall, oo-o-l

3 Common Business Letter Salutations and Closings

Dear Sir

Dear Madam

Yours truly

Sincerely yours

Yours very truly

Very truly yours

◉ Note: Although the expressions *Dear Sir*, *Dear Madam*, and *Yours truly* are considered too impersonal by letter-writing experts, they are still used by many dictators. Therefore, special abbreviations have been provided for them.

Reading and Writing Practice

Suggestion: Before you begin your work on the letters that follow, turn to page 10 and read the procedures outlined there for reading and writing shorthand. To make the most rapid progress, follow those procedures carefully.

4 Brief-Form Review Letter This letter reviews the brief forms you have studied thus far.

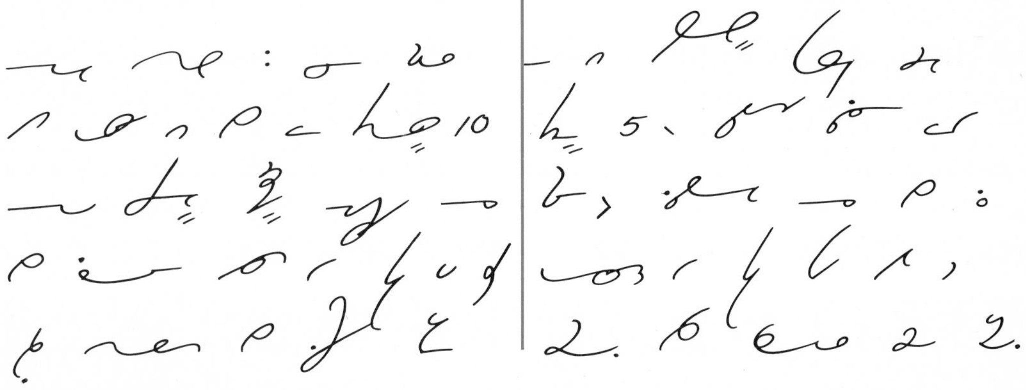

[87]

5

[74]

6

[60]

7

15

[76]

8

[80]

9

[66]

Principles

1 Brief Forms Here is another group of nine brief forms for very common words. Learn them well!

would	this	them
for	good	which
there (their)	they	be,* by

**Be* is also used as a word beginning in words such as *believe* and *because.*

Spell: be-l-e-v, believe

believe	because	begin

2 Word Ending -ly The common word ending *-ly* is represented by the *e* circle.

Spell: l-a-t-lē, lately

lately	mainly	mostly
nearly	plainly	only
badly	briefly	highly
costly	namely	daily

◉ *Observe that in* highly *the small circle for* -ly *is written inside the large circle; that in* daily *it is added to the other side of the* d *after the* a *has been written.*

3 Amounts and Quantities When you take dictation in the business office, you will frequently have occasion to write amounts and quantities. Here are some devices that will enable you to write them rapidly.

600		$12		$3.40	
8,000		$3,000		8 percent	
800,000		$700,000		7 o'clock	

◉ *Observe that the* n *for* hundred *and the* ith *for* thousand *are placed* underneath *the figure.*

Reading and Writing Practice

4 Brief-Form Letter The following letter contains one or more illustrations of the brief forms in this lesson.

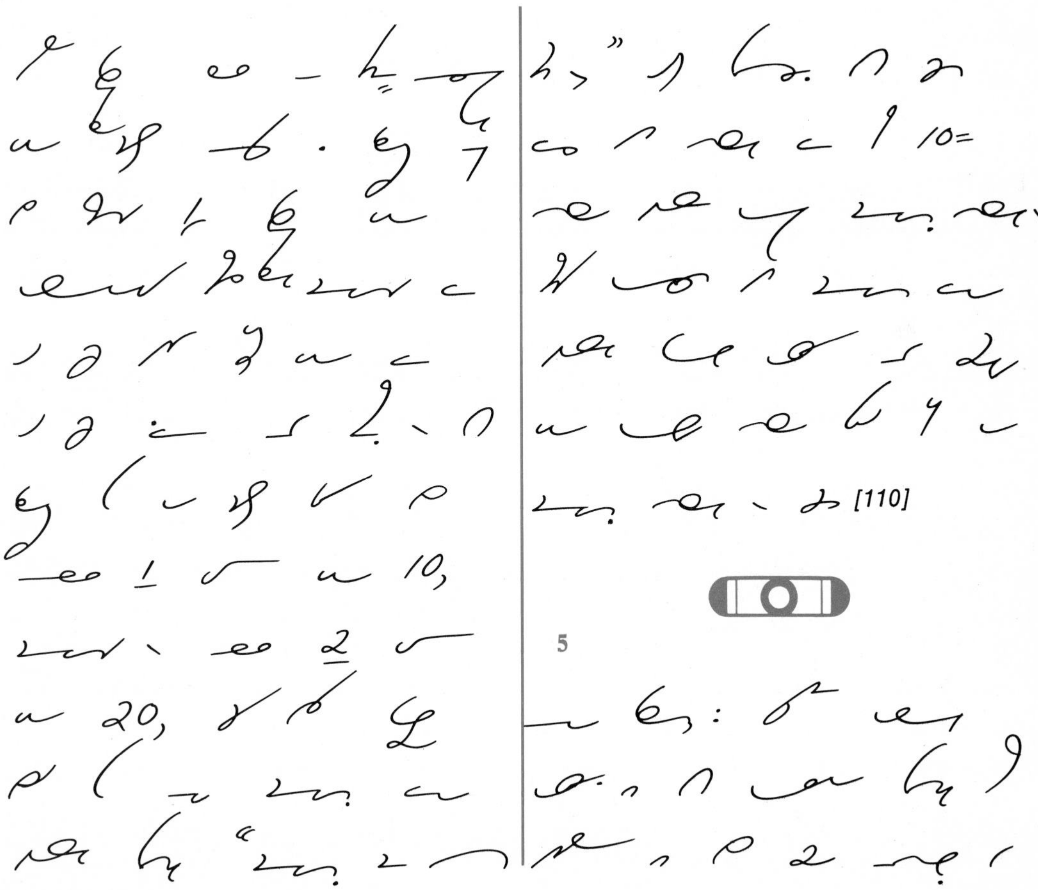

[146]

6

[89]

7

[95]

8

[84]

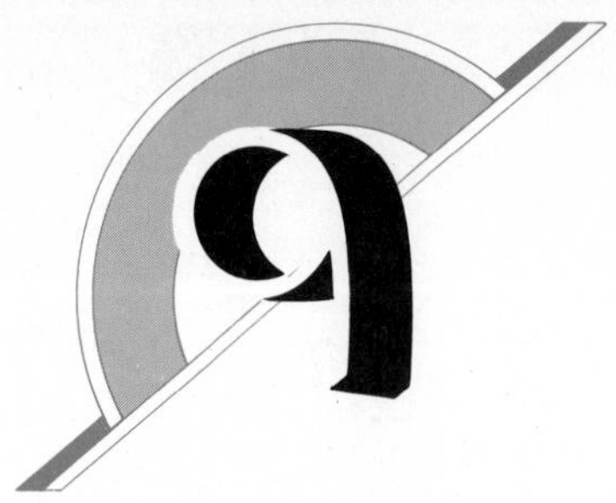

Principles

1 **Word Ending -tion** The word ending *-tion* (sometimes spelled *-sion, -cian,* or *-shion*) is represented by *ish.*

Spell: a-k-shun, action

action	operation	national
occasion	physician	nationally
election	fashion	cautioned
position	nations	inflation

2 **Word Endings -cient, -ciency** The word ending *-cient* (or *-tient*) is represented by *ish-t*; *-ciency*, by *ish-s-e.*

Spell: p-a-shun-t, patient

e-f-e-shun-s-e, efficiency

patient	ancient	efficiency
patiently	efficient	proficiency

3 **T for To in Phrases** In phrases, *to* is represented by *t* when it is followed by a downstroke.

to have	to check	to sell
to be	to buy	to serve
to say	to plan	to charge
to see	to place	to change

Reading and Writing Practice

4. **Brief-Form Review Letter** The following letter reviews the brief forms you studied in Lesson 8 as well as many brief forms you learned in Lessons 3 and 5.

[138]

5

[90]

6

[88]

[113]

7

8

[104]

9

[108]

10

[57]

Principles

1 Nd The shorthand strokes for *n-d* are joined without an angle to form the *nd* blend, as in *signed.*

Nd

Compare: sign signed

Spell: s-ī-end, signed; end-o-r-s, endorse

land	friend	kind
planned	spend	mind
trained	happened	bind
errand	brand	endorse

2 Nt The stroke that represents *nd* also represents *nt,* as in *sent.*

Spell: s-e-ent, sent; ent-oo, into

sent	printed	agent
rent	painted	vacant
prevent	planted	into
current	parents	entire

3 Ses The sound of *ses,* as in *senses,* is represented by joining the two forms of *s.*

Compare: sense senses

face faces

Spell: s-e-n-sez, senses

places	causes	reduces
prices	chances	produces
addresses	increases	cases
glasses	necessary	services

4 **Sis, Sus** The similar sounds of *sis*, as in *sister*, and *sus*, as in *versus*, are also represented by joining the two forms of *s*.

Spell: sez-t-r, sister; v-e-r-sez, versus

sister	assist	analysis
basis	insist	versus

Reading and Writing Practice

5 **Brief-Form Review Letter** This letter reviews the brief forms you studied in Lesson 8 as well as many of those in previous lessons.

15, 15

(703) 555-5176 [138]

6

4 5 2

[137]

7

10 4 4 2

[103]

8

520/

50

50

555-

1187-

[101]

[92]

9

Principles

1 Brief Forms Here are nine more brief forms for very common words.

when		after		and	
were		could		from	
send		should		street	

2 Rd The combination *rd* is represented by writing the *r* with an upward turn at the finish.

Compare: assure assured

Spell: a-ish-oo-ärd, assured; h-e-ärd, heard

assured		toward		record	
hired		guard		hardest	
insured		guarded		heard	

3 Ld The combination *ld* is represented by writing the *l* with an upward turn at the finish.

Compare: mail mailed

Spell: m-a-eld, mailed; o-eld, old

mailed		failed		build	
old		filled		builder	
sold		told		folded	

4 Been in Phrases The word *been* is represented by *b* after *have, has, had.*

have been	had been	I could have been
I have been	I have not been	I should have been
you have been	it has been	had not been

5 Able in Phrases The word *able* is represented by *a* after *be* or *been.*

I have been able	I should be able
I have not been able	you will be able
you have been able	you should be able
you have not been able	I may be able

Reading and Writing Practice

6 Brief-Form Letter The following letter contains one or more illustrations of the brief forms presented in this lesson.

150

[167]

7

[89]

8

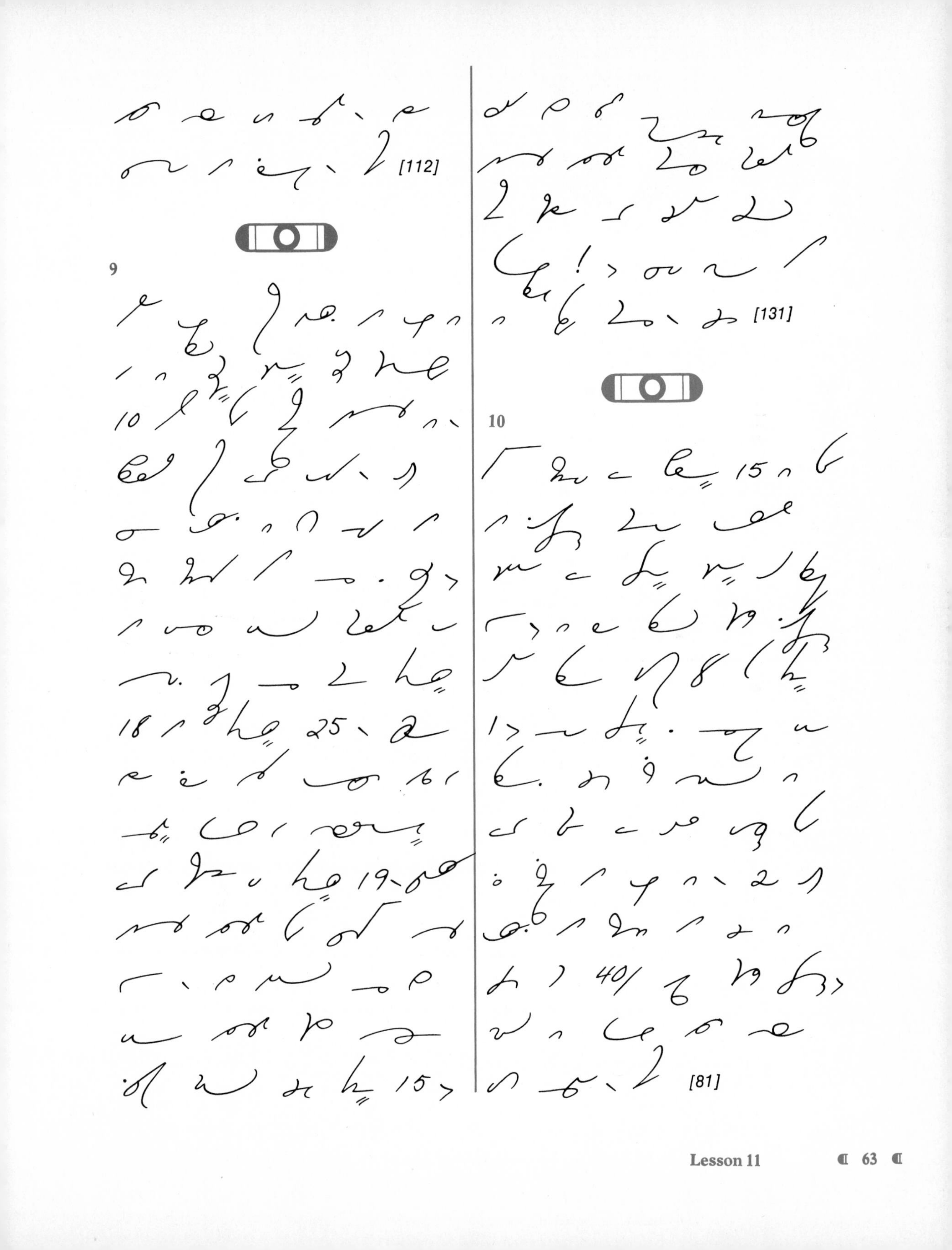

[112]

9

[131]

10

[81]

RECALL

Lesson 12 is another "breather"; it presents no new devices for you to learn. It reviews the shorthand strokes you learned in previous lessons.

Principles of Joining

The following principles deal with the joinings of the two forms of *s*.

1 At the beginning and end of words, the comma *s* is used before and after *f, v, k, gay*; the left *s*, before and after *p, b, r, l*.

saves sips series

seeks globes rags

2 The comma *s* is used before *t, d, n, m, o*; the left *s* is used after those strokes.

stones solos needs

3 The comma *s* is used before and after *ish, chay, j*.

sessions reaches stages

4 The comma *s* is used in words consisting of *s* and a circle vowel or *s* and *ith* and a circle vowel.

say these seethe

5 Gregg Shorthand is equally legible whether it is written on ruled or unruled paper; consequently, you need not worry about the exact placement of your outlines on the printed lines in your notebook. The main purpose of the printed lines in your notebook is to keep you from wandering uphill and downhill as you write.

However, so that all outlines may be uniformly placed in the shorthand books from which you study, this general rule has been followed:

The base of the first consonant of a word is placed on the line of writing. When *s* comes before a downstroke, however, the downstroke is placed on the line of writing.

name	safe	pace
dealer	chief	space

6 **Recall Chart** The following chart contains the brief forms presented in Chapter 2 and illustrations of the shorthand principles you studied in Chapters 1 and 2. Can you read the chart in 6 minutes or less?

BRIEF FORMS

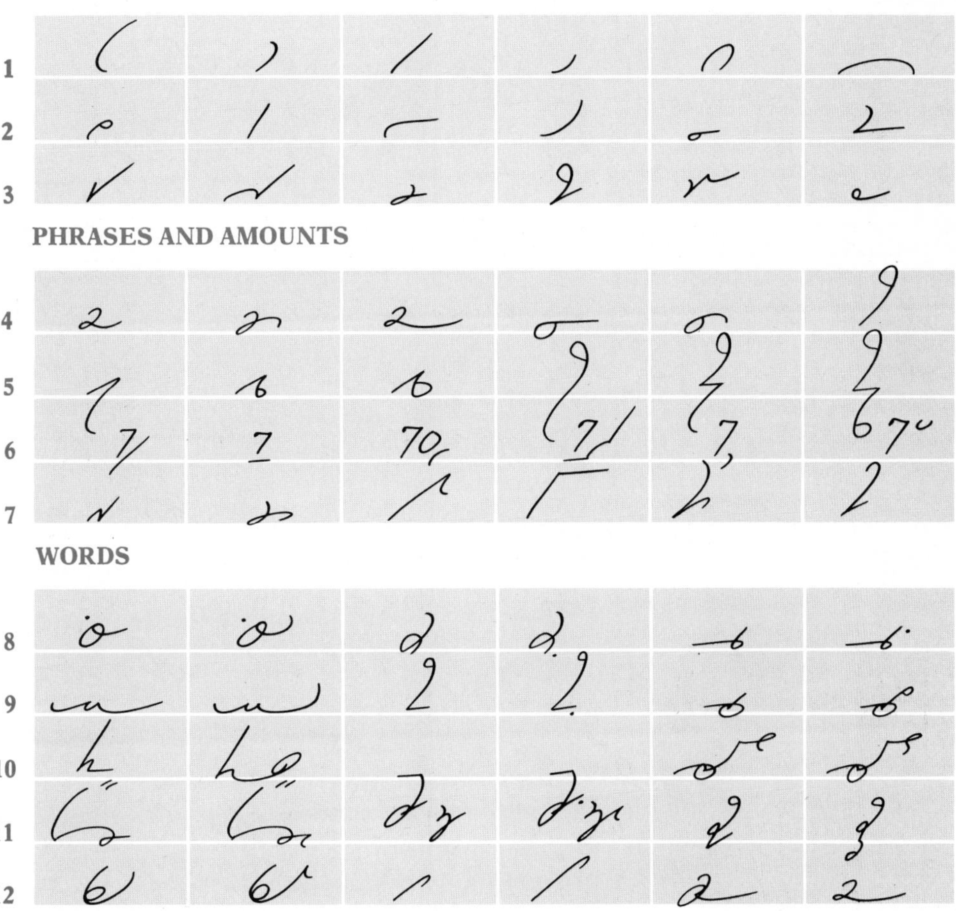

Reading and Writing Practice

7 Brief-Form Review Letter

[107]

8

1975

15/ 20/

33⅓ 20/

5

1978

18 19

[144]

9

[84]

10

[65]

11

[74]

3 MEASURING YOUR SHORTHAND SKILL

The term *words a minute* can be misleading. The term is meaningful only as a measuring device while you are learning Gregg Shorthand. In order to increase your speed from 60 words a minute, you need to set a measurable higher goal for yourself—probably 80 words a minute.

A speed of 80 words a minute doesn't necessarily mean that 80 actual words are dictated every 60 seconds. In order to equalize short and long words such as *the* and *unnecessarily*, the sounds dictated are broken down into syllables that are timed to determine your dictation speed.

Studies have shown that for standard dictation a typical word contains about 1.4 syllables. Therefore, a speed of 80 words a minute is equal to 112 syllables a minute (80 x 1.4).

What is an "adequate" shorthand skill? We hear that the average business dictation speed is approximately 80 words a minute, and some studies have shown this to be true. Be sure to note the word *average*. If your employer dictates at an *average* rate of 80 words a minute, your dictation speed should be 100 words a minute or more because some portions of the dictation will be much faster than others. Obviously, a short, simple letter is easier to write than a long, technical one. A rate of 120 words a minute means little if the dictated material is very short and simple. This rate does mean something if you can write for a sustained period of several minutes on new material.

Despite the fact that the business-entry level dictation speed is 80 words a minute, don't be satisfied with attaining just that speed. Aim for a rate of 120 words a minute—or higher—and you will be able to take dictation from almost any executive at any time.

Principles

1 Brief Forms

work	circular	enclose
yesterday	order	was
glad	soon	thank

2 Brief-Form Derivatives and Phrases

thanks	gladly	thank you
worked	ordered	thank you for

◉ *Observe:* ☐ 1 Thanks *is written with a disjoined left* s *in the dot position.*
☐ 2 *The* d *representing the past tense of* order *is joined with a jog.*
☐ 3 *The dot in* thank *is omitted in phrases.*

3 U, OO

The hook that represents the sound of *oo,* as in *to,* also represents the vowel sounds in *does* and *book.*

U

Spell: d-oo-s, does

does	none	us
drug	number	just
up	enough	adjust
product	must	precious

◉ *Observe:* ☐ 1 *The hook in the words in the second column is turned on its side.*
☐ 2 *The* oo-s *in the words in the third column is joined without an angle.*

OO

Spell: b-oo-k, book

book		put		pull	
cook		push		stood	
look		foot		sugar	
took		full		wood	

Building Transcription Skills

4 BUSINESS VOCABULARY BUILDER

As a stenographer or secretary, you will constantly be dealing with words. Consequently, the larger the vocabulary you have at your command, the easier your task will be when taking dictation and transcribing.

To help you build your vocabulary at the same time that you are learning shorthand, a Business Vocabulary Builder is provided in Lesson 13 and in many of the lessons that follow. The Business Vocabulary Builder consists of brief definitions of business words and expressions, selected from the Reading and Writing Practice of the lesson, that may be unfamiliar to you.

Be sure to read each Business Vocabulary Builder before you begin your work on the Reading and Writing Practice that follows it.

Business Vocabulary Builder

nursing home An establishment where care is provided for the aged or sick who are unable to take care of themselves properly.

utmost The most possible; the greatest amount.

copywriters Those who write advertising or publicity copy.

Reading and Writing Practice

5 Brief-Form Letter

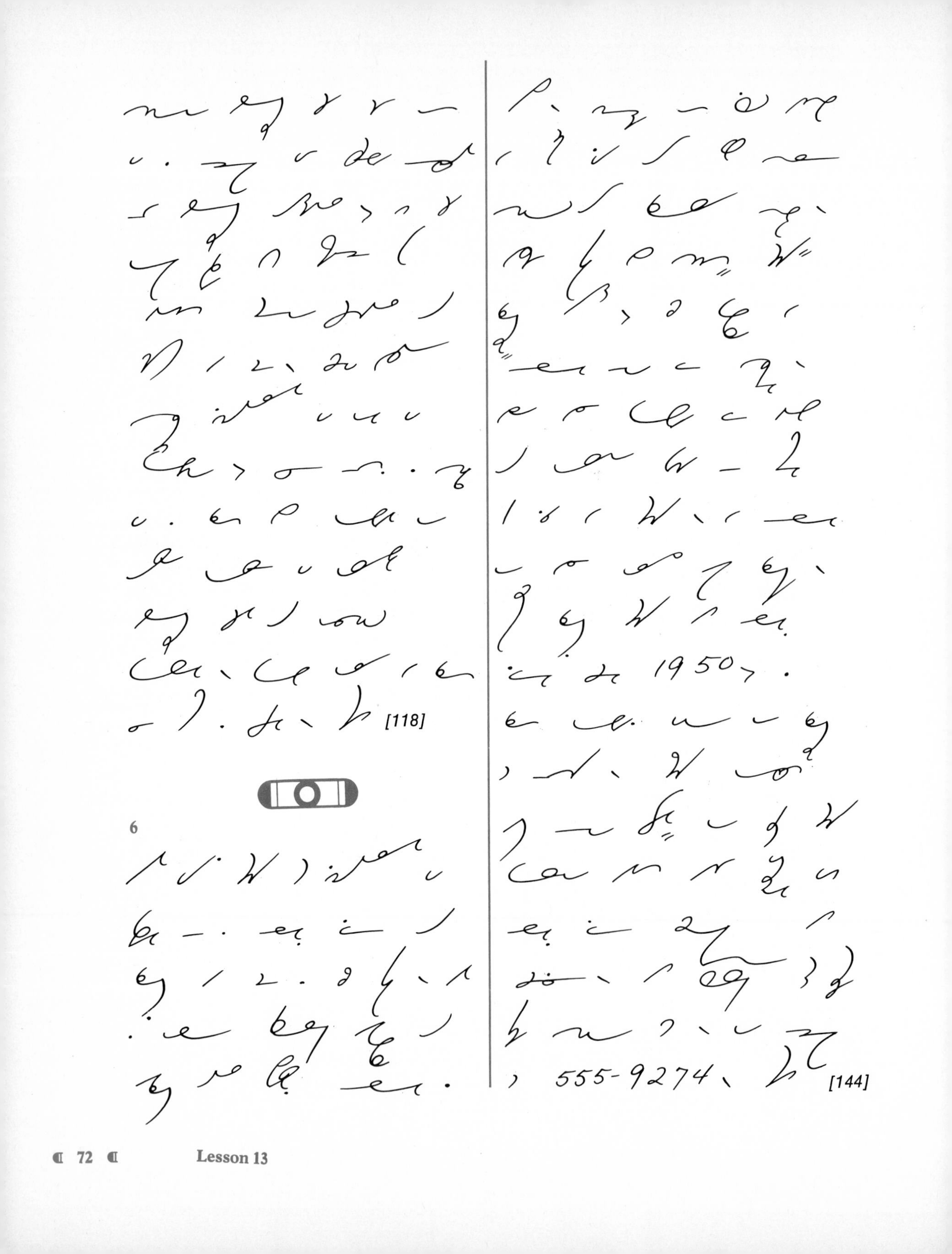

[118]

6

1950.

555-9274.

[144]

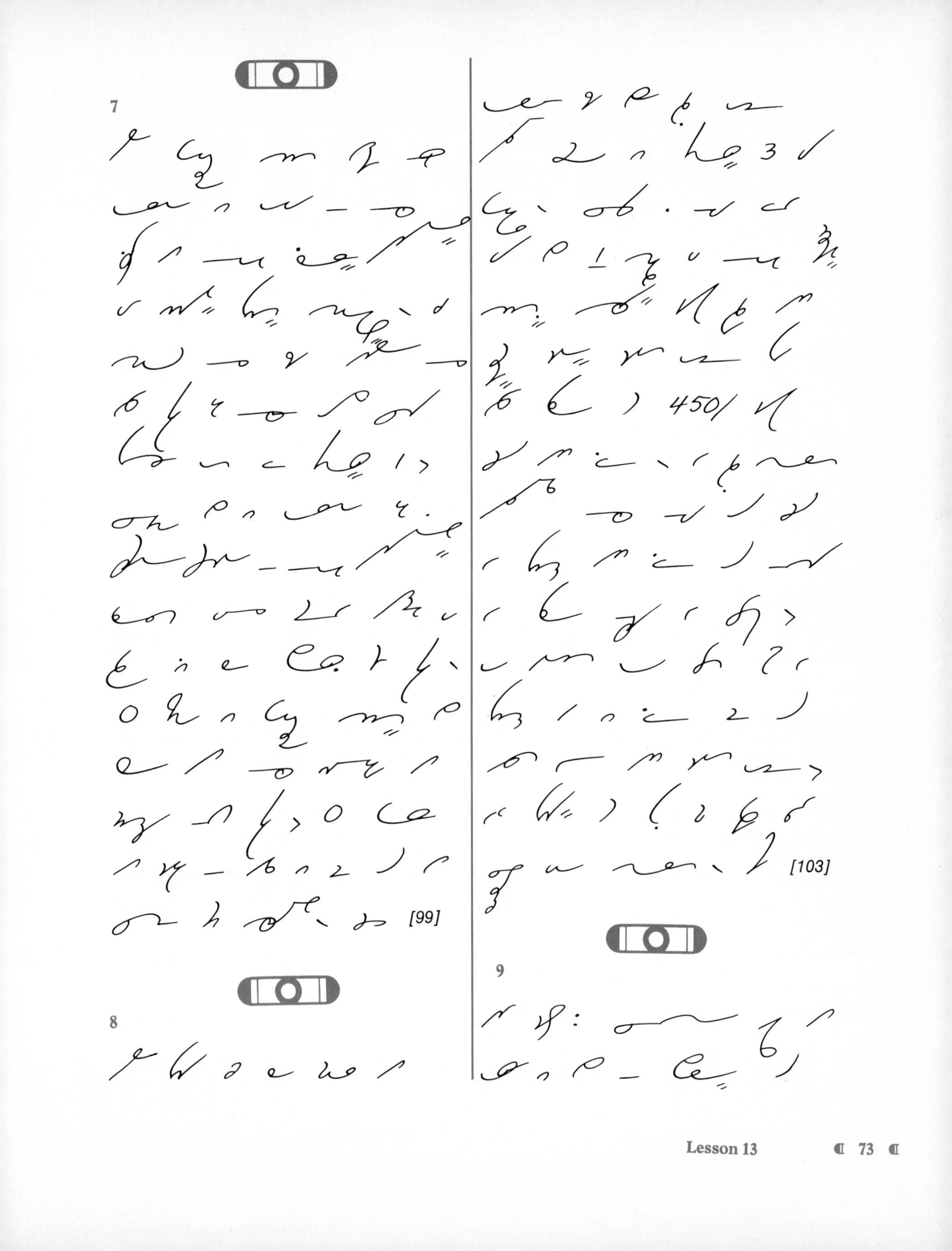

7

[99]

8

[103]

9

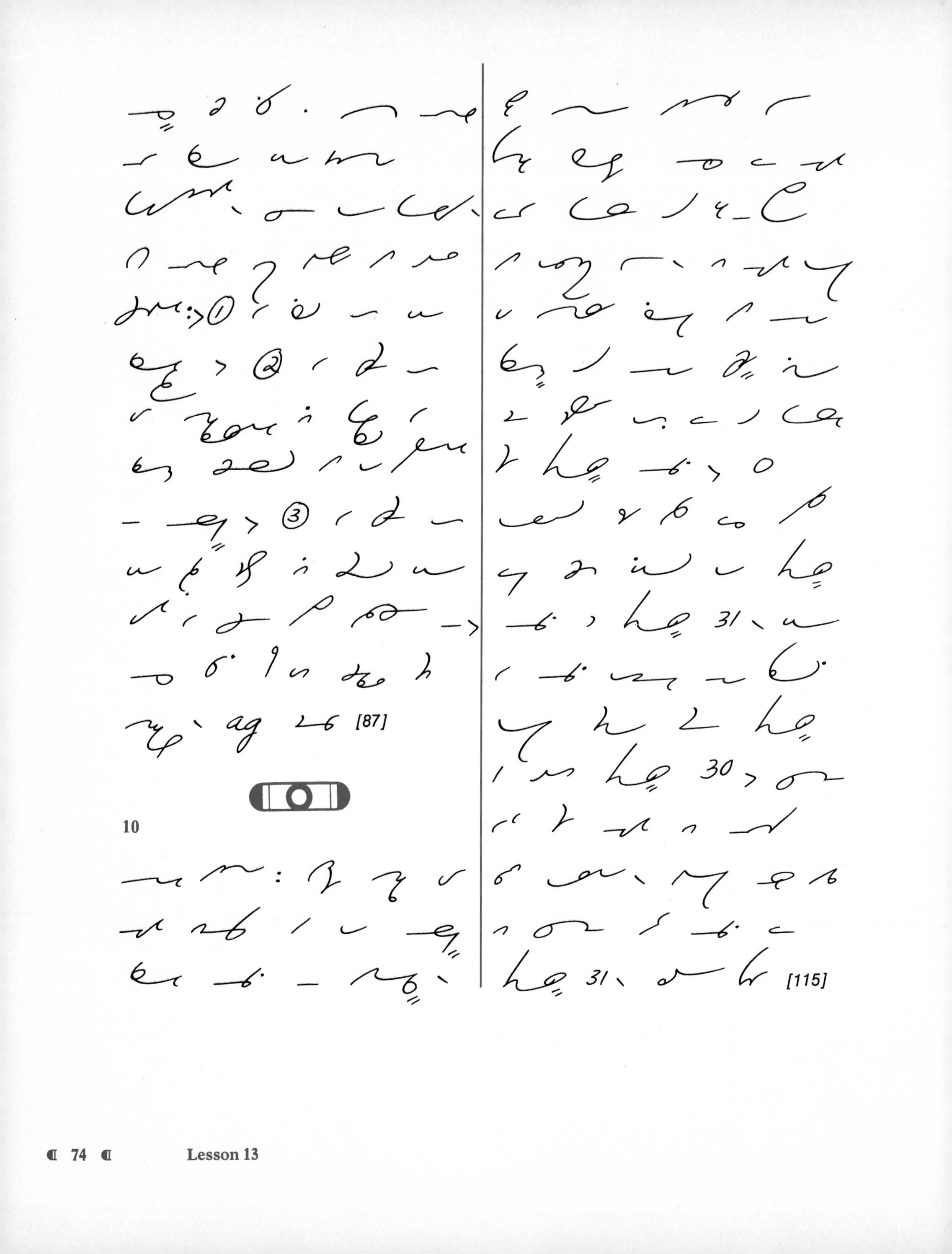

[87]

10

31

30

31

[115]

Principles

1 **W in the Body of a Word** When the sound of *w* occurs in the body of a word, as in *quick,* it is represented by a short dash underneath the vowel following the *w* sound. The dash is inserted after the rest of the outline has been written.

Spell: k-oo-e-k, quick

quick	between	qualify
quote	square	hardware
quit	twice	roadway
equip	twine	always

2 **Ted** The combination *ted* is represented by joining *t* and *d* into one long upward stroke.

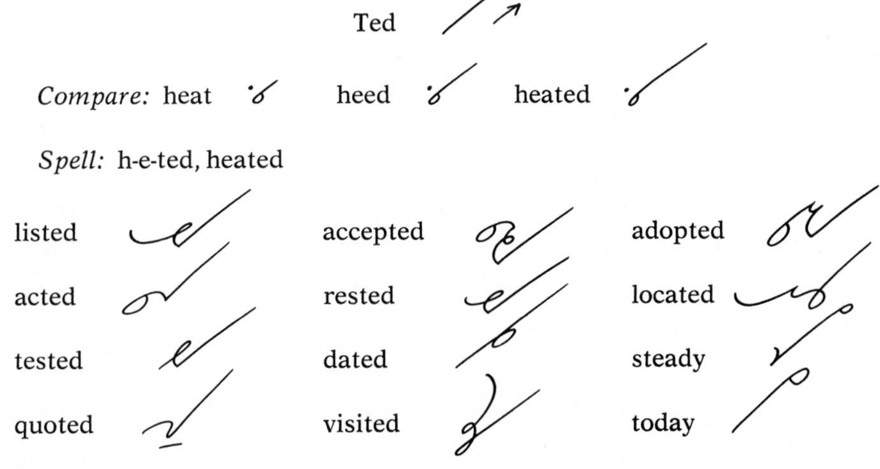

3 Ded, Dit, Det The long stroke that represents *ted* also represents *ded* and the similar sounds of *dit* and *det*.

Spell: gay-ī-ded, guided; det-a-l, detail

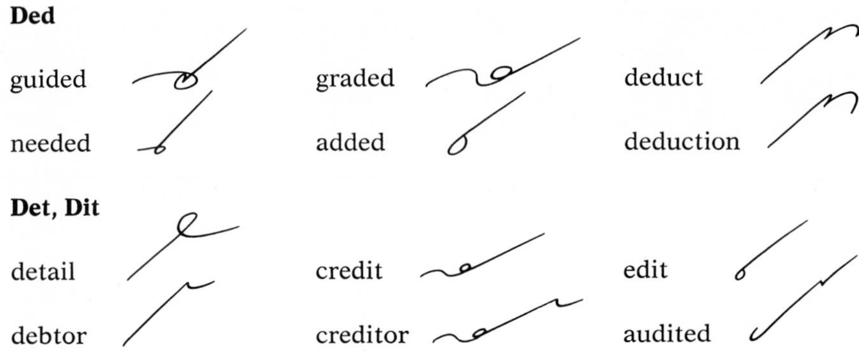

◉ *Observe that the* d *representing the past tense in* audited *is joined to* dit *with a jog.*

Building Transcription Skills

4 Business Vocabulary Builder

Twin Cities Minneapolis and St. Paul, Minnesota.
premises A tract of land with a building or buildings on it.
toll A great price.
queries Questions.

Reading and Writing Practice

5 Brief-Form Review Letter

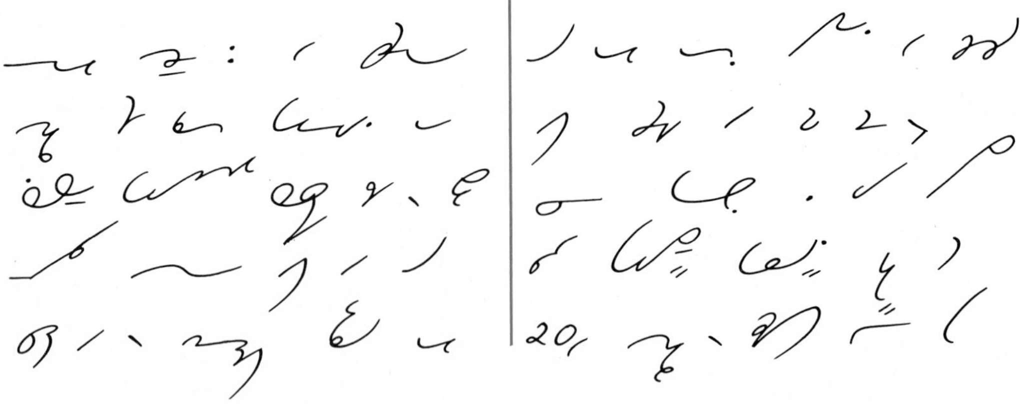

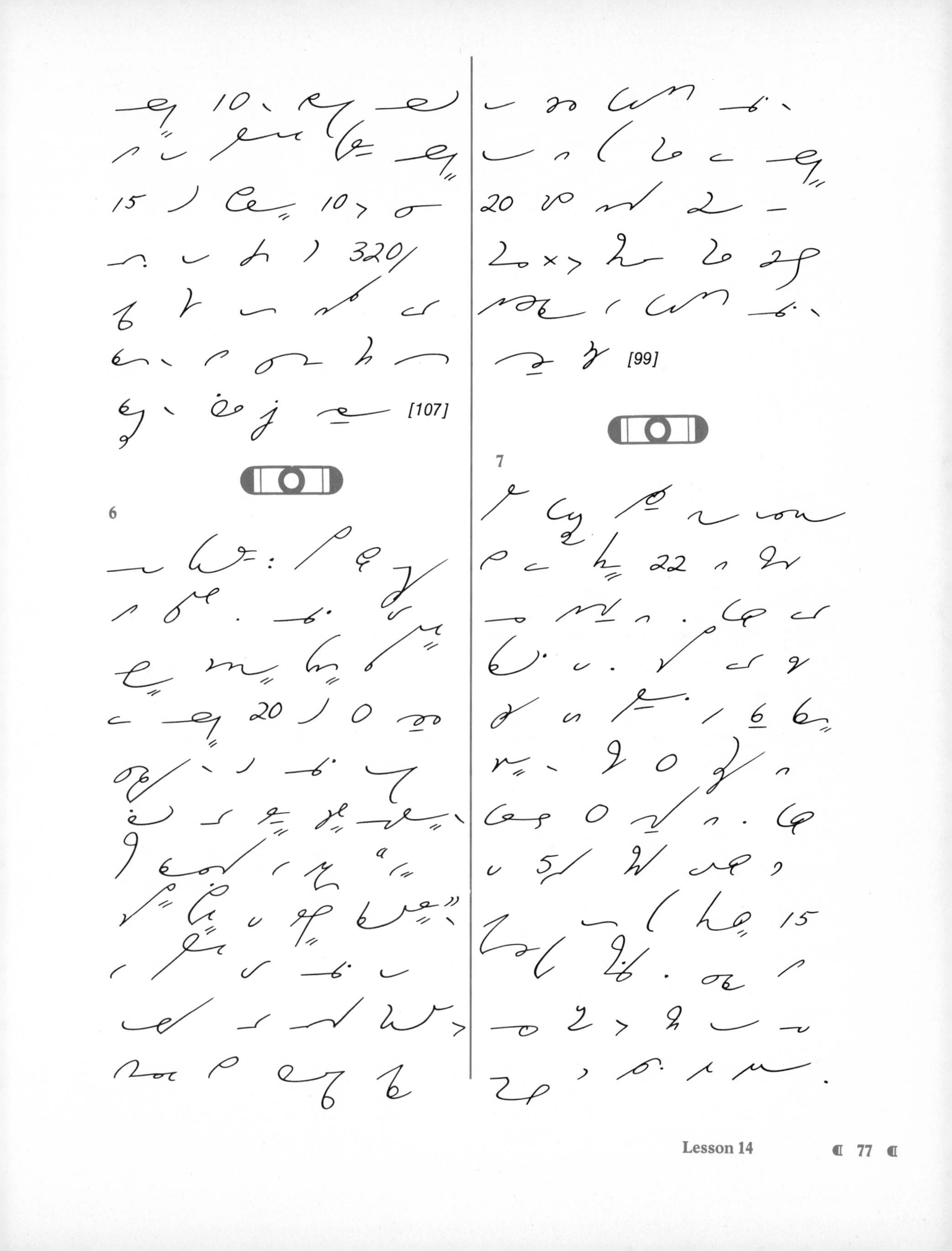

[107]

[99]

6

7

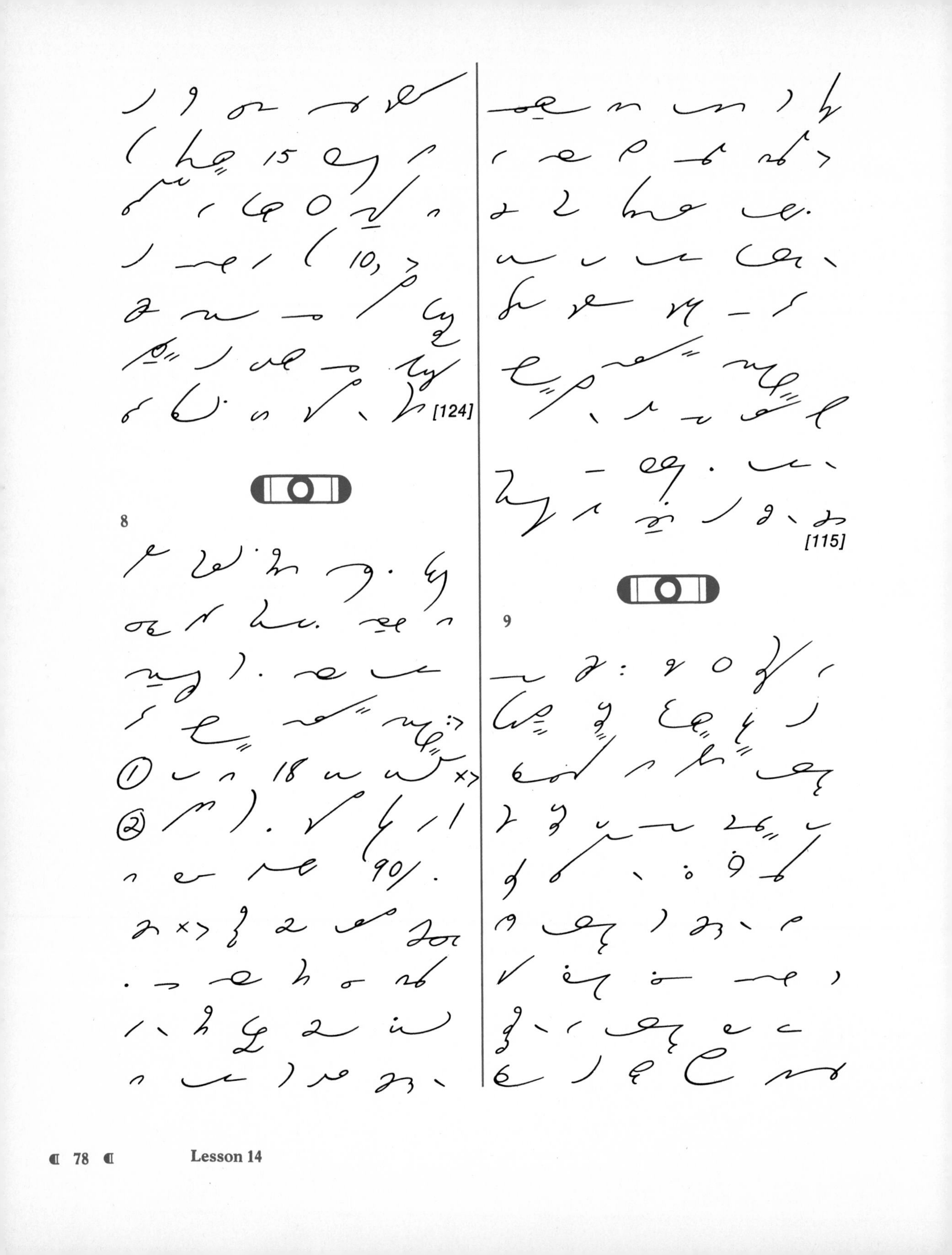

[124]

8

[115]

9

85/ 555-8702

85/ [78]

10

[90]

STUDY-HABIT CHECKLIST

No doubt as a conscientious student you do your home assignments regularly. Do you, however, derive the greatest benefit from the time you devote to practice?

You do if you practice in a quiet place where you can concentrate.

You don't if you practice with one eye on the television and the other on your text!

You do if, once you have started your assignment, you do not leave your desk or table until you have completed it.

You don't if you are constantly interrupted during your practice.

Principles

1 Brief Forms

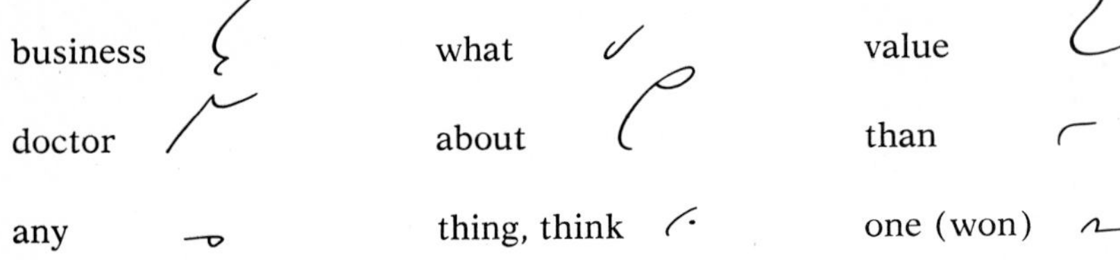

business	what	value
doctor	about	than
any	thing, think	one (won)

2 Brief-Form Derivatives

things, thinks	anything	businesses
thinking	once	businessman

◉ *Observe:* ☐ **1** *A disjoined left* s *is used to express* things, thinks.
☐ **2** *The plural of* business *is formed by adding another left* s.

3 Word Ending -ble The word ending-*ble* is represented by *b*.

Spell: p-o-s-bul, possible

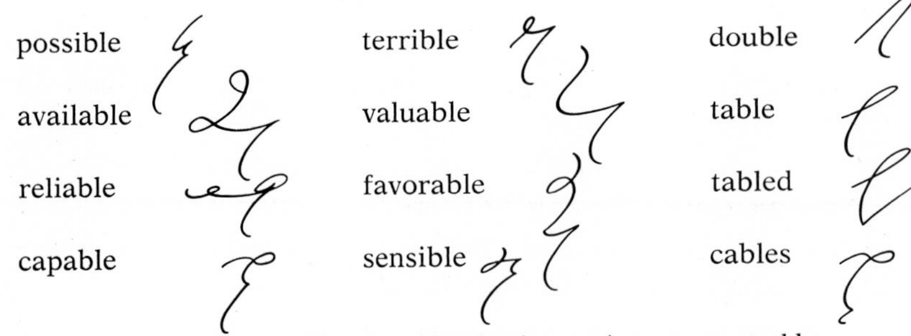

possible	terrible	double
available	valuable	table
reliable	favorable	tabled
capable	sensible	cables

4 Word Beginning Re- The word beginning *re-* is represented by *r*.

Spell: re-s-e-v, receive

receive	revise	reasonable

reply

repair

reappear

research

reception

rearrange

replace

receipt

reopen

Building Transcription Skills

5 Business Vocabulary Builder

sizable Very large.

jeopardize Place in great peril.

resolve Find an answer to.

Reading and Writing Practice

6 Brief-Form Letter

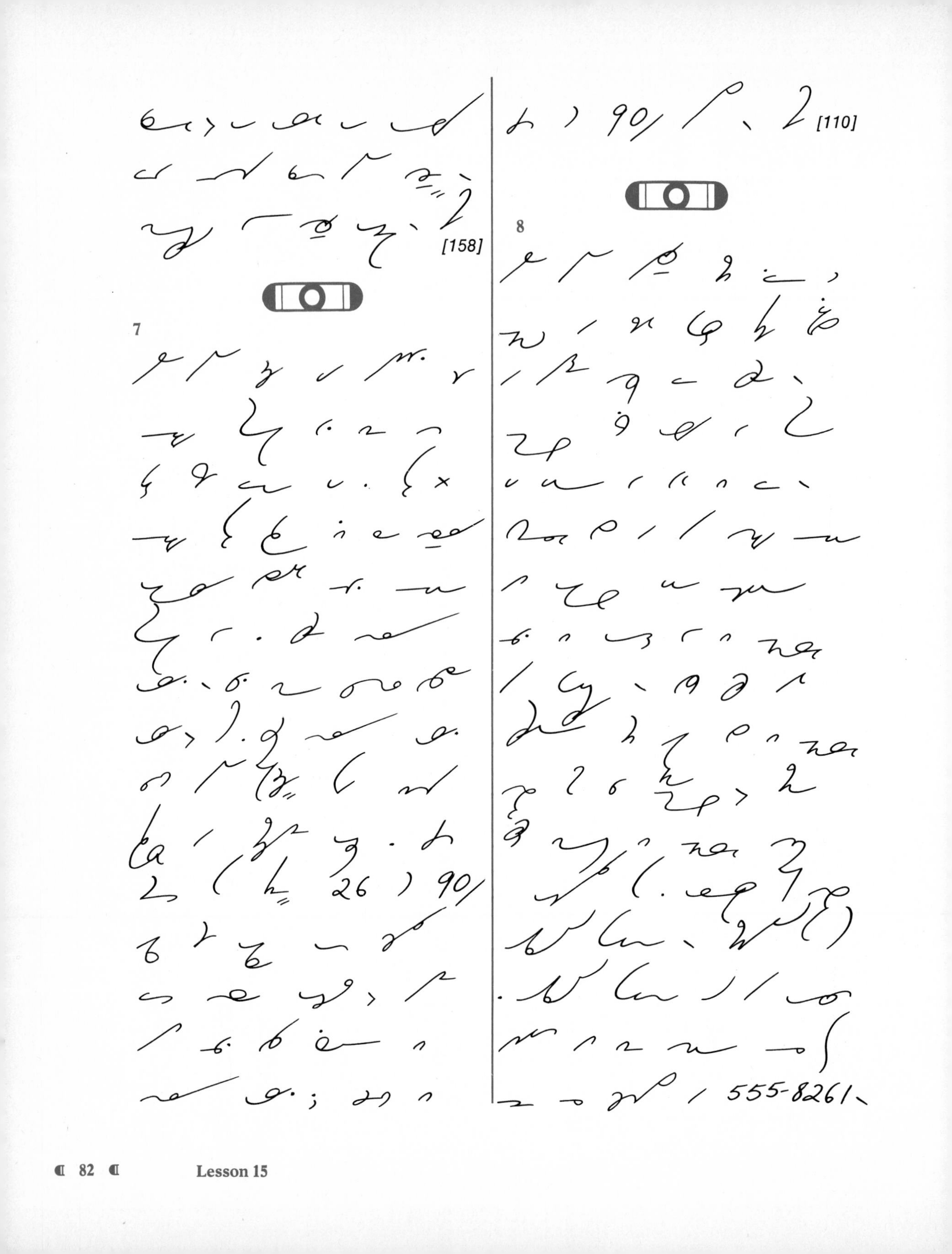

[158]

7

26 90

90 [110]

8

555-8261

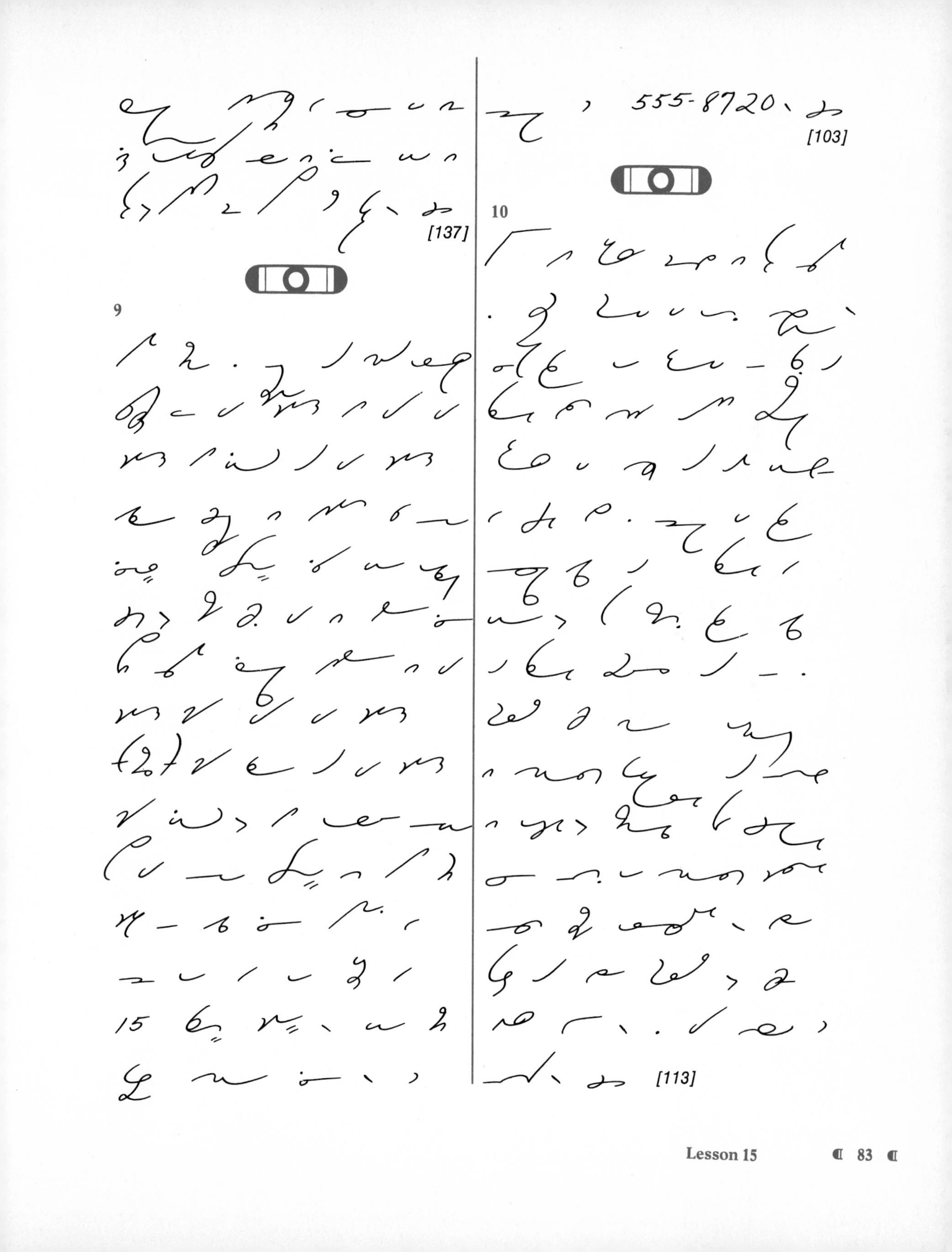

555-8720.

[137]

[103]

9

(2)

15

10

[113]

Principles

1 **Oi** The sound of *oi*, as in *toy*, is represented by [shorthand outline].

Spell: b-oi, boy

boy		oil		annoy	
toy		spoil		point	
join		boil		appoint	

2 **Men** The sound of *men* is represented by joining *m* and *n* into one long forward stroke.

Men

Compare: knee me many

Spell: men-e, many

men		mentioned		businessmen	
meant		women		mended	
mental		salesmen		immense	

3 **Min, Mon, Man** The similar sounding combinations *min, mon,* and *man* are also represented by the long forward stroke that represents *men*.

Spell: men-e-t, minute; men-r, manner

minute		month		manner	
minimum		money		manage	

4 Ye, Ya *Ye*, as in *year*, is represented by the *e* circle; *ya*, as in *yard*, by the *a* circle.

Spell: e-r, year; a-ärd, yard

Ye

year   yellow   yield

yet   yes   yielded

Ya

yard   yarn   Yale

Building Transcription Skills

5 Business Vocabulary Builder

solicit Try to obtain; ask for.

pledges *(noun)* Binding promises or agreements.

eligible Qualified to be chosen.

hazard A source of danger.

Reading and Writing Practice

6 Brief-Form Review Letter

[152]

7

[141]

8

[82]

9

[93]

10

[97]

Principles

1 **Brief Forms** When you have learned the following eight brief forms, you will have learned more than half the brief forms of Gregg Shorthand.

gentlemen company short

morning manufacture important, importance

where next

2 **Word Beginnings Per-, Pur-** The word beginnings *per-, pur-* are represented by *p-r*.

Spell: pur-s-n, person; pur-chay-a-s, purchase

Per-

person perfect persist

personal permanent perhaps

permit personnel persuade

Pur-

purchase purple purpose

3 **Word Beginnings De-, Di-** The word beginnings *de-, di-* are represented by *d*.

Spell: de-l-a, delay; de-r-e-k-t, direct

De-

delay deposit decide

deserve	deliver	decision
desirable	depended	design

Di-

direct	direction	directly

Building Transcription Skills

4 **SIMILAR-WORDS DRILL**

The English language contains many groups of words that sound alike, but each member of the group is spelled differently and has its own meaning.

Example: sent (dispatched); **scent** (a smell); **cent** (a coin).

In addition, there are many groups of words that sound almost alike.

Example: defer (to put off); **differ** (to disagree).

The secretary who is not alert may, while transcribing, select the wrong member of the group, with the result that the transcript makes no sense.

In this lesson and in a number of other lessons that follow, you will find a Similar-Words Drill that will call to your attention similar words which may cause the unwary transcriber to stumble.

Study these words carefully.

SIMILAR-WORDS DRILL • personal, personnel

personal Individual; private; pertaining to the person or body.

He is traveling on *personal* business.
You should watch your *personal* appearance with care.

personnel The people who work for a firm; the staff.

Yesterday I read your *personnel* policies booklet.
You can rely on our *personnel* to give you good service.

5 **wildcat strike** A work stoppage that does not have the approval of the union.

Business Vocabulary Builder

imaginative Having creative ability.

deadline A time or date before which something must be done.

Reading and Writing Practice

6 Brief-Form Letter

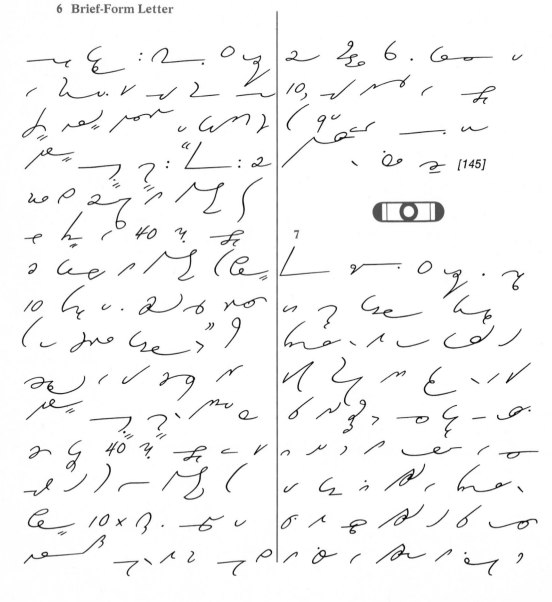

[145]

7

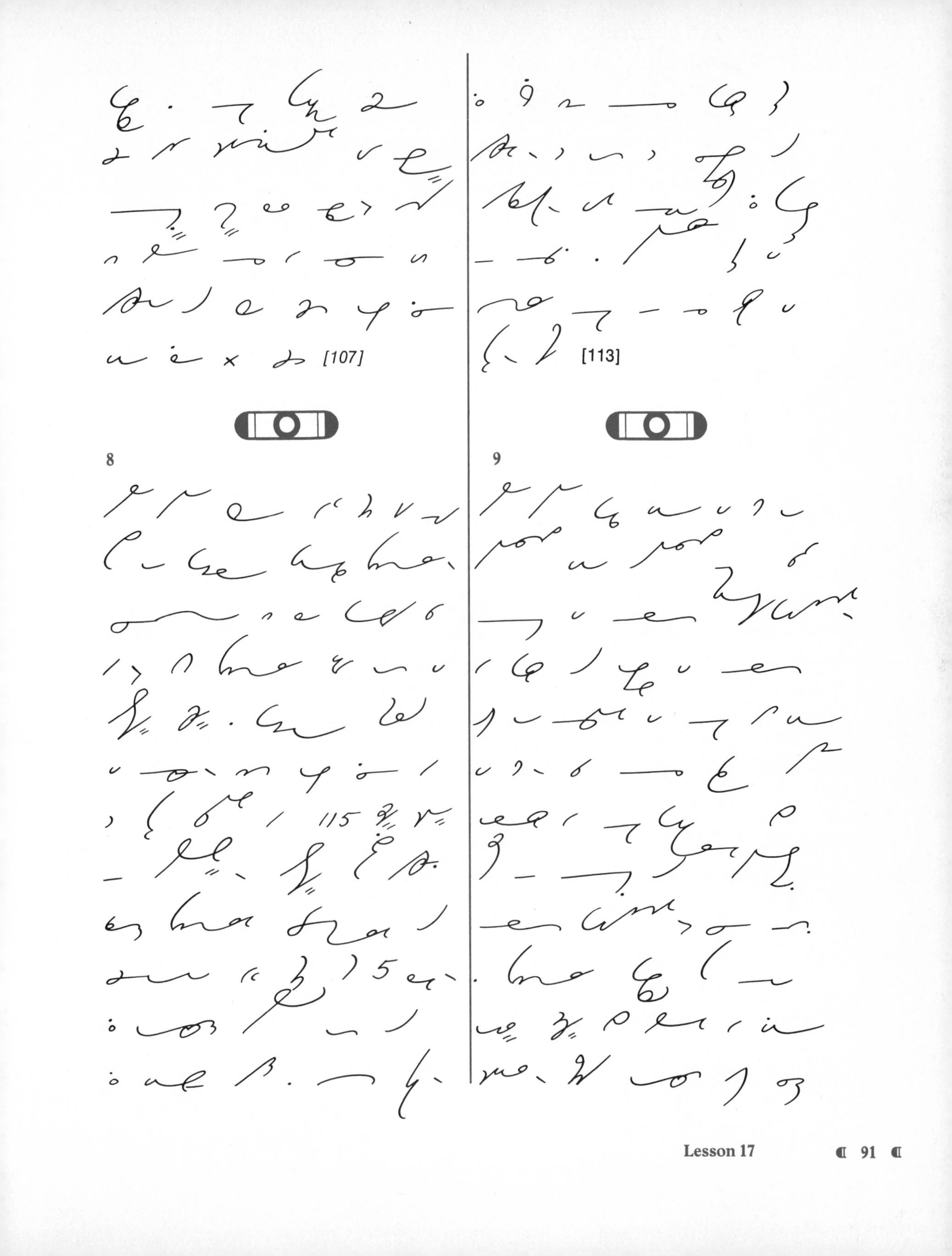

[107]

[113]

8

115 … 5

9

[103]

10

[93]

11

[104]

RECALL

Lesson 18 is another "breather." It contains no new shorthand devices for you to learn. In this lesson you will find: (1) several principles of joining, (2) a recall chart, (3) a Reading and Writing Practice that you will find interesting and informative.

Principles of Joining

1 At the beginning of a word and after *k*, *gay*, or a downstroke, the combination *oo-s* is written without an angle.

husky gust just

but

loose does rust

2 The word beginning *re-* is represented by *r* before a downstroke or a vowel.

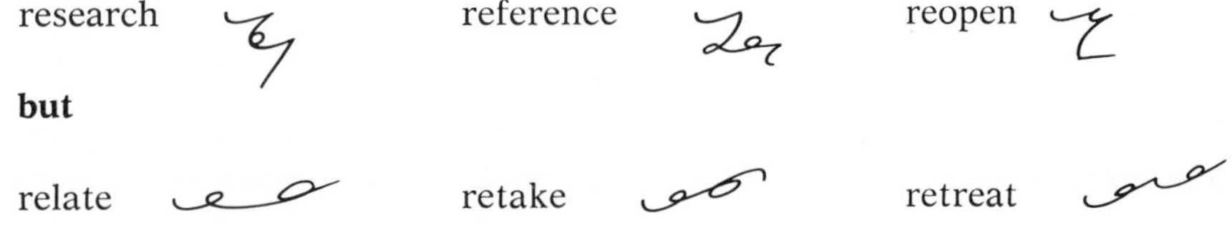

research reference reopen

but

relate retake retreat

3 The word beginnings *de-*, *di-* are represented by *d* except before *k* or *gay*.

depressed deliver direction

but

declare decay degrade

4 As you have perhaps already noticed from your study of Lessons 1 through 17, the past tense of a verb is formed by adding the stroke for the sound that is heard in the past tense. In some words the past tense has the sound of *t*, as in *baked*; in others, it has the sound of *d*, as in *saved*. In some words, the past tense is incorporated in a blend, as in *planned, feared, mailed.*

baked saved feared

missed planned mailed

5 **Recall Chart** The following chart reviews the brief forms of Chapter 3 as well as the shorthand devices you studied in Chapters 1, 2, and 3.

The chart contains 96 words and phrases. Can you read it in 8 minutes or less?

BRIEF FORMS AND DERIVATIVES

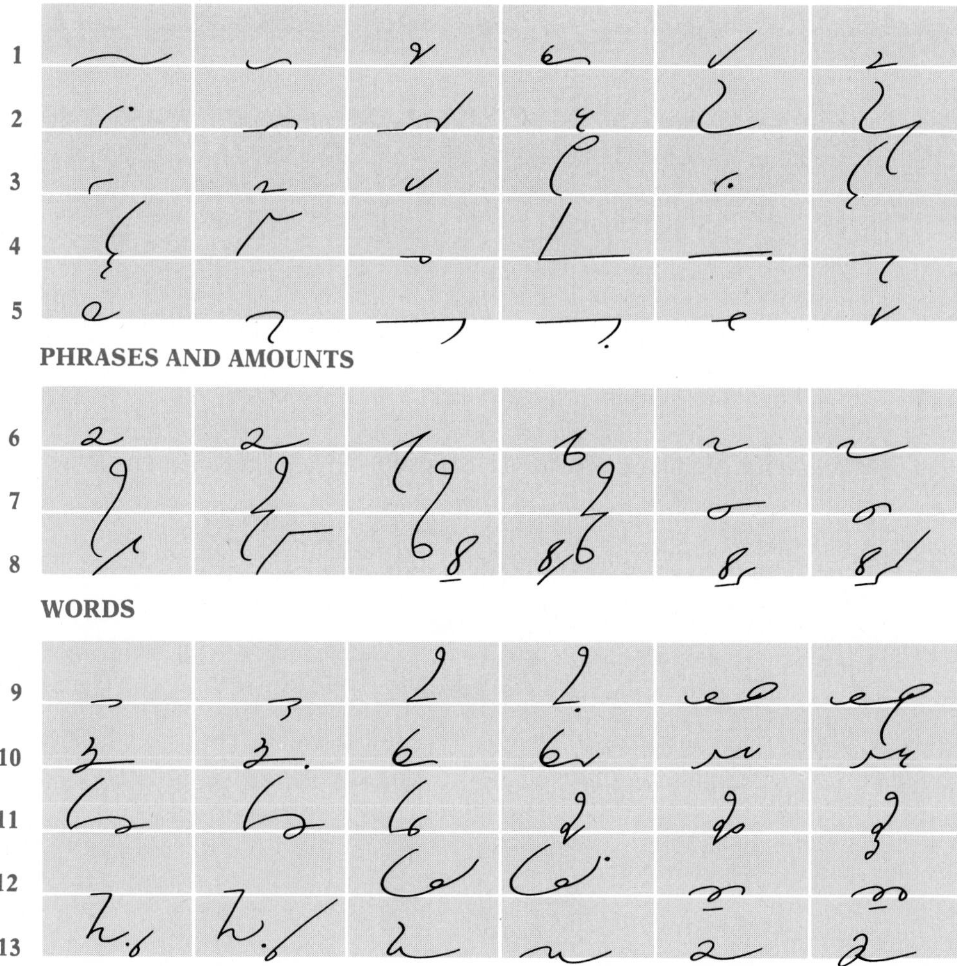

1
2
3
4
5

PHRASES AND AMOUNTS

6
7
8

WORDS

9
10
11
12
13

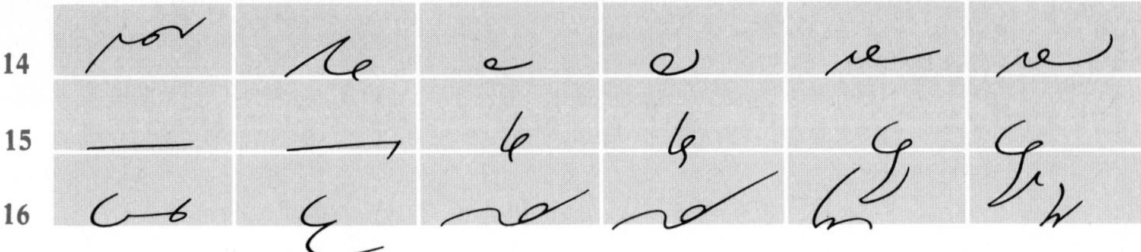

Building Transcription Skills

6 Business Vocabulary Builder

absorb Take in or take up, like a sponge.

emerges Comes out of.

passive Not active or operating.

Reading and Writing Practice

Reading Scoreboard One of the factors in measuring shorthand growth is the rate at which you can read shorthand. Here is an opportunity for you to measure your reading speed on the *first reading* of the material in Lesson 18. The following table will help you determine how rapidly you can read shorthand.

LESSON 18 CONTAINS 531 WORDS

If you read Lesson 18 in	your reading rate is
20 minutes	**27 words a minute**
24 minutes	**22 words a minute**
28 minutes	**19 words a minute**
32 minutes	**17 words a minute**
36 minutes	**15 words a minute**
40 minutes	**13 words a minute**

If you can read through Lesson 18 the first time in less than 20 minutes, you are doing well indeed. If you take considerably longer than 40 minutes, here are some questions you should ask yourself:

☐ **1** Am I spelling each outline I cannot read immediately?

☐ **2** Am I spending too much time deciphering an outline that I cannot read even after spelling it?

☐ **3** Should I perhaps reread the directions for reading shorthand on page 10?

After you have determined your reading rate, make a record of it in some convenient place. You can then watch your reading rate grow as you time yourself on the Reading Scoreboards in later lessons.

7 Be a Good Listener

There are

Speed of Talking and Listening.

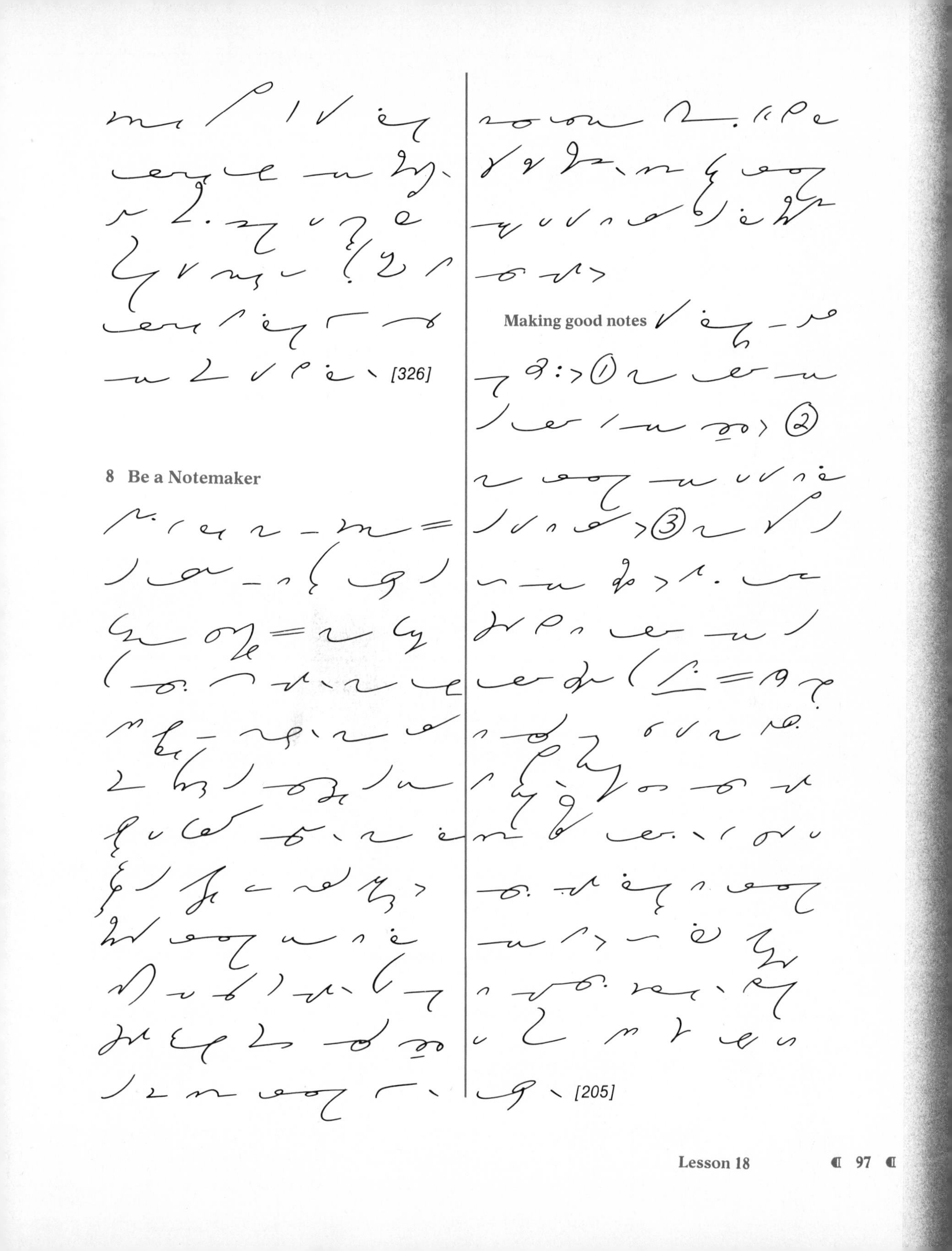

[326]

8 Be a Notemaker

Making good notes

[205]

4 YOUR COLLEGE EDUCATION—A DEFINITE PLUS

When you are considered for a secretarial position, your basic skills will of course be evaluated. But your general educational background is an important factor that will also be considered.

You will be a more valuable employee if you have more than your basic skills and a high school diploma to offer because of the additional knowledge you can bring to a job. A secretary who is a college graduate has a wider range of knowledge and greater familiarity with areas common to all businesses—economics, finance, management, and general business organization. Moreover, you will be considered a mature, sophisticated individual.

You—not just your employer—will benefit from your college education. Because you can bring added knowledge and training to the job, a prospective employer will be willing to hire you for a high-level secretarial position at a high starting salary. Once you are hired, you will be given greater opportunities for advancement.

Although you will have a college degree, it must be supplemented by performance. Once you're on the job, you will have to prove yourself by carrying out your assigned duties efficiently, effectively, and willingly. Your educational background will lose its value if you do not back it up with on-the-job performance.

Make the most of your time in college. Your education will not only make you more interesting to others; it will also widen your horizons and help you to obtain a good, profitable job.

Principles

1 Brief Forms Here is another group of brief forms—only six this time.

part	Ms.	opportunity
present	advertise	immediate

2 U The sound of *u*, as in *use*, is represented by .

Spell: u-s, use

use	review	unite
few	unit	pure
view	unique	acute

3 Word Ending -ment The word ending *-ment* is represented by *m*.

Spell: p-a-ment, payment

payment	department	settlement
management	equipment	treatment
shipment	movement	element
advertisement	replacement	assignment

◉ *Observe that in* assignment, *the* m *is joined to the* n *with a jog.*

4 Word Ending -tial The word ending *-tial* (also spelled *-cial*) is represented by *ish.*

Spell: s-p-e-shul, special

special	financial	initial
especial	social	initially
partial	official	initialed

Building Transcription Skills

5 SPELLING

When you look at the letter on page 102, you get a very favorable first impression. The letter is tastefully positioned; the right-hand margin is even; the date, inside address, and closing are all in their proper places. When you scan the letter casually, you find that it makes good sense and apparently represents what the dictator said.

But that favorable first impression will vanish when you read the letter carefully. In fact, you will quickly realize that it will never be signed and that the dictator will have some harsh words for the stenographer who transcribed the letter. Why? It contains several misspelled words. No business executive will knowingly sign a letter that contains a misspelled word!

If you are to succeed as a secretary, your letters must not only be accurate transcripts of what your employer dictated, but they must also be free of spelling errors. A secretary who regularly submits letters for the employer's signature that contain spelling errors will not be a secretary long!

To make sure that you will be able to spell correctly when you have completed your shorthand course, you will from this point on give special attention to spelling in each Reading and Writing Practice.

As you read the Reading and Writing Practice, you will occasionally find shorthand outlines printed in color. These outlines represent words that stenographers and secretaries often misspell. When you encounter an outline printed in color, finish reading the sentence in which it occurs; then glance at the margin, where you will find the word in type, properly spelled and syllabicated.

Spell the word aloud if possible, pausing slightly after each word division. (The word divisions indicated are those given in *Webster's New Collegiate Dictionary*.)

6 Business Vocabulary Builder

unique The only one of its kind.

car accessories Items such as radios, heaters, tire chains, and so on.

installment One part of a repayment plan.

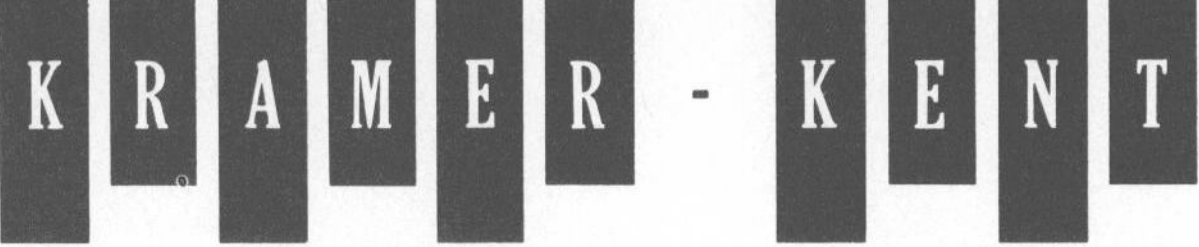

10 MAGNOLIA STREET • LOUISVILLE • KENTUCKY • 40205

September 22, 19--

Miss Jane Smith
112 Main Avenue
Seattle, WA 98117

Dear Miss Smith:

It is a comfortible feeling to know that the heating system in your home does not have to depend on the elements. Snow and ice cannot leave you shiverring when you heat with gas. It travels under ground.

The dependability of gas is only one of its many virtues. A gas heat system costs less to instal and less to operate. It needs lots less serviceing, and it lasts longer. It has no odor and makes no filmy deposits that cause extra work.

No wonder more than 400,000 users of other feuls changed to gas last year.

Why not let us show you how easy it is to instal gas heat in your home.

Yours truely,

Thomas A. Frost

Thomas A. Frost
Sales Manager

TAF:re

Can you find all the errors in this letter?

Reading and Writing Practice

7 Brief-Form Letter

spe·cial

pur·chased

ac·ces·so·ries

20 5 5 81, 62, 5 555-9864 [201]

8

in·stall·ment

15 6

cou·pon

ful·fill

book·keep·ing

[163]

Di·rec·tor

ef·fi·cient

[145]

9

Fi·nan·cial

10

[61]

Principles

1 Ow The sound of *ow*, as in *now*, is written .

Spell: n-ow, now

now	south	how
down	loud	house
sound	account	ounce
found	round	crowd

2 Word Ending -ther The word ending *-ther*, as in *other*, is represented by *ith*.

Spell: oo-ther, other

other	mother	either
another	gather	bother
whether (weather)	brother	bothered

3 Word Beginning Con- The word beginning *con-*, as in *confer*, is represented by *k*.

Spell: con-f-e-r, confer

confer	considerable	concrete
concert	control	contract
convey	convince	contest

4 Word Beginning Com- The word beginning *com-*, as in *complete,* is also represented by *k*.

Spell: com-p-l-e-t, complete

complete compliment combine
computer compare accomplish

5 Con-, Com- Followed by a Vowel When *con-, com-* are followed by a vowel, these word beginnings are represented by *kn* or *km*.

connect commit commercial
connection commerce accommodate

Building Transcription Skills

6 Business Vocabulary Builder

complimentary Flattering; free.
convey Give or deliver to another.
conserve Avoid wasteful use of; save.

Reading and Writing Practice

7 Brief-Form Review Letter

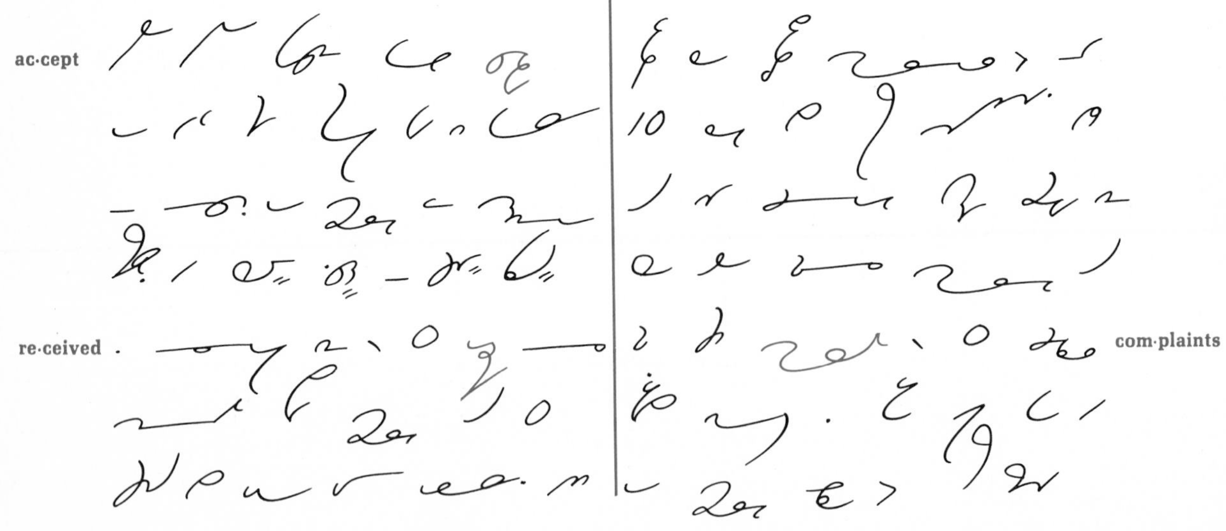

250
[131]

8

con·ven·tion

an·nounce·ment

pro·fi·cien·cy

ac·com·plish·ments

[118]

9

unique

com·plete

555-1818

ma·jor

[143]

[119]

10

cri·sis

11

amounts

slipped

con·crete

[94]

Principles

1 Brief Forms

advantage — several — ever, every
suggest — out — very

2 Ten By rounding off the angle between *t-n*, we obtain the fluent *ten* blend.

Ten

Spell: ten-d, tend; k-o-ten, cotton

tend — potential — bulletin
attend — competent — stand
attention — consistent — cotton
tentative — straighten — tonight

3 Den The stroke that represents *t-n* also represents *d-n*.

Spell: den-ī, deny

deny — evidence — danger
dentist — condense — dinner
sudden — president — guidance

4 Tain The stroke that represents *t-n, d-n* also represents *-tain*.

Spell: o-b-tain, obtain

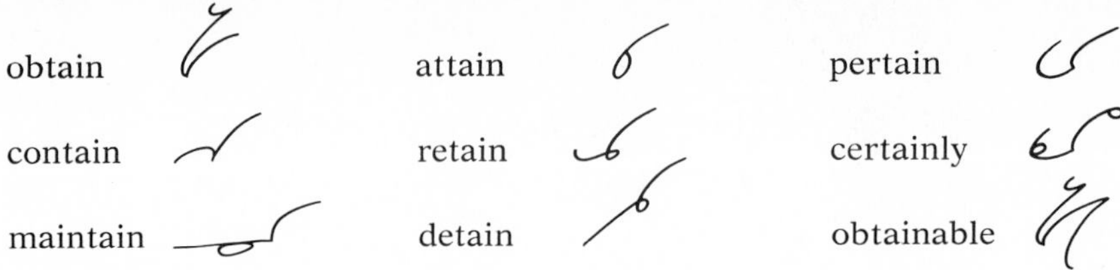

Building Transcription Skills

5 Business Vocabulary Builder

residential Pertaining to the home or residence.

materialize Come into existence; appear.

anticipate Foresee and deal with in advance.

Reading and Writing Practice

6 Brief-Form Letter

in·stall·ing

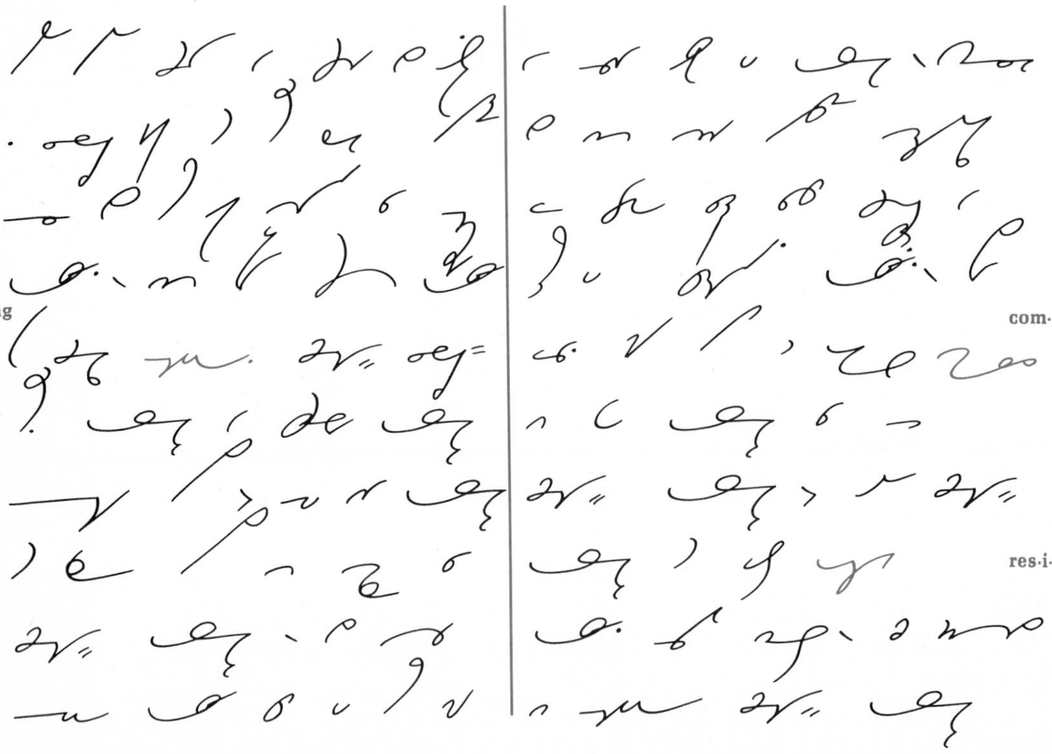

com·plete·ly

res·i·den·tial

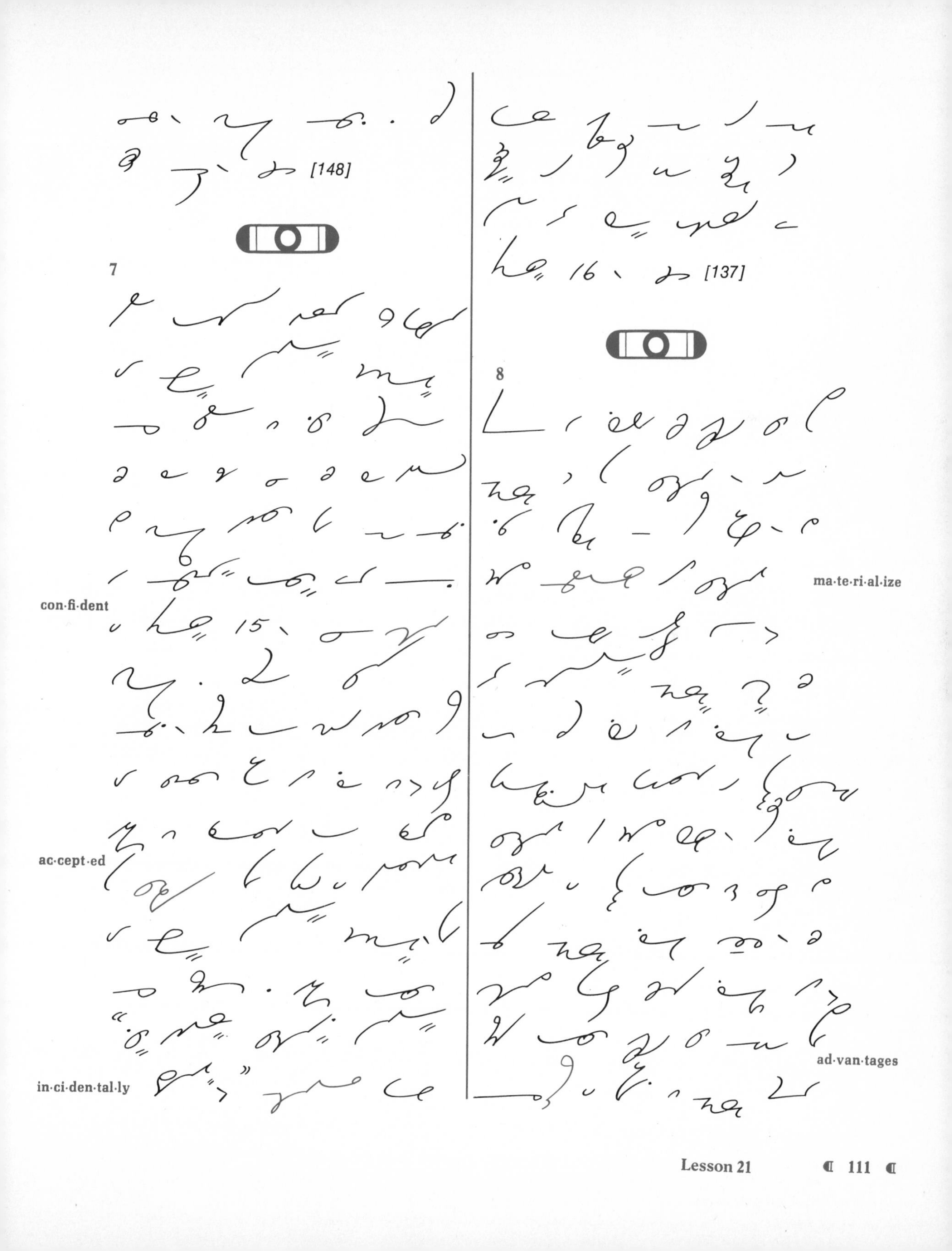

[148]

7

con·fi·dent

ac·cept·ed

in·ci·den·tal·ly

[137]

8

ma·te·ri·al·ize

ad·van·tages

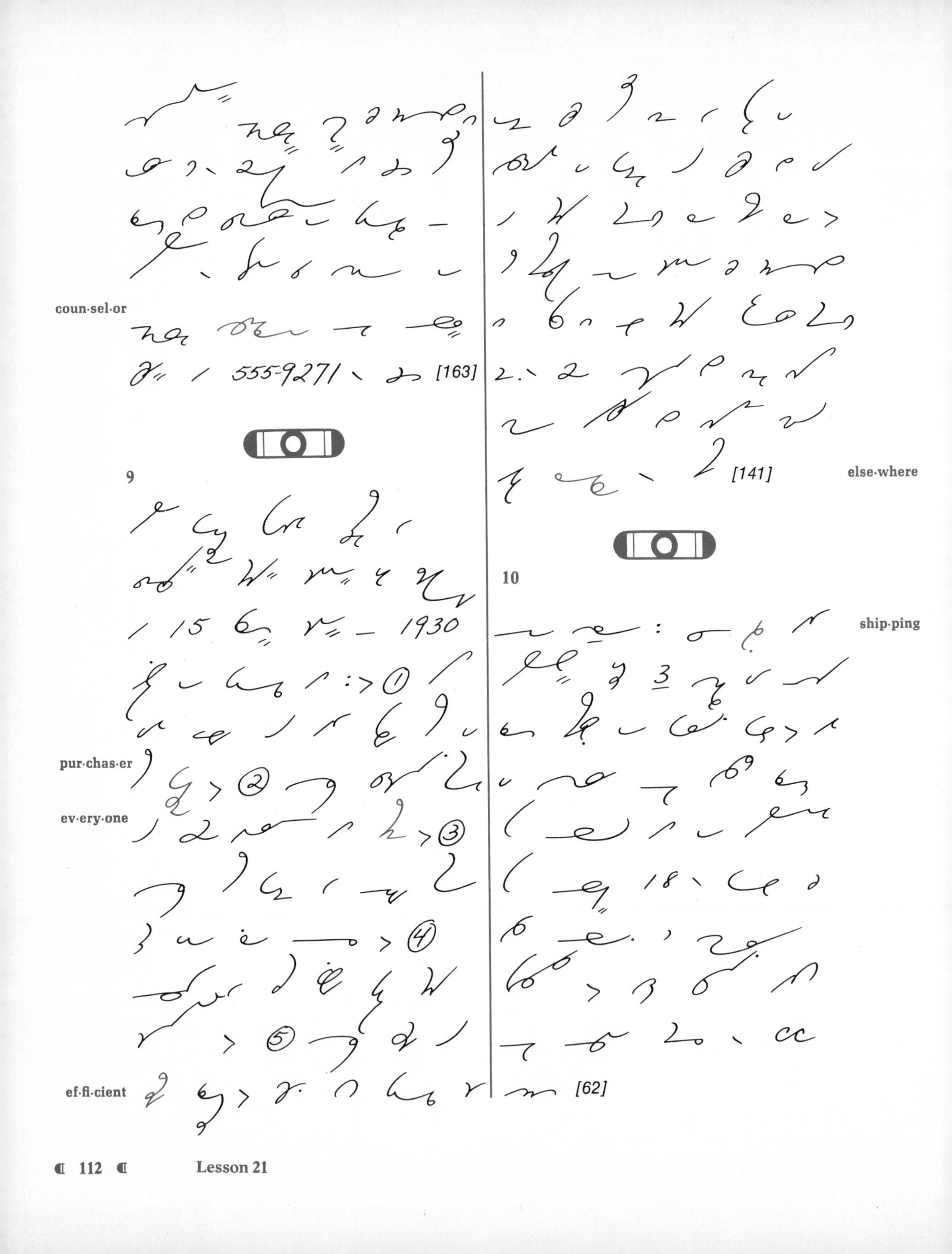

coun·sel·or

555-9271 [163]

9

15 1930

(1) (2) (3) (4) (5)

pur·chas·er

ev·ery·one

ef·fi·cient

2.

[141]

else·where

10

ship·ping

3

18

cc

[62]

Principles

1 Tem By rounding off the angle between *t-m*, we obtain the fluent *tem* blend.

Tem

Compare: ten tem

Spell: tem-p-r, temper

temper attempt estimate

temporary item customer

system contemplate tomorrow

2 Dem The stroke that represents *t-m* also represents *d-m*.

Spell: dem-a-end, demand; m-e-dem, medium

demand seldom domestic

demonstrate freedom damage

demonstration random medium

3 Business Abbreviations Here are additional salutations and closings often used in business letters.

Dear Mrs. Dear Miss Cordially yours

Dear Mr. Dear Ms. Yours sincerely

4 **Useful Phrases** With the *ten* and *tem* blends, we can form three very useful phrases.

to know | to me | to make

5 **Days of the Week**

Sunday

Monday

Tuesday

Wednesday

Thursday

Friday

Saturday

6 **Months of the Year** You are already familiar with the shorthand forms for several of the months as they are written in full. Here are all 12 months.

January

February

March

April

May

June

July

August

September

October

November

December

Building Transcription Skills

7 **Business Vocabulary Builder**

contemplate Consider; think of doing.

surpass Go beyond.

contagious Catching.

irreparably Permanently damaged; not able to be repaired.

Reading and Writing Practice

8 **Brief-Form Review Letter**

do·mes·tic

tem·po·rary

ten·ants

30

25

150

31

60

[184]

9

[132]

10

10 … 10 … [118]

shop·ping

nour·ish·ing

erod·ing

11

250/ … 30 … [105]

law·yer

ir·rep·a·ra·bly

12

[117]

13

[89]

SHORTHAND READING CHECKLIST

When you read shorthand, be sure to:

■ 1 Read aloud so that you know that you are concentrating on each outline that you read.

■ 2 Spell each outline that you cannot immediately read.

■ 3 Reread each lesson a second time.

■ 4 Occasionally reread the suggestions for reading shorthand given on pages 10 and 12.

Principles

1 Brief Forms After this group, you have only four more groups to learn.

acknowledge		time		organize	
general		question		over*	

*The outline for *over* is written above the following shorthand stroke. It is also used as a prefix form, as in:

oversight		overdo		overcame	

2 Def, Dif By rounding off the angle between *d-f*, we obtain the fluent *def, dif* blend.

Def, Dif

Spell: def-ī, defy; def-r, differ

defy		define		differ	
defied		definite		different	
defeat		defect		difference	

3 Div, Dev The stroke that represents *def, dif* also represents *div* and *dev*.

Spell: div-ī-d, divide; dev-o-t, devote

divide		dividend		devote	
division		develop		devotion	

4 Ea, Ia The sounds of *ea,* as in *create,* and *ia,* as in *piano,* are represented by a large circle with a dot placed within it.

Spell: k-r-eah-t, create

create		appropriate		piano	
area		appreciate		brilliant	
recreation		aviation		initiate	

Building Transcription Skills

5 SIMILAR-WORDS DRILL ● to, too, two

to *(preposition)* In the direction of. (*To* is also the sign of the infinitive.)

15

I gave the book *to* Kay.
I will go back *to* work on May 15.

too Also; more than enough.

I, *too,* have a college degree.
You make *too* many telephone calls.

two One plus one.

I will need *two* days to finish the job.

6 Business Vocabulary Builder

creative Having the ability to produce through imagination.
recreational Relating to the refreshment of strength or spirit after work.
appropriation An amount of money set aside for a specific purpose.

Reading and Writing Practice

7 Brief-Form Letter

may·or

cam·paign·ing

cit·i·zens

[141]

8

1950

its

com·plete·ly

copy·ing

[171]

9

As·so·ciates

urge

[163]

10

de·vel·op·ing

too

ac·knowl·edg·ment

pro·ceed

[177]

11

ef·fec·tive

15

[68]

12

Feb·ru·ary

1960

dur·ing

50

4

5

[101]

RECALL

In Lesson 24 you will have no new shorthand devices to learn; you will have a little time to "digest" the devices that you studied in previous lessons. In Lesson 24 you will find a new feature—Accuracy Practice—that will help you improve your shorthand writing style.

Accuracy Practice

The speed and accuracy with which you will be able to transcribe your shorthand notes will depend on how well you write them. If you follow the suggestions given in this lesson when you work with each Accuracy Practice, you will soon find that you can read your own notes with greater ease and facility.

So that you may have a clear picture of the proper shapes of the shorthand strokes that you are studying, enlarged models of the alphabetic characters and of the typical joinings are given, together with a short explanation of the things that you should keep in mind as you practice.

To get the most out of each Accuracy Practice, follow this simple procedure:

☐ **a** Read the explanations carefully.

☐ **b** Study the model to see the application of each explanation.

☐ **c** Write the first outline in the Practice Drill.

☐ **d** Compare what you have written with the enlarged model.

☐ **e** Write three or four more copies of the outline, trying to improve your outline with each writing.

☐ **f** Repeat this procedure with the remaining outlines in the Practice Drill.

1 **R** **L** **K** **G**

To write these strokes accurately:

☐ **a** Start and finish each one on the same level of writing.

☐ **b** Make the **beginning** of the curve in **r** and **l** deep. Make the **end** of the curve in **k** and **g** deep.

☐ **c** Make the **l** and **g** considerably longer than **r** and **k**.

Practice Drill

Are-our-hour, will-well, can, good.
Air, lay, ache, gate.

2 **K-r** **R-k** **G-l**

To write these combinations accurately:

☐ **a** Make the curves rather flat.

☐ **b** Make the combinations **kr** and **rk** somewhat shorter than the combined length of **r** and **k** when written separately.

☐ **c** Make the combination **gl** somewhat shorter than the combined length of **g** and **l** when written separately.

Practice Drill

Cream, crate, maker, mark, dark.
Gleam, glean, glare, eagle.

3 **Recall Chart** This chart contains the brief forms in Chapter 4 and illustrations of all the shorthand devices you have studied in Chapters 1 through 4.

The chart contains 96 shorthand outlines. Can you read the entire chart in 7 minutes or less?

WORDS

1

2

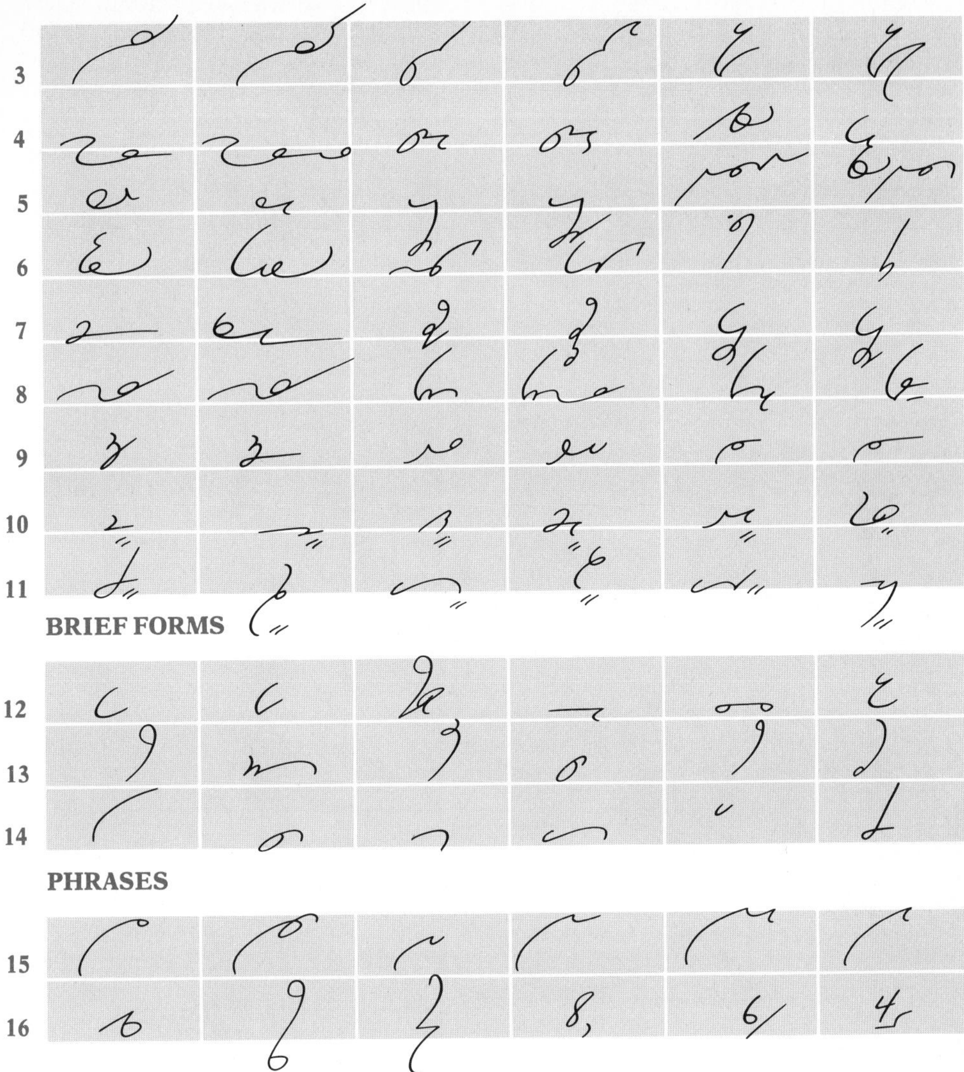

Building Transcription Skills

4 Business Vocabulary Builder

reputable Held in high esteem.
corrective Tending to right something that is wrong.
timid Shy; lacking in boldness.

Reading and Writing Practice

5 The Rights of a Consumer

com·plaints

re·venge

When to Complain.

rep·u·ta·ble

im·me·di·ate·ly

cus·tom·ers

Where to Complain.

pur·chase

cor·rec·tive

re·ceipts

tim·id

What Next?

str·in·gent

Identifying Problems.

vic·tim

de·ceived

fraud

le·git·i·mate

val·id

[607]

5 JOB SELECTION

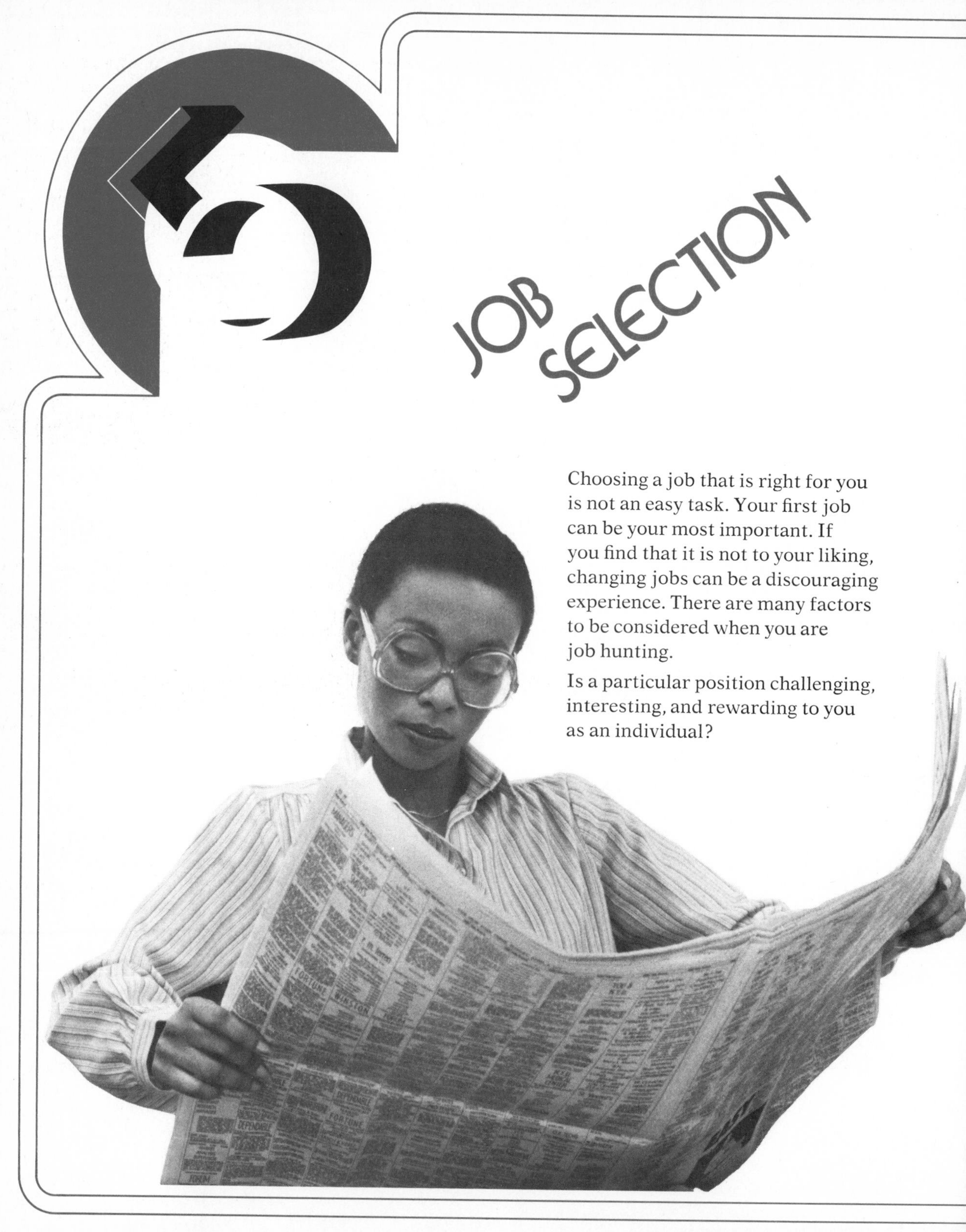

Choosing a job that is right for you is not an easy task. Your first job can be your most important. If you find that it is not to your liking, changing jobs can be a discouraging experience. There are many factors to be considered when you are job hunting.

Is a particular position challenging, interesting, and rewarding to you as an individual?

Are you interested in the field of publishing or banking or medicine?

Do you like what you've heard about a particular company you may have in mind?

Would you prefer being a small fish in the large pond of a nationwide corporation, or would you rather be in a small firm such as a local real estate agency?

If you live in the suburbs, do you want to travel into the city every day?

What are your chances for advancement, both professionally and financially?

Are you interested in special fringe benefits such as the reduced travel rates offered by airlines as well as the vacation, insurance, and hospitalization benefits offered by many organizations?

Finally, what is the starting salary? Since beginning salaries are basically equal in a particular area, this should not be your first or sole consideration; future opportunity for increases is the thing to consider. During an interview, you will probably be told the starting salary. Don't ask unless it is obvious that the interviewer is not going to bring up the subject.

Well-trained, skilled secretaries can *choose* the fields in which they wish to work because of the great demand for such people. The decision is yours.

Principles

1 Brief Forms

envelope	state	success
difficult	satisfy, satisfactory	wish
progress	request	under*

*The outline for *under* is written above the following shorthand stroke. It is also used as a prefix form, as in:

underneath	undertake	undermine

2 Cities and States In your work as a secretary, you will frequently have occasion to write geographical expressions. Here are a few important cities and states.

Cities

New York	Boston	Los Angeles
Chicago	Philadelphia	St. Louis

States

Michigan	Massachusetts	Missouri
Illinois	Pennsylvania	California

3 Useful Business Phrases The following phrases are used in business so frequently that special forms have been provided for them.

as soon as		to do		let us	
as soon as possible		of course		I hope	

Building Transcription Skills

4 Business Vocabulary Builder

influential Having the power to sway or convince.

tentative Not final; uncertain.

tailored Made to fit a special need or purpose.

Reading and Writing Practice

5 Brief-Form Letter

el·i·gi·ble

[188]

6

30

Bu·reau

90

[153]

7

[74]

8

fac·to·ry

com·ply

[125]

9

[130]

10

kitch·en

[105]

Principles

1 **Long Ī and a Following Vowel** Any vowel following long ī is represented by a small circle within a large circle.

Compare: signs science

Spell: t-r-īah-l, trial

trial	drier	compliance
dial	client	reliance
prior	quiet	appliances

2 **Word Beginnings En-, Un-** The word beginnings *en-, un-* are represented by *n.*

En-

Spell: en-j-oi, enjoy

enjoy	engagement	endanger
engrave	engine	encourage
endeavor	enlarge	encouragement

Un-

Spell: un-t-e-l, until

until	unfair	unfilled
unless	unpaid	unreasonable
undue	uncertain	undoubtedly

3 In-, En-, Un- Followed by a Vowel When *in-, en-, un-* are followed by a vowel, they are written in full.

innovation   enact   unable

4 Useful Business Phrases Here are six more frequently used business phrases.

more than   to us   your order

we hope   let me   you ordered

Building Transcription Skills

5 Business Vocabulary Builder

enlarged Made bigger.

fragile Easily broken or destroyed.

enlightening Furnishing knowledge or information.

Reading and Writing Practice

6 Brief-Form Review Letter

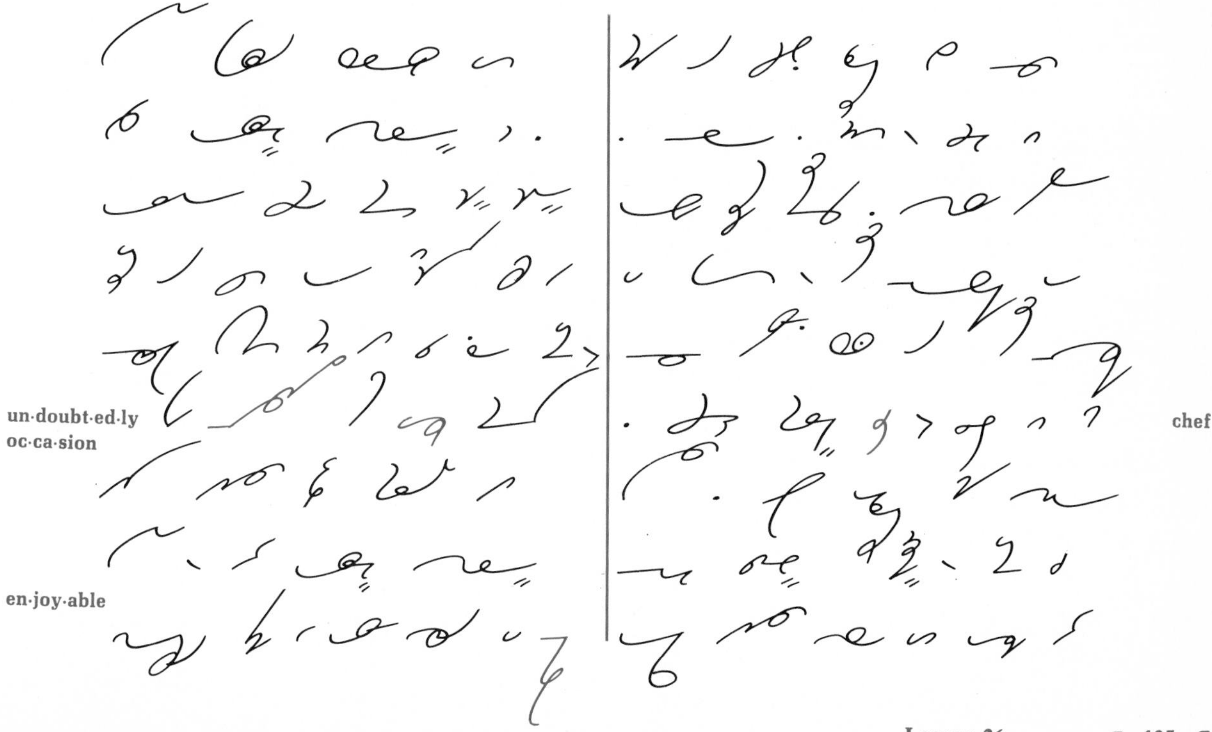

cal·en·dar

[178]

guar·an·tee

[138]

7

bag·gage

un·ques·tioned

8

de·vote

praise

[124]

9

un·col·lect·ible

350/

en·deav·ors

pri·or

los·ing

de·mise

in·ev·i·ta·ble

[200]

10

[27]

Principles

1 Brief Forms After you have learned the following brief forms, you will have only two more groups to go!

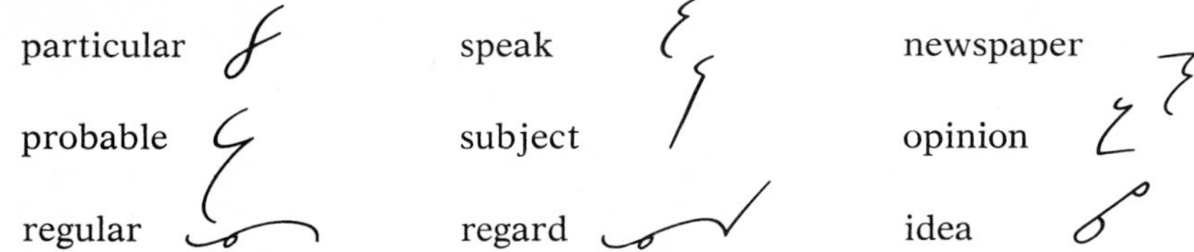

particular	speak	newspaper
probable	subject	opinion
regular	regard	idea

2 Ng The sound of *ng,* as in *sing,* is written 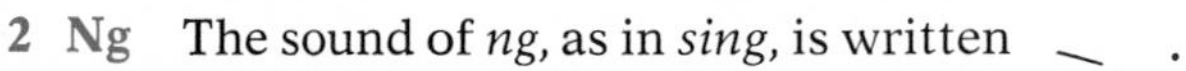.

Compare: seen sing

Spell: s-e-ing, sing

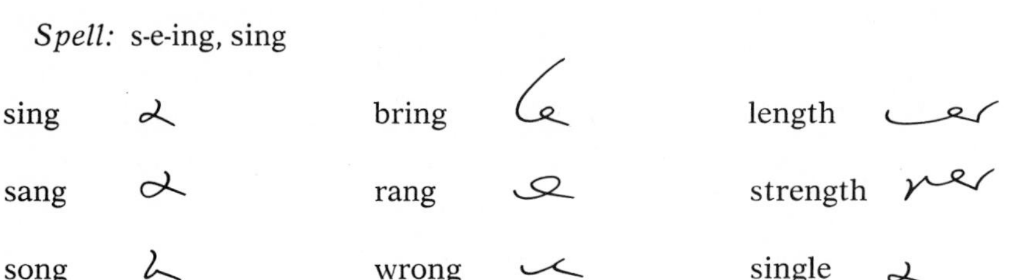

sing	bring	length
sang	rang	strength
song	wrong	single

3 Ngk The sound of *ngk,* as in *sink,* is written .

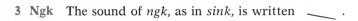

Compare: seem sink

Spell: r-a-ink, rank

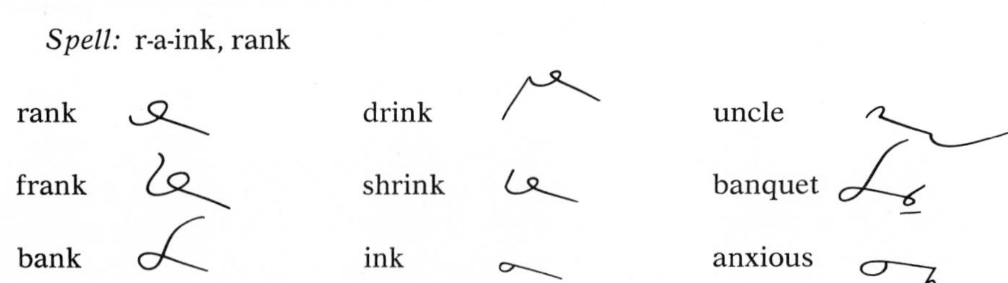

rank	drink	uncle
frank	shrink	banquet
bank	ink	anxious

4 Omission of Vowel Preceding -tion When *t, d, n,* or *m* is followed by *-ition* or *-ation,* the circle is omitted.

addition, quotation, permission, edition, combination, commission, notation, reputation, estimation

Building Transcription Skills

5 Business Vocabulary Builder

greenhouses Glassed buildings used for cultivating and protecting plants.

automation A technique often using electronic devices that take the place of human effort.

heirs Those who are entitled to inherit.

Reading and Writing Practice

6 Brief-Form Letter

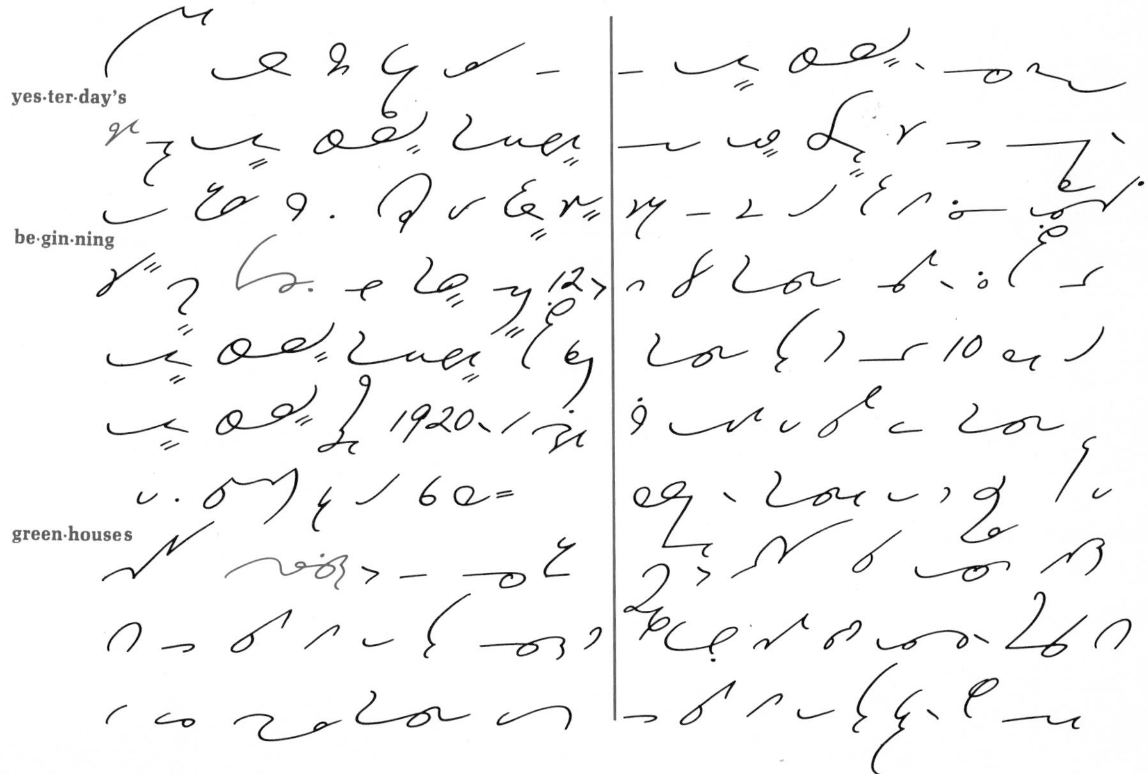

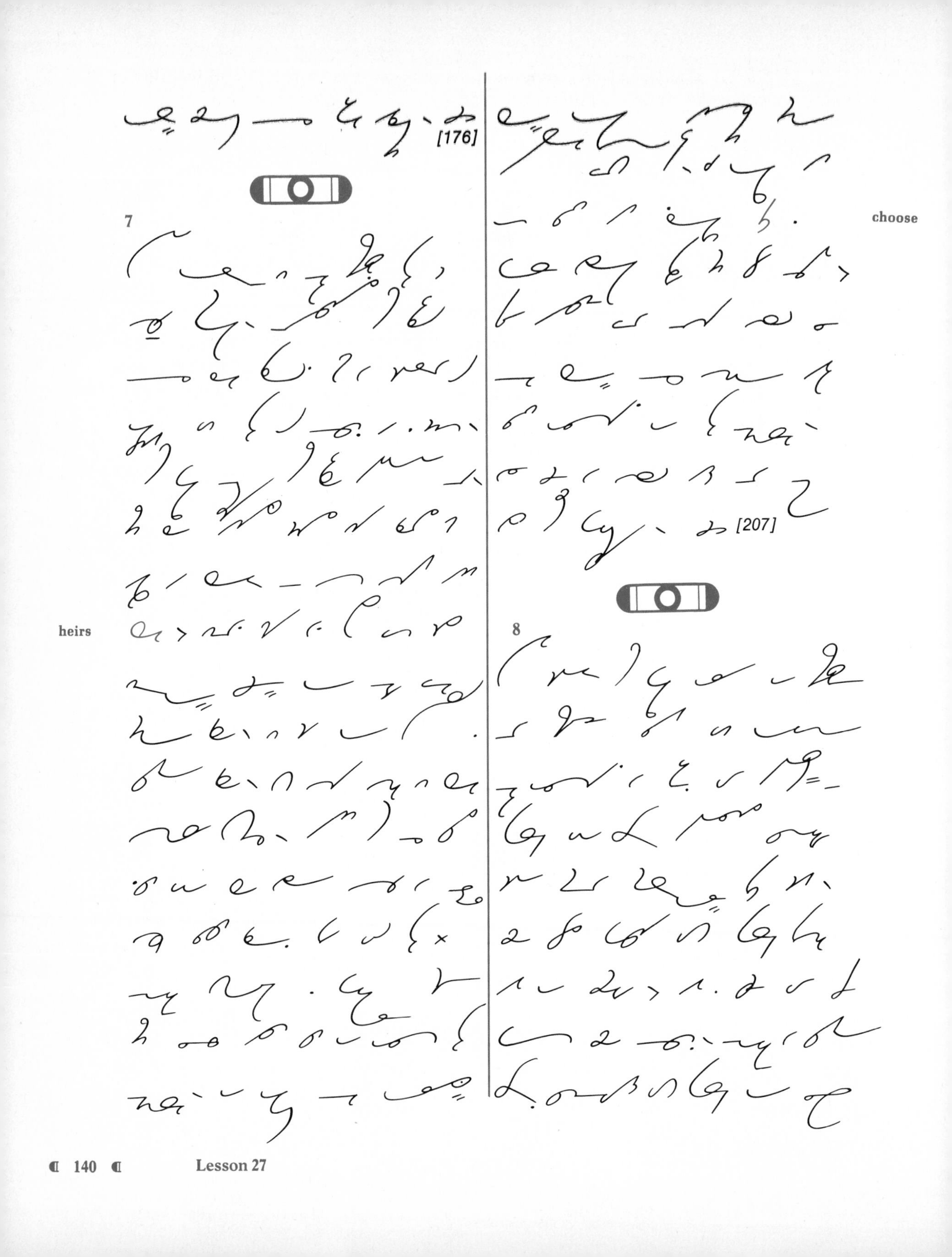

[176]

7

heirs

choose

[207]

8

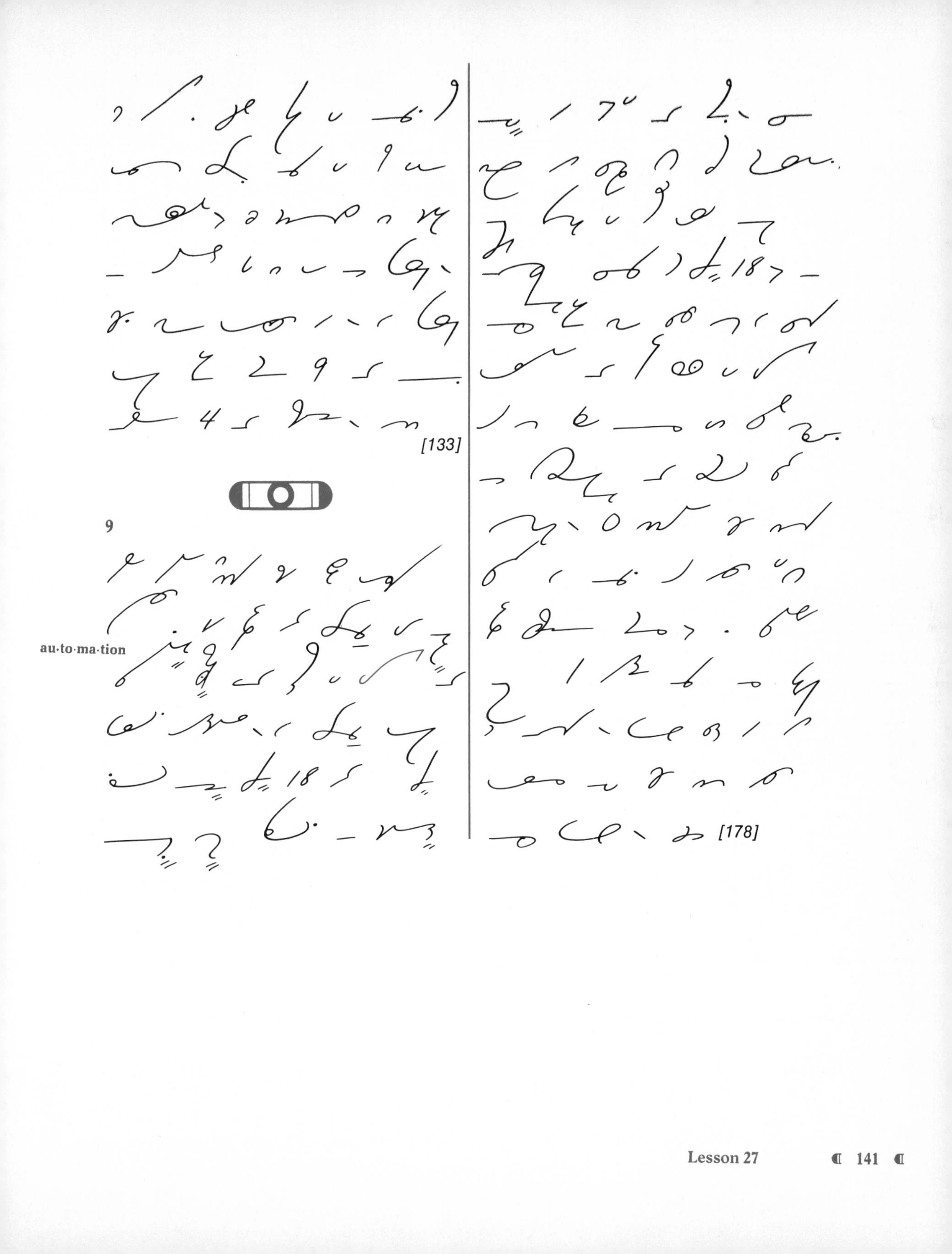

[133]

9

au·to·ma·tion

[178]

Principles

1 Ah, Aw A dot is used for *a* in words that begin *ah* and *aw*.

Spell: a-h-e-d, ahead; a-oo-a, away

ahead	awaken	awoke
away	awakened	award

2 X The letter *x* is represented by an *s* written with a slight backward slant.

Compare: miss mix

fees fix

Spell: t-a-ex, tax; t-a-exes, taxes

tax	relax	indexes
taxes	relaxes	approximate
box	relaxation	complex

3 Omission of Short U In the body of a word, the sound of short *u*, as in *fun*, is omitted before *n*, *m*, or a straight downstroke.

Before N

fun	done	lunch
begun	son (sun)	front

Before M

sum (some)   come   income

summer   become   column

Before a Straight Downstroke

rush   touch   judged

brushed   much   budget

Building Transcription Skills

4 Business Vocabulary Builder

perplexing Baffling; difficult to solve.

conscientious Governed by the desire to do the right and proper thing.

vouch To give a guarantee; to verify.

Reading and Writing Practice

5 Brief-Form Review Letter

aware

ten·ta·tive

agen·da

Phoe·nix

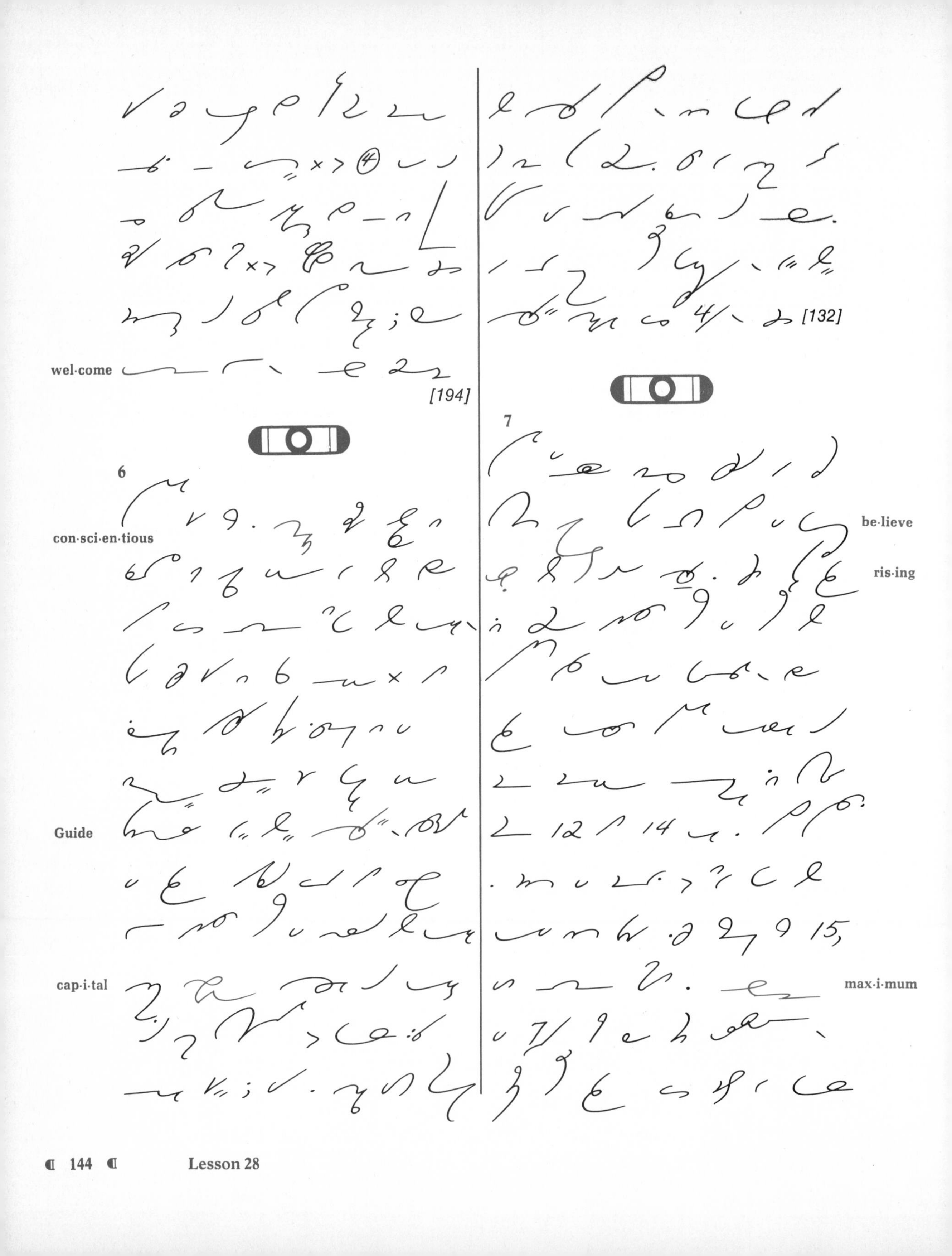

wel·come

[194]

6

con·sci·en·tious

Guide

cap·i·tal

[132]

7

be·lieve

ris·ing

max·i·mum

[150]

8

[156]

9

sim·ply

spa

de·vot·ed

com·plete·ly

as·sis·tant

com·mer·cial

vouch

555-6402

[123]

10

par·tic·u·lar·ly

hon·est

fraud

house·hold

(1) (2) (3) (4) (5)

[164]

Principles

1 Brief Forms

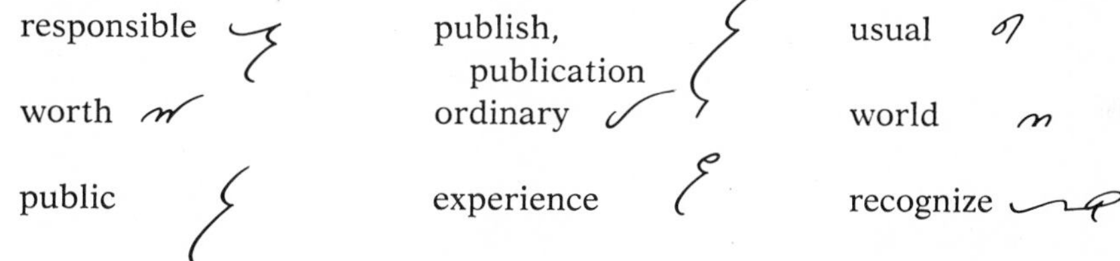

responsible	publish, publication	usual
worth	ordinary	world
public	experience	recognize

2 Word Beginning Ex-

The word beginning *ex-* is represented by *e-s*.

Spell: ex-t-r-a, extra

extra	expenses	excuse
examine	expert	extensive
extremely	excellent	exception

3 Word Ending -ful

The word ending *-ful* is represented by *f*.

Spell: k-a-r-ful, careful

careful	useful	helpful
doubtful	thoughtful	helpfully
grateful	beautiful	helpfulness

4 Word Endings -cal, -cle

The word endings *-cal, -cle* are represented by a disjoined *k*.

Spell: k-e-m-ical, chemical

chemical	logical	technical
medical	political	physically
identical	typical	articles

Building Transcription Skills

5 SIMILAR-WORDS DRILL • write, right

write To put words on paper.

I will *write* you about my plans.

right *(noun)* Something to which one has a just claim; *(adjective)* correct; *(adverb)* directly.

You have a *right* to expect good service from us.
Do you have the *right* time?
They are going *right* home after the meeting.

6 Business Vocabulary Builder

remote Far away; out of the way.

atlas A book of maps.

endorsement Approval.

Reading and Writing Practice

7 Brief-Form Letter

ev·ery·where

ex·traor·di·nary

equip·ment

write

[212]

8

bi·cy·cles

ex·cel·lent

[193]

9

edi·tion

prac·ti·cal

[116]

10

de·but

as·sur·ance

en·cour·age·ment

right

[167]

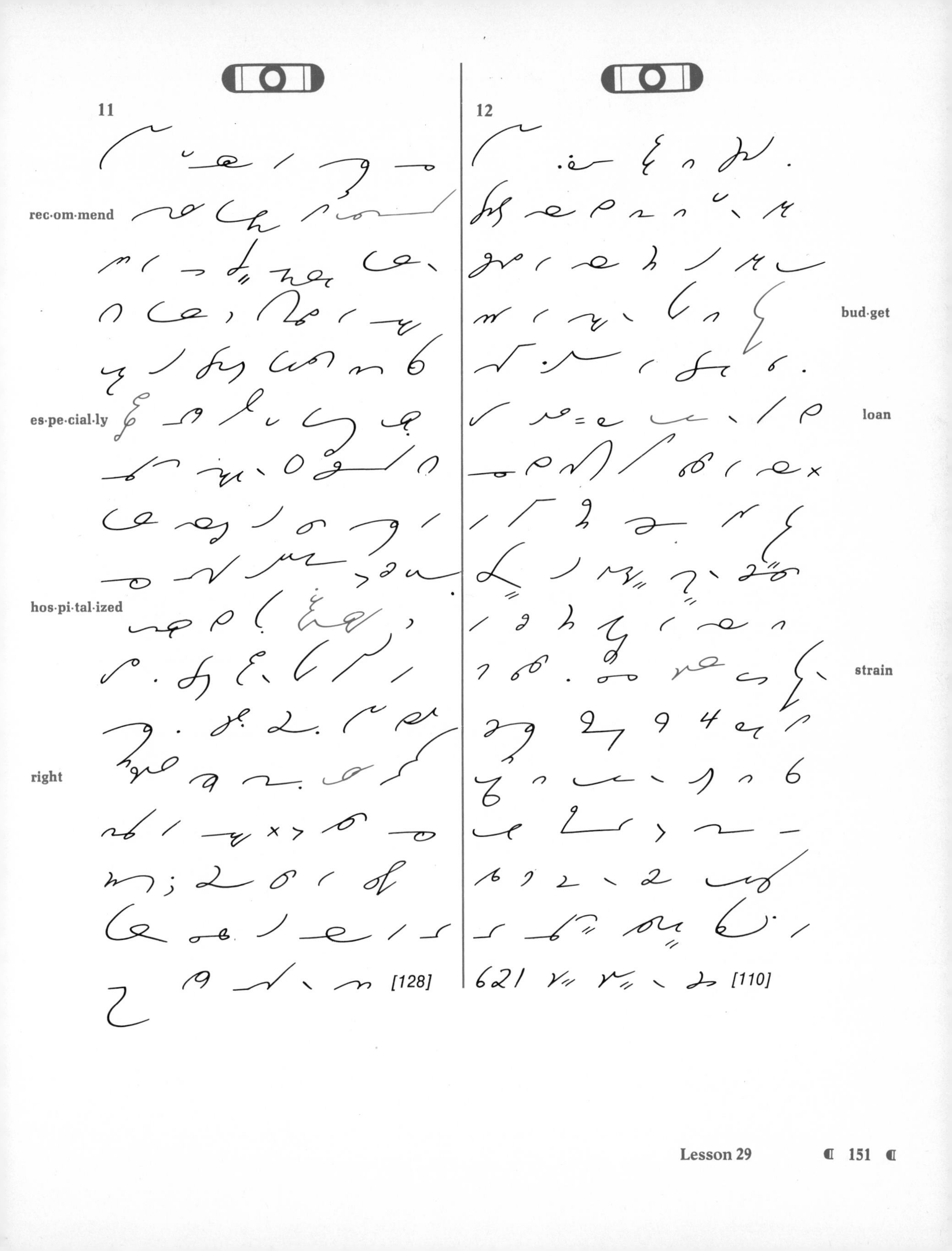

11

rec·om·mend

es·pe·cial·ly

hos·pi·tal·ized

right

[128]

12

bud·get

loan

strain

[110]

RECALL

There are no new shorthand strokes or principles in Lesson 30. In this lesson you will find an Accuracy Practice devoted to the curved strokes of Gregg Shorthand, a Recall Chart, and a Reading and Writing Practice.

Accuracy Practice

To get the most benefit from the Accuracy Practice, be sure to follow the procedures suggested on page 123.

1 **B** **V** **P** **F** **S**

To write these strokes accurately:

☐ **a** Give them approximately the slant indicated by the dotted lines.

☐ **b** Make the curve deep at the **beginning** of **v**, **f**, comma **s**; make the curve deep at the **end** of **b**, **p**, left **s**.

Practice Drill

Pay, spare, business, bears, stairs, sphere, leaves, briefs.

2 **P-r** **P-l** **B-r** **B-l**

To write these combinations accurately:

☐ **a** Write each without a pause between the first and second letter of each combination.

☐ **b** Watch your proportions carefully.

Practice Drill

Pray, press, prim, please, plan, place, plea.
Brim, bread, bridge, blame, bless, blast.

3 **F-r** **F-l**

To write the combinations accurately:

☐ Write them with one sweep of the pen, with no stop between the **f** and the **r** or **l**.

Practice Drill

Free, freeze, frame, flee, flame, flap.

4 **Recall Chart** This chart contains all the brief forms and phrases presented in Chapter 5 and illustrations of the word-building principles you studied in Chapters 1 through 5.

Can you read the entire chart in 6 minutes or less?

BRIEF FORMS, DERIVATIVES, AND PHRASES

1
2
3
4
5
6
7

WORDS

8
9
10
11
12
13
14
15
16

Building Transcription Skills

5 Business Vocabulary Builder	**currency** Paper money, coins, and other mediums of exchange that are in circulation.
	basic Fundamental; essential.
	withdraw Take out.

Reading and Writing Practice

Reading Scoreboard The previous Reading Scoreboard appeared in Lesson 18. If you have been studying each Reading and Writing Practice faithfully, you have no doubt increased your reading speed. Measure that increase on your first reading of the material in Lesson 30. The following table will help you:

LESSON 30 CONTAINS 572 WORDS	
If you read Lesson 30 in	your reading rate is
19 minutes	**30 words a minute**
21 minutes	**27 words a minute**
22 minutes	**25 words a minute**
24 minutes	**23 words a minute**
27 minutes	**21 words a minute**
31 minutes	**18 words a minute**
38 minutes	**15 words a minute**

If you can read Lesson 30 in 19 minutes or less, you are doing well. If you take considerably longer than 38 minutes, perhaps you should review your homework procedures. For example, are you:

- ☐ **1** Practicing in a quiet place at home?
- ☐ **2** Practicing without the radio or television set on?
- ☐ **3** Spelling aloud any words that you cannot read immediately?

6 Our Money

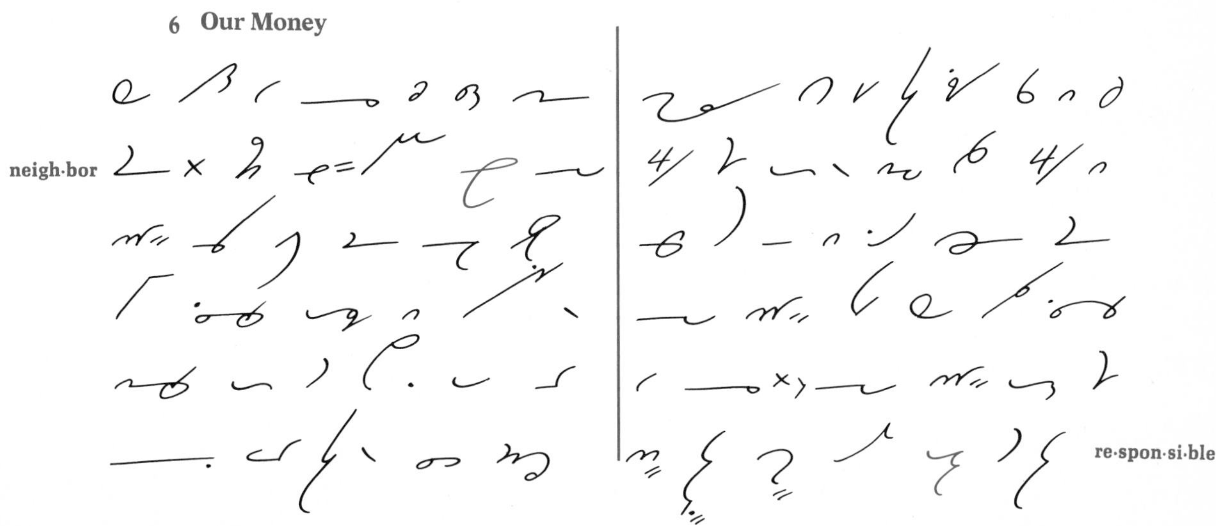

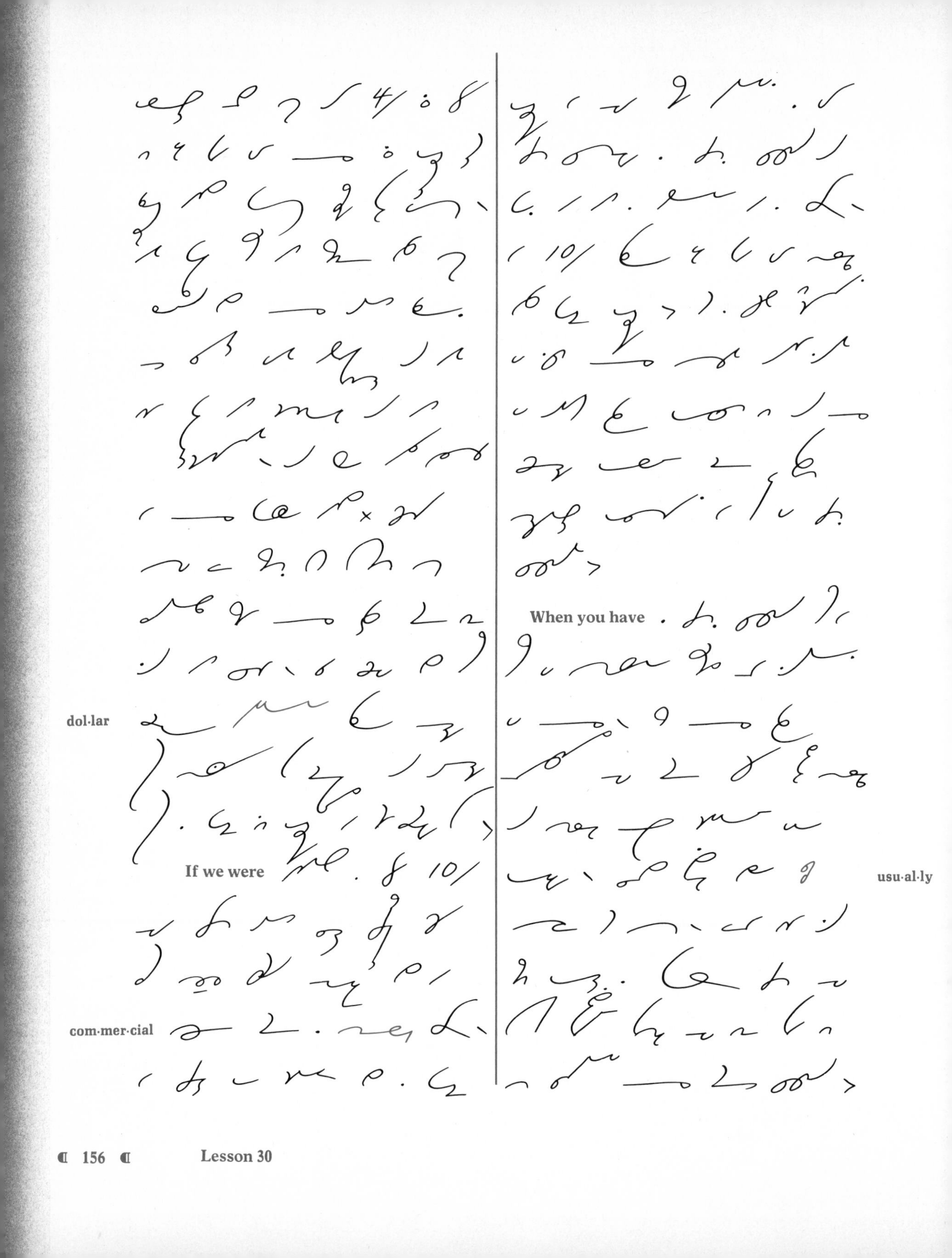

dol·lar

If we were

com·mer·cial

When you have

usu·al·ly

per·son·al·ly

A checking

ne·ces·si·ty

[572]

PROPORTION CHECKLIST

You can read your shorthand notes fluently if you are careful of proportions. In your shorthand writing, be sure to:

■ **1** Make the large *a* circle huge; the small *e* circle tiny.

■ **2** Make the straight strokes very straight and the curves very deep.

■ **3** Make the *o* and *oo* hooks deep and narrow.

■ **4** Make short strokes, such as *t* and *n,* very short and long strokes, such as *ted* and *men,* very long.

6 SPECIALIZATION

Why specialize? Because specialists—heart specialists, corporate-law specialists, engineering specialists—are looking for *other* specialists to help them in their work.

Training in specialized fields is becoming more frequent for secretaries. Colleges and private business schools offer courses in the scientific, technology, legal, and medical fields. These courses, in

addition to teaching the basic secretarial skills, help students become familiar with the terminology and procedures needed to perform well in specific jobs.

Students now have a greater number of textbooks available to them to help them become proficient in their chosen field. For example, legal secretarial students are instructed in the special procedures used in a legal office, the vocabulary used in correspondence and legal documents, and legal research. They are also taught the special shorthand outlines used in legal dictation.

Once on the job, there are many reference books available that will prove invaluable to the new specialized secretary. There are also a number of national organizations for these secretaries.

Because specialized secretaries have extra training to offer an employer, they are often paid higher salaries than they might get in a general business organization. Such people also gain a certain amount of prestige and recognition for their talents.

If your interests point you in a particular direction, specialization might be the key to a rewarding job.

Principles

1 Brief Forms This is the last group of brief forms you will learn!

never
quantity
executive

throughout
object
character

govern
correspond, correspondence

2 Word Ending -ure The word ending *-ure* is represented by *r*.

Spell: f-a-l-r, failure

failure
future

feature
featured

nature
natural

3 Word Ending -ual The word ending *-ual* is represented by *l*.

Spell: a-k-t-l, actual

actual
gradual

schedule
scheduled

equal
equally

Building Transcription Skills

4 PUNCTUATION PRACTICE

An efficient secretary must, as you have already learned, be able to take dictation at a reasonable speed and be able to spell. Another "must" for the efficient secretary is the ability to punctuate correctly. Most business executives rely on their secretaries to supply the proper punctuation when they transcribe. Because the inclusion or omission of a punctuation mark may completely alter the meaning of a sentence, it is important that you know when and where to use each punctuation mark.

To sharpen your punctuation skill, you will hereafter give special attention to punctuation in each Reading and Writing Practice.

In the lessons ahead you will review nine of the most common uses of the comma. Each time one of these uses of the comma occurs in the Reading and Writing Practice, it will be encircled in the shorthand, thus calling it forcefully to your attention.

PRACTICE SUGGESTIONS

If you follow these simple suggestions in your homework practice, your ability to punctuate should improve noticeably.

☐ **1** Read carefully the explanation of each comma usage (for example, the explanation of the parenthetical comma given below) to be sure that you understand it. You will encounter a number of illustrations of each comma usage in the Reading and Writing Practice exercises, so that eventually you will acquire the knack of applying each of them correctly.

☐ **2** Continue to read and copy each Reading and Writing Practice as you have done before. However, add these two important steps:

☐ **a** Each time you see an encircled comma in the Reading and Writing Practice, note the reason for its use, which is indicated directly above the comma.

☐ **b** As you copy the Reading and Writing Practice in your shorthand notebook, insert the commas in your shorthand notes, encircling them as was done in the textbook.

PUNCTUATION PRACTICE ● , parenthetical

A word or a phrase or a clause that is used parenthetically (that is, one not necessary to the grammatical completeness of the sentence) should be set off by commas.

If the parenthetical expression occurs at the end of the sentence, only one comma is necessary.

There is, of course, *a small application fee.*

Never hesitate to let us know, Mr. Smith, *when our organization can help you.*

We will be happy to serve you, Mrs. Martinez.

Each time a parenthetical expression occurs in the Reading and Writing Practice, it will be indicated thus in the shorthand: par (,)

5 **Business Vocabulary Builder**

deprived Taken from; denied something.
ravages Violent, destructive effects.
vivid Strong or clear; sharp.

Reading and Writing Practice

6 Brief-Form Letter

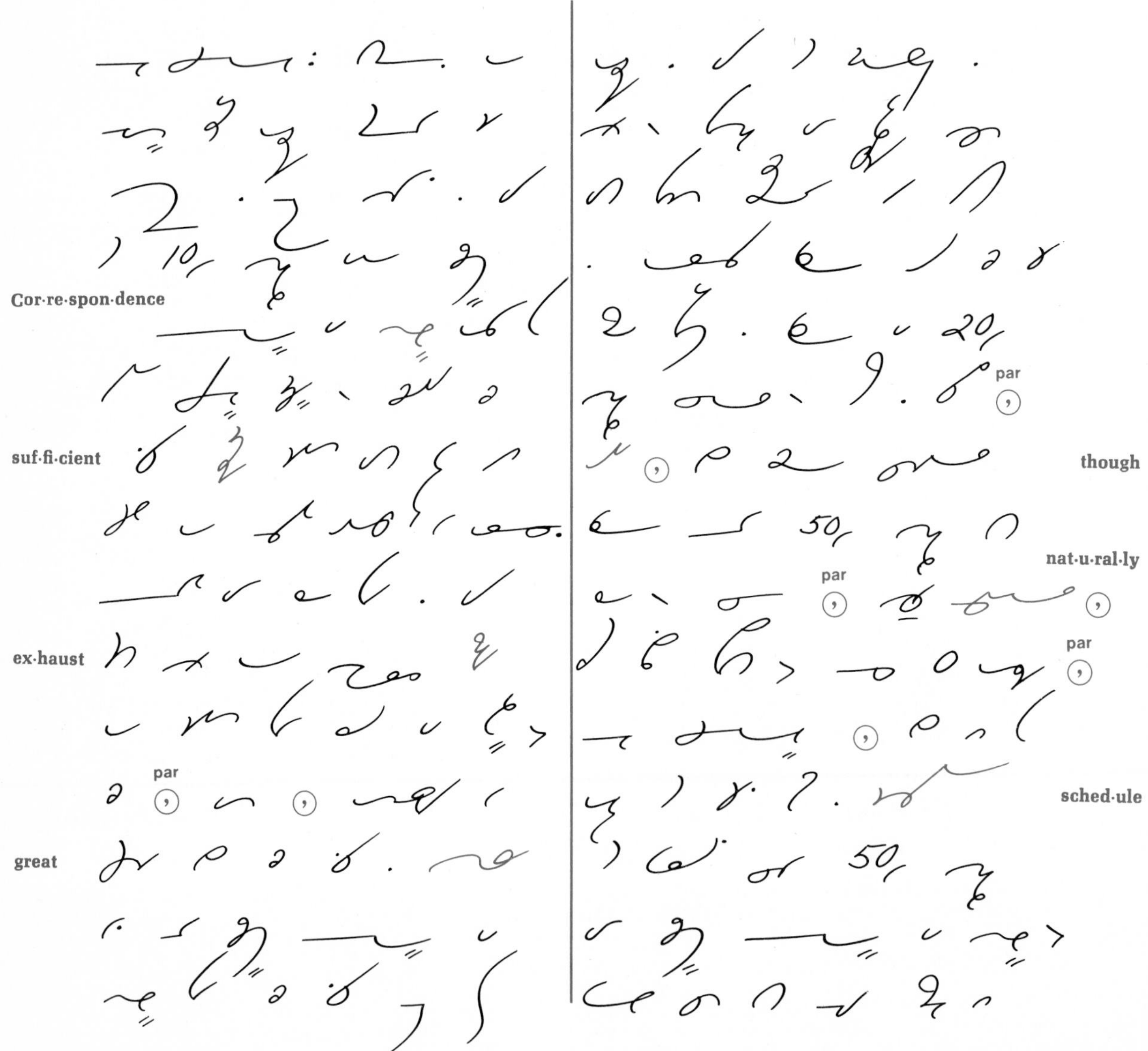

[217]

7

ex·cel·lent

par

prob·a·bly

pur·sue

[101]

8

sec·tion

par

par

ar·range
ap·point·ment

[136]

9

par

even·tu·al·ly

de·prived

rep·re·sen·ta·tives

par

[180]

10

[34]

Principles

1 Word Ending -ily The word ending *-ily* is represented by a narrow loop.

Compare: steady   steadily

Spell: r-e-d-ily, readily

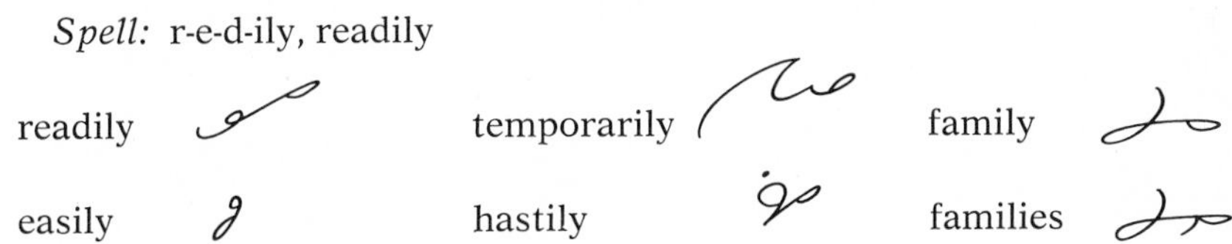

readily   temporarily   family

easily   hastily   families

◉ *Observe the special joining of* s *in* families. *This joining helps form an outline that is easily read.*

2 Word Beginning Al- The word beginning *al-* is represented by the shorthand letter *o*.

Spell: all-t-r, alter

alter   altogether   also

altered   almost   almanac

3 Word Beginnings Dis-, Des- The word beginnings *dis-*, *des-* are represented by *d-s*.

Spell: dis-k-oo-s, discuss; dis-k-r-ī-b, describe

Dis-

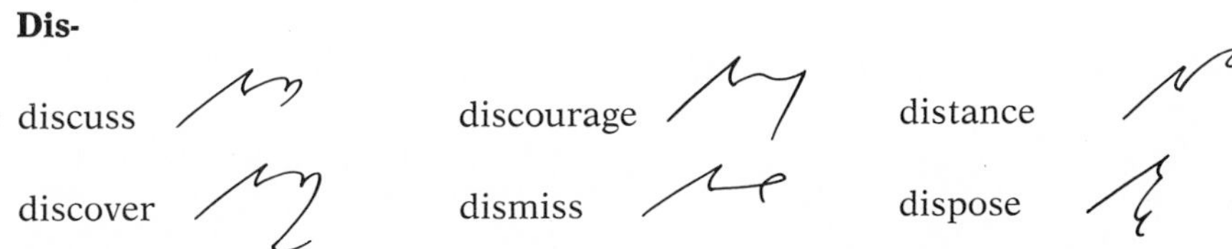

discuss   discourage   distance

discover   dismiss   dispose

Des-

describe despite desperate

description destination destroy

Building Transcription Skills

4 PUNCTUATION PRACTICE ● , apposition

An expression in apposition (that is, a word or a phrase or a clause that identifies or explains another word or term) should be set off by commas. When the expression in apposition occurs at the end of a sentence, only one comma is necessary.

My employer, Ms. Mildred H. O'Brien, *is out of town.*

The book, Human Relations, *is now for sale.*

The meeting is scheduled for Wednesday, June 23.

Each time an expression in apposition appears in the Reading and Writing Practice, it will be indicated thus in the shorthand: ap ,

---

5 Business Vocabulary Builder

bench The office or dignity of a judge.

extensive Wide; considerable.

unbiased Not favoring one side or the other; fair.

temporarily For a short time; not permanently.

Reading and Writing Practice

6 Brief-Form Review Letter

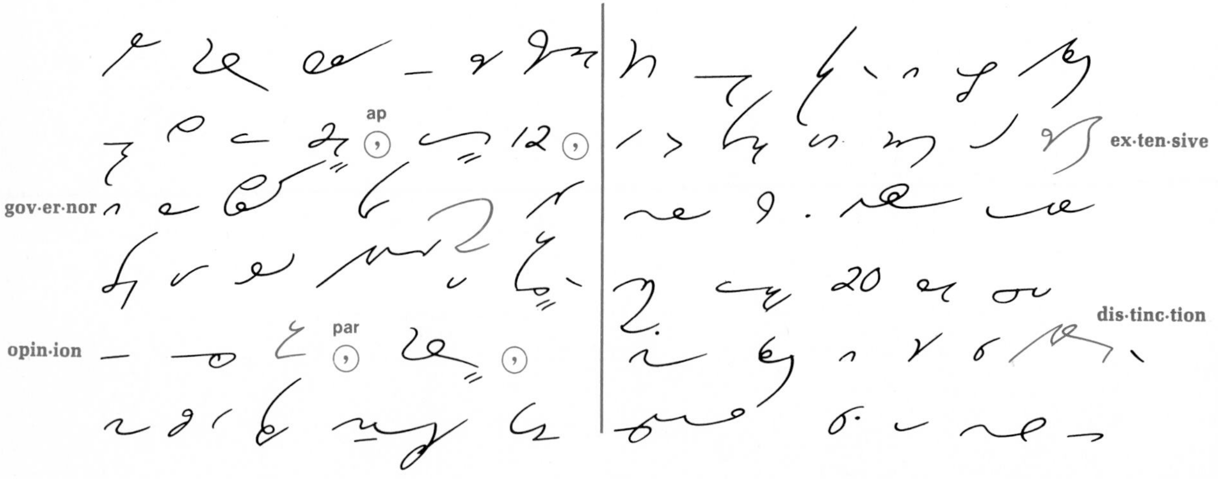

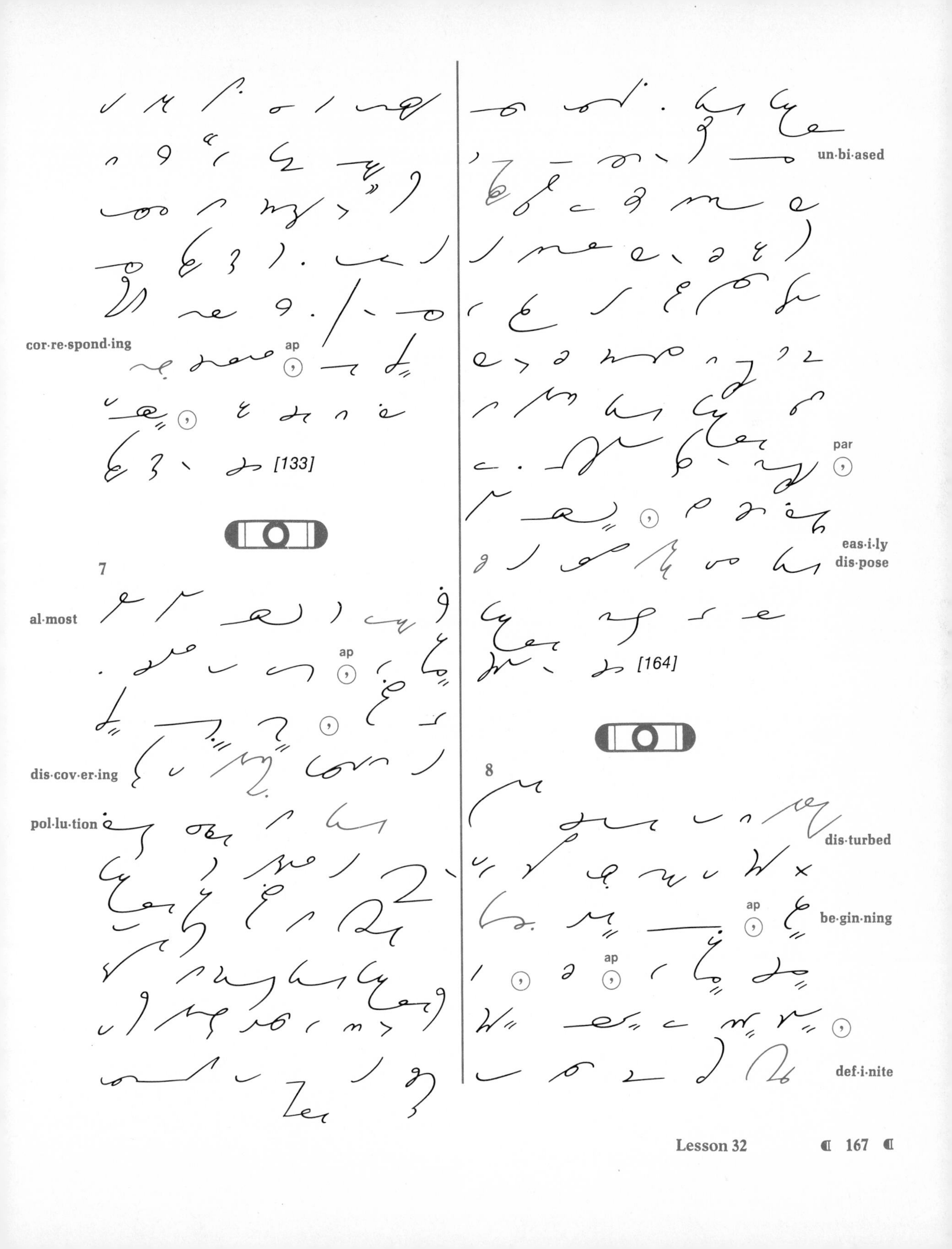

cor·re·spond·ing

ap

[133]

7

al·most

ap

dis·cov·er·ing

pol·lu·tion

un·bi·ased

par

eas·i·ly
dis·pose

[164]

8

dis·turbed

ap

be·gin·ning

ap

def·i·nite

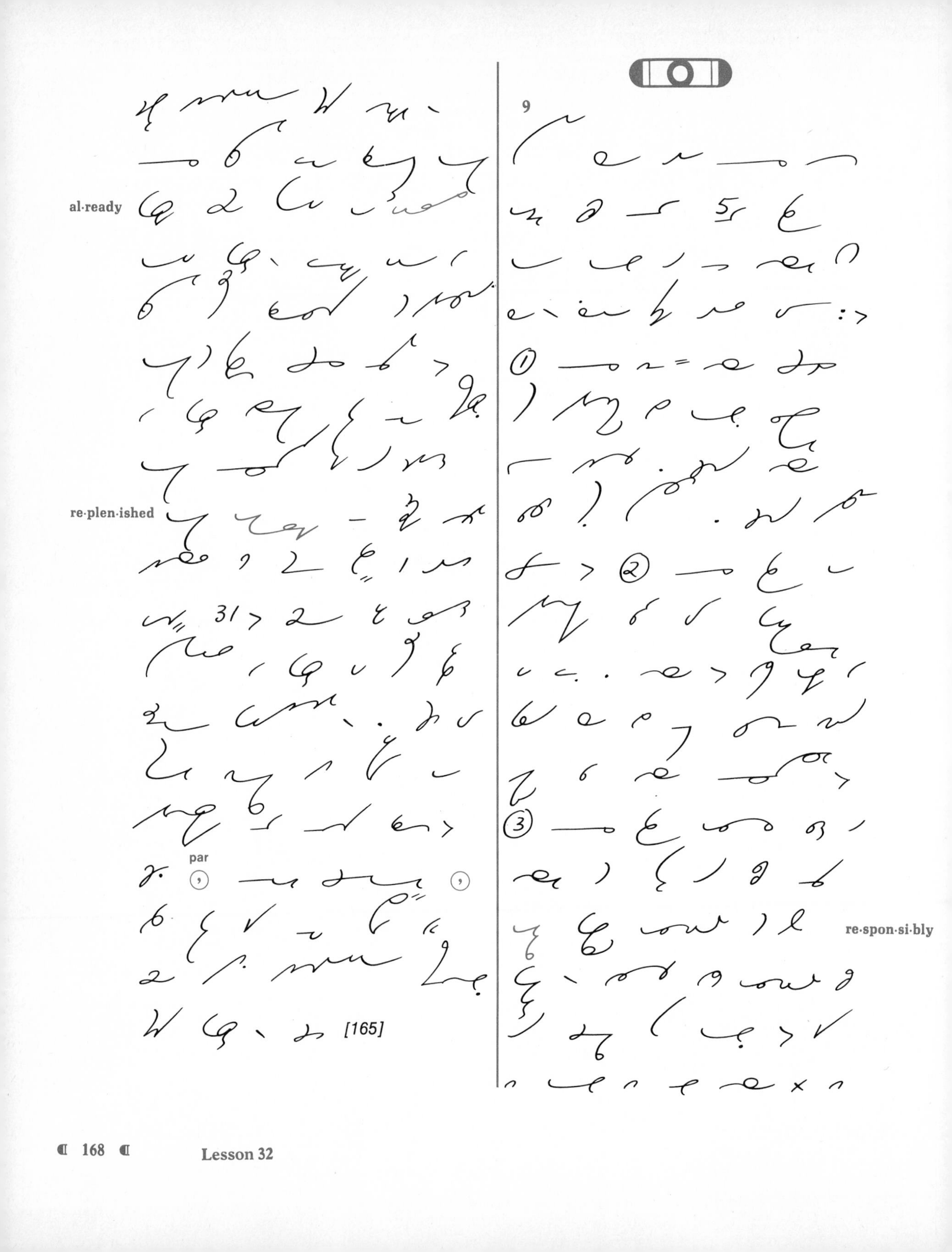

al·ready

re·plen·ished

31

par

[165]

9

5

re·spon·si·bly

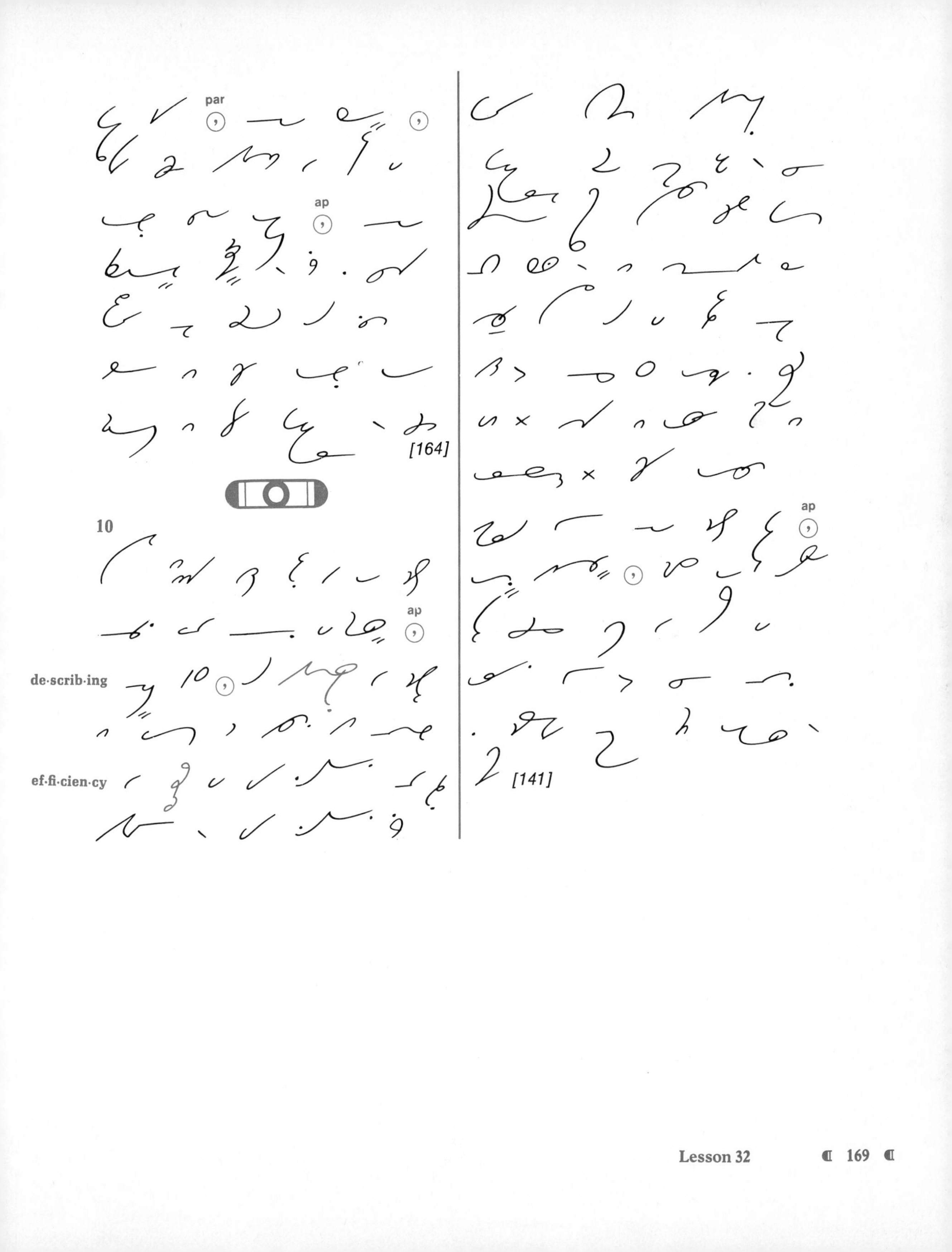

par

ap

[164]

10

ap

de·scrib·ing

ef·fi·cien·cy

ap

[141]

Principles

1 Word Beginnings For-, Fore- The word beginnings *for-, fore-* are represented by *f*.

Spell: for-gay-e-t, forget

forget	form	forerunner
forgive	inform	forlorn
effort	information	forever

◉ *Observe:* ☐ **1** *The* f *is joined with an angle to* r *or* l, *as in* forerunner *and* forlorn, *to indicate that it represents a word beginning.*
☐ **2** *The* f *is disjoined if the following character is a vowel, as in* forever.

2 Word Beginning Fur- The word beginning *fur-* is also represented by *f*.

Spell: fur-n-ish, furnish

furnish	furniture	further
furnished	furnace	furthermore

3 Ago in Phrases In expressions of time, *ago* is represented by *gay*.

days ago	years ago	several days ago
weeks ago	months ago	few days ago

Building Transcription Skills

4 PUNCTUATION PRACTICE ● , series

When the last member of a series of three or more items is preceded by *and* or *or*, place a comma before the conjunction as well as between the other items.

I need a desk, a chair, and a table.

I saw Kay on July 18, on July 19, and again on July 30.

I need someone to take dictation, to answer the telephone, and to greet callers.

Note: Some authorities prefer to omit the comma before the conjunction. In your shorthand books, however, the comma will be inserted before the conjunction.

Each time a series occurs in the Reading and Writing Practice, it will be indicated thus in the shorthand: ser (,)

5 Business Vocabulary Builder

informally Casually; without ceremony.

gracious Having charm and good taste; pleasing.

forecasting Predicting.

suites Groups of rooms occupied as units; apartments.

Reading and Writing Practice

6 Brief-Form Review Letter

ap (,) (,) par (,) ser (,) (,) par (,) (,)

Cor·re·spon·dence

dis·ap·point·ing

ex·hausted

ware·houses

readi·ly

[198]

7

per·son·al

par

for·mer

ap

ac·cepted

re·spon·si·ble

gov·ern·ment

ser

some·time

par

[113]

8

ser

ex·traor·di·nary

gra·cious

ser

de·sign·er

par

[130]

9

fur·ther·more

else

de·scribe

[113]

ap

ser

con·sid·er·able

ap

au·di·ence

[156] en·gage·ment

10

an·nu·al

11

lei·sure

in·stalled

ser

suites

ser

[186]

UP-AND-DOWN CHECKLIST

Always write the following strokes upward.

- 1 and — their-there
- 2 it-at — would

Always write the following strokes downward.

- 1 is-his — for — have
- 2 she — which

Principles

1 Want in Phrases In phrases, *want* is represented by the *nt* blend.

I want · I wanted · if you want

you want · he wants · do you want

2 Ort The *r* is omitted in the sound *ort.*

Spell: re-p-o-t, report

report · quart · sort

export · quarterly · portable

3 R Omitted in -ern, -erm The *r* is omitted in the combinations *tern, term, thern, therm, dern.*

Spell: t-e-n, turn

turn · term · southern

return · terms · thermometer

western · determined · modern

4 Md By rounding off the angle between *m-d,* we obtain the fluent *md* blend.

Md

Compare: blame · blamed

Spell: b-l-a-emd, blamed

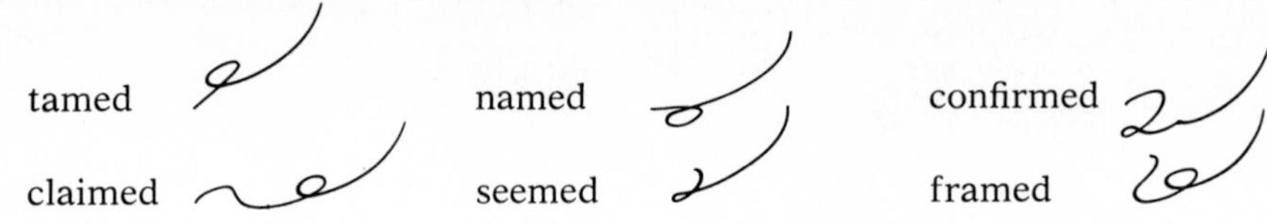

tamed named confirmed

claimed seemed framed

5 Mt The stroke that represents *md* also represents *mt.*

Spell: p-r-o-emt, prompt

prompt promptly empty

Building Transcription Skills

6 Business Vocabulary Builder

quarterly Four times a year.

contention A point advanced in an argument or debate.

terminal A carrier station or depot or airport.

Reading and Writing Practice

7 Brief-Form Review Letter

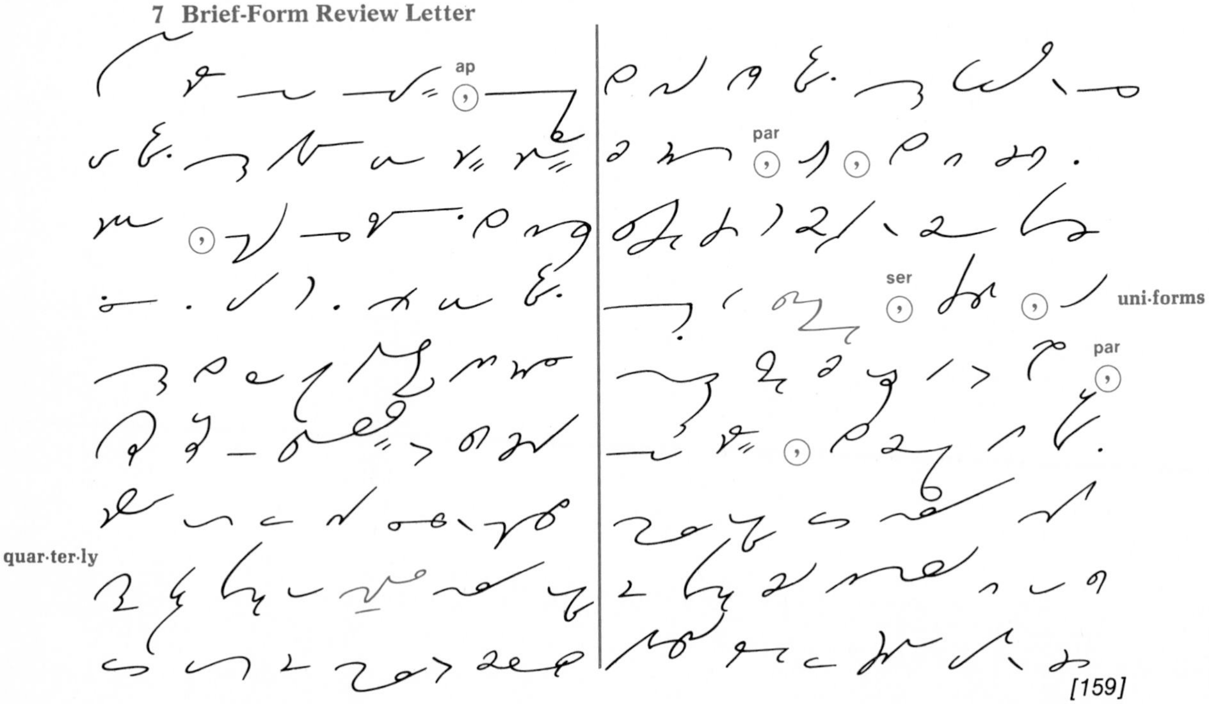

ap

par

ser

uni·forms

par

quar·ter·ly

[159]

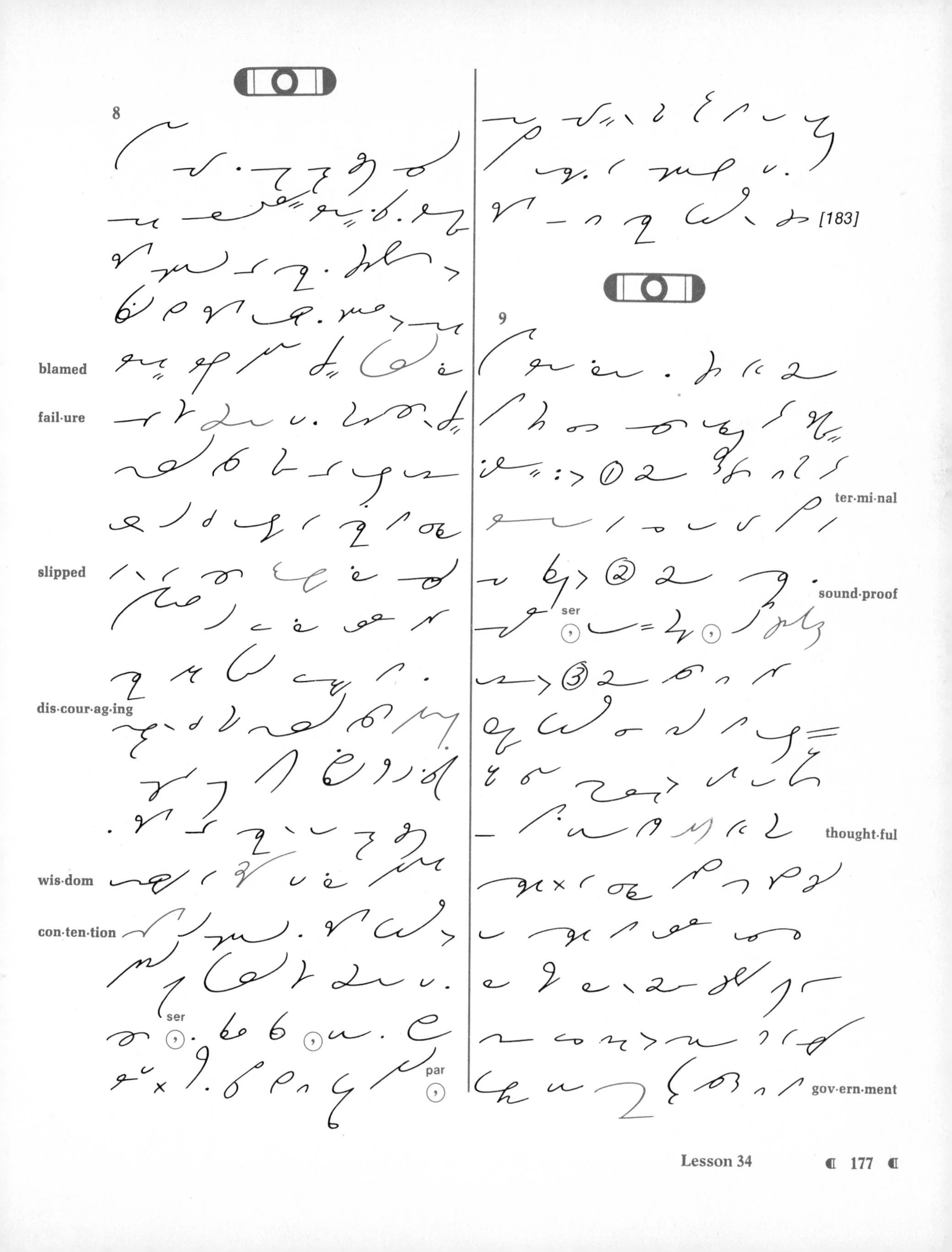

8

blamed

fail·ure

slipped

dis·cour·ag·ing

wis·dom

con·ten·tion

ser

par

[183]

9

ter·mi·nal

sound·proof

ser

thought·ful

gov·ern·ment

par

[137]

10

Wednes·day

Feb·ru·ary

ap

de·scribed

ra·di·a·tion

ef·fect

re·gard·ing

par

in·stalled

par

[161]

11

ser

ser

suc·cess·ful

pro·gres·sive

par

[96]

Principles

1 **Word Beginnings Inter-, Intr-, Enter-, Entr-** These similar-sounding word beginnings (and the word *enter*) are represented by a disjoined *n*. These disjoined word beginnings, as well as other disjoined word beginnings that you will study in later lessons, are placed above the line of writing close to the remainder of the word.

Inter-

Spell: inter-s-t, interest

interest international interrupt
interview interval internal

Intr-

Spell: intro-d-oo-s, introduce

introduce intruder intricate

Enter-

Spell: enter-ing, entering

entering entertain enterprise
entered entertainment enterprising

Entr-

Spell: enter-n-s, entrance

entrance entrances entrant

2 Word Ending -ings The word ending *-ings* is represented by a disjoined left *s*.

Spell: s-a-v-ings, savings

savings | furnishings | proceedings
openings | earnings | hearings

3 Omission of Words in Phrases It is often possible to omit one or more unimportant words in a shorthand phrase. In the phrase *one of the,* for example, the word *of* is omitted; we write *one the.* When transcribing, the stenographer would insert *of,* as the phrase would make no sense without that word.

one of the | some of the | many of the
one of them | up to date | in the future
some of our | in the world | two or three

Building Transcription Skills

4 SIMILAR-WORDS DRILL ● addition, edition

addition Anything added.

She will be a valuable *addition* to our staff.

edition All the copies of a book or periodical printed at one time.

It will appear in the next *edition* of our newspaper.

5 Business Vocabulary Builder

unduly Unnecessarily; too much.

interior The inside of something.

initiative A first step.

Reading and Writing Practice

6 Brief-Form Review Letter

cor·re·spond·ing

de·light·ful

grasp

ad·di·tion

in·ter·view

ser

par

par

[147]

un·du·ly

de·layed

ser

par

[128]

7

8

de·scrip·tion

edi·tion

ap

ap

ap·peals

par

ex·cept

555-1876

com·plete

ac·tu·al·ly

par

[143]

9

in·ter·sec·tions

en·trance

ap·par·ent·ly

ini·tia·tive

par

ap·pro·pri·a·tion

rec·om·mend

award·ing

[195]

10

in·for·ma·tive

ser

ap

past·ry chefs

ap

par

de·vices

[174]

11

ap

ser

en·ter·pris·ing

mes·sage

ar·ti·cles

ser

par

[104]

RECALL

Lesson 36 is another breather. In Lesson 36 you will find the last principle of joining, a chart that contains a review of many shorthand devices you studied in Lessons 1 through 35, an Accuracy Practice, and a Reading and Writing Practice.

Principles of Joining

1 The word endings *-ure* and *-ual* are represented by *r* and *l* except when those endings are preceded by a downstroke.

nature procedure creature

annual gradual equal

but

pressure treasure ensure

casual visual visually

Accuracy Practice

2 **O** **On** **Sho** **Non**

To write these combinations accurately:

☐ **a** Keep the **o** hook narrow, being sure that the **beginning** and **end** are on the same level of writing as indicated by the dotted line.

☐ **b** Keep the **o** in **on** and **sho** parallel with the consonant, as indicated by the dotted line.

☐ **c** Make the **beginning** of the **o** in **non** retrace the **end** of the first **n**.

☐ **d** Avoid a point at the **curved** part indicated by the arrows.

Practice Drill

Of, know, low, own, home, hot, known, moan, shown.

3 **OO** **Noo** **Noom**

To write these combinations accurately:

☐ **a** Keep the **oo** hook narrow and deep.

☐ **b** Keep the **beginning** and **end** of the hook on the same level of writing.

☐ **c** In **noo** and **noom**, keep the hook parallel with the straight line that precedes it.

☐ **d** In **noom**, retrace the **beginning** of the **m** on the bottom of the **oo** hook.

☐ **e** Avoid a point at the places indicated by arrows.

Practice Drill

You, yours truly, you would, to, do, noon, moon, renew.

4 **Hard** **Hailed**

To write these combinations accurately:

☐ **a** Give the **end** of the **r** and the **end** of the **l** a lift upward.

☐ **b** Do not lift the **end** too soon, or the strokes may resemble the **nd**, **md** combinations.

Practice Drill

Neared, feared, cheered, dared, hold, sold, bold.

5 **Recall Chart** This chart provides a review of most of the shorthand devices you studied in previous lessons. It contains 84 outlines. Can you read the entire chart in 5 minutes?

BRIEF FORMS AND DERIVATIVES

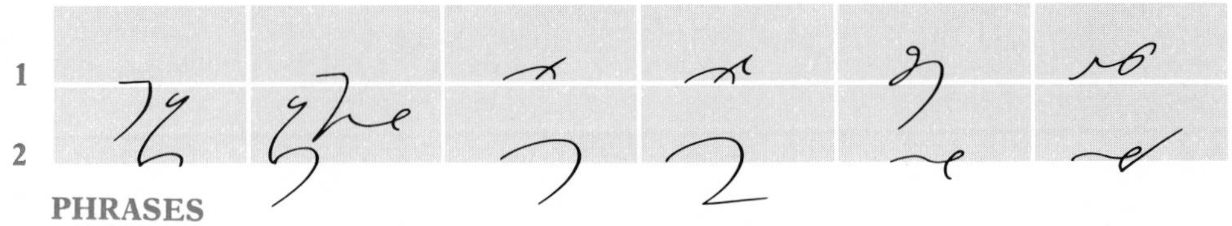

1

2

PHRASES

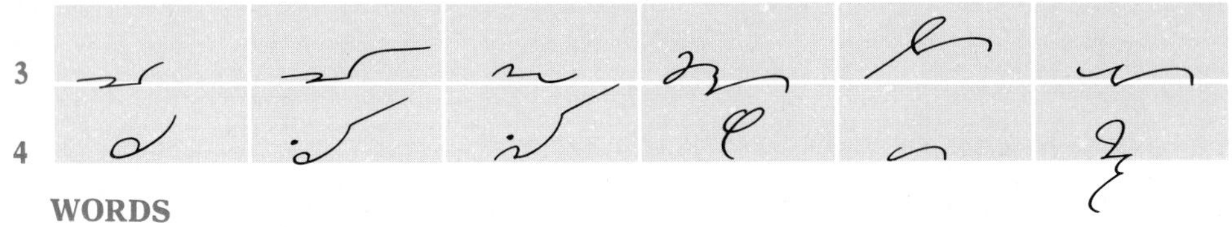

3

4

WORDS

5

6

7

8

9

10

11

12

13

14

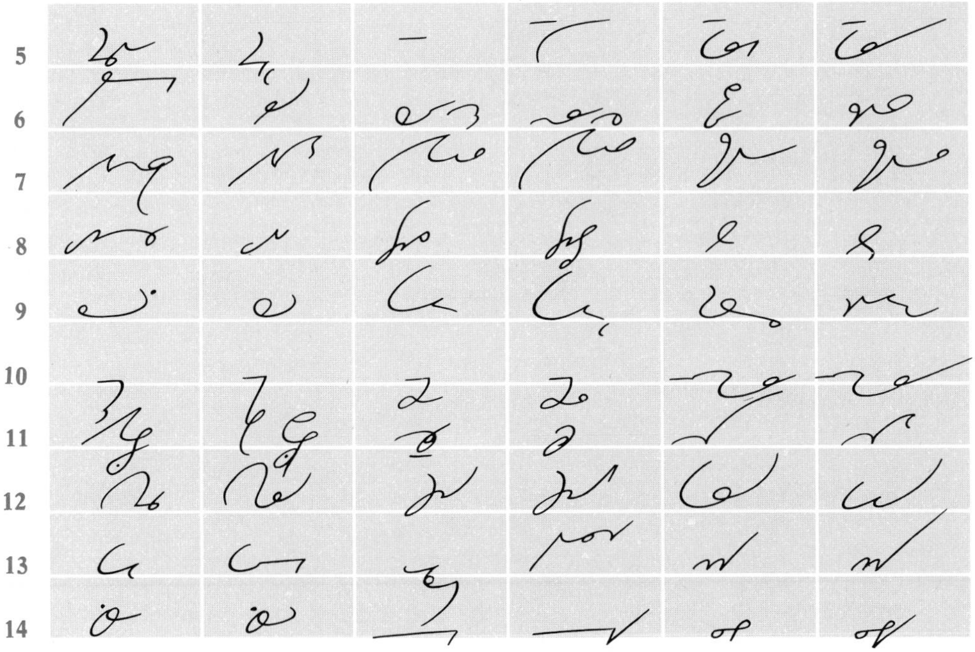

Building Transcription Skills

6 Business Vocabulary Builder

screening *(verb)* Keeping out that which is unneeded or unwanted.

sensitive Delicately aware of the feelings of others.

undercurrents Hidden pressures or feelings often contrary to the ones publicly shown.

soothe Bring comfort or reassurance to.

Reading and Writing Practice

7 The Administrative Secretary

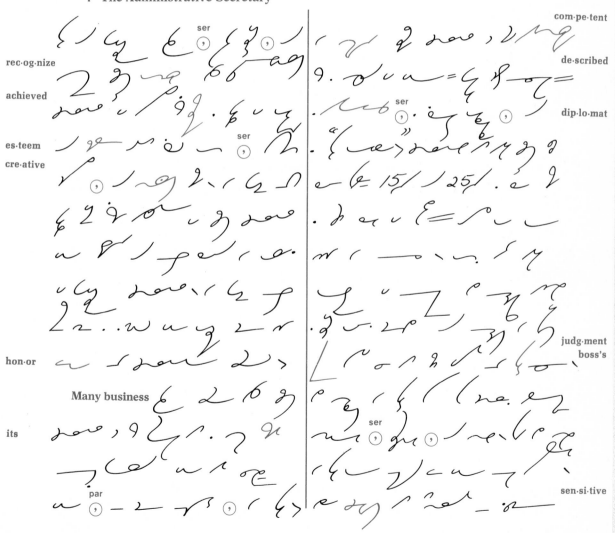

ser

rec·og·nize

achieved

ser

es·teem

cre·ative

hon·or

Many business

its

par

com·pe·tent

de·scribed

ser

dip·lo·mat

judg·ment

boss's

ser

sen·si·tive

A secretary

an·tic·i·pate

ser

ser

con·vey

ser

soothe

ser

cor·re·spon·dence

10,

15,

15,

3

60,

as·sis·tants

plan·ning

ap

Throughout the

par

though

[674]

8 The Follow Through

sat·is·fac·to·ri·ly

re·ceive

dil·i·gence

par

par

ini·ti·ate

Do not accept

ex·pend

[204]

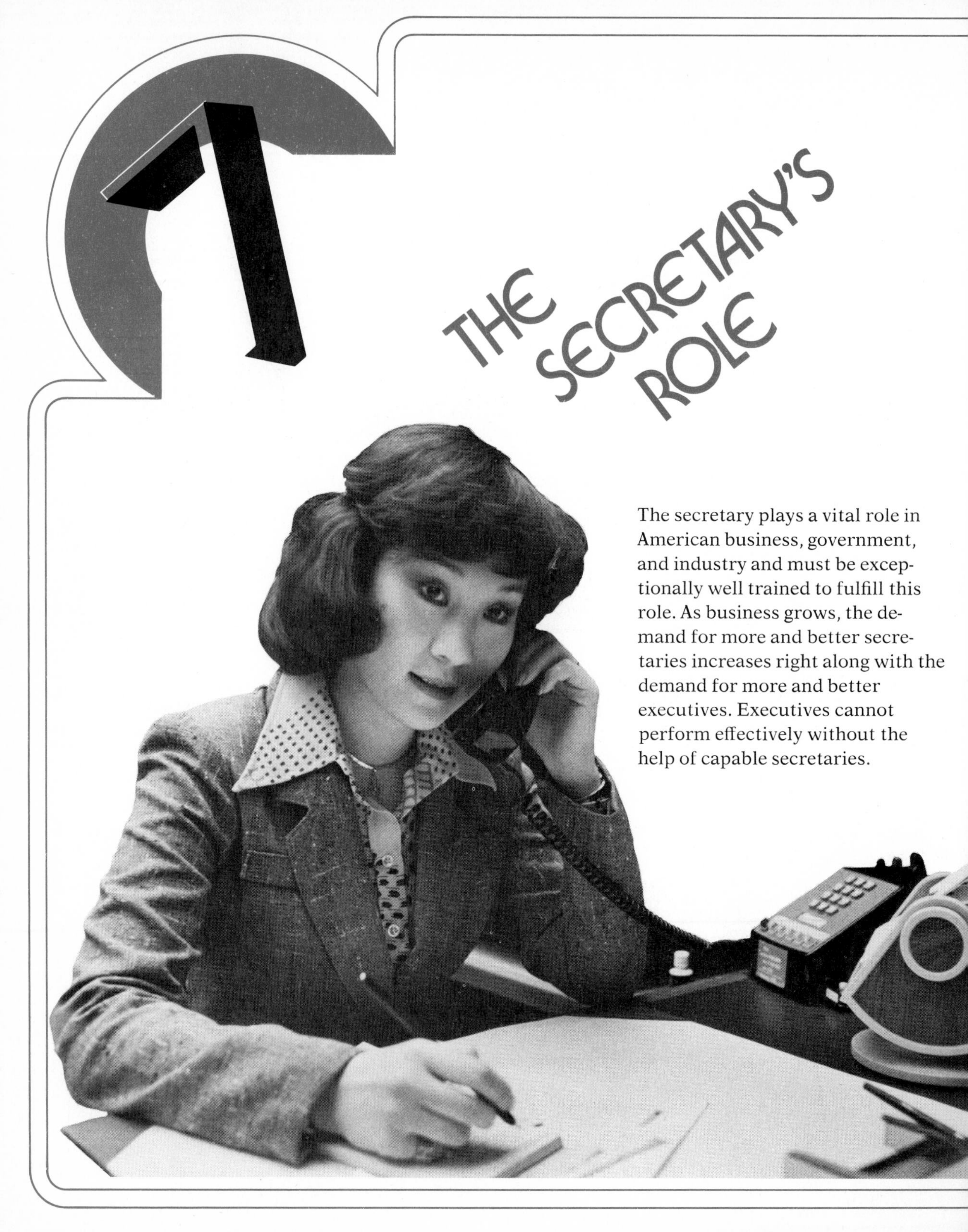

1 THE SECRETARY'S ROLE

The secretary plays a vital role in American business, government, and industry and must be exceptionally well trained to fulfill this role. As business grows, the demand for more and better secretaries increases right along with the demand for more and better executives. Executives cannot perform effectively without the help of capable secretaries.

The secretary does more than answer the telephone and take and transcribe dictation. Keeping track of appointments, writing letters and reports, doing research, arranging for and reporting on meetings, maintaining an efficient records system, and following up on pending business all fall within the realm of the secretary's duties.

One of the most important functions of today's secretary is that of public relations specialist. Because the secretary is in constant contact with people—executives, top management, subordinates, personnel from other organizations, and the general public—there is an opportunity to make an important contribution. Communications from these people include suggestions, ideas, and complaints in both oral and written form.

The secretary works closely with those who direct the activities of any enterprise and aids in many of the innumerable management decisions that are made every day.

Performing all these duties requires the skill of a professional, one who is an important member of the management team.

Principles

1 Word Ending -ingly The word ending *-ingly* is represented by a disjoined *e* circle.

Spell: n-o-ingly, knowingly

knowingly increasingly seemingly
accordingly surprisingly exceedingly

2 Word Beginning Im- The word beginning *im-* is represented by *m*.

Spell: im-p-o-s, impose

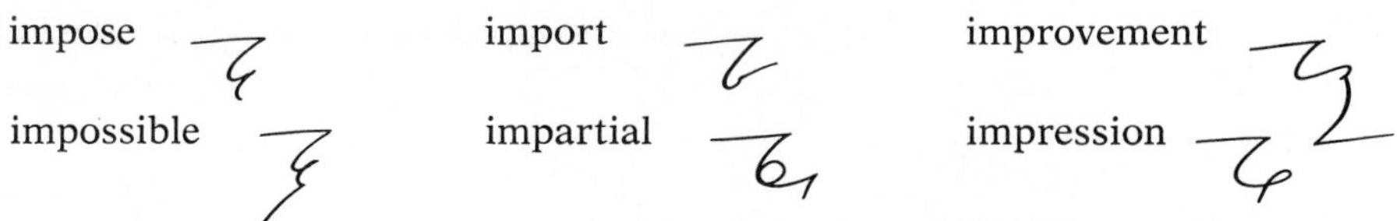

impose import improvement
impossible impartial impression

3 Word Beginning Em- The word beginning *em-* is also represented by *m*.

Spell: em-p-l-oi, employ

employ emphasis empire
employment emphasize embarrass

4 Im-, Em- Followed by a Vowel When *im-, em-* are followed by a vowel, they are written in full.

immodest immortal emotional

5 Omission of Minor Vowel When two vowel sounds come together, the minor vowel may be omitted.

serious	period	situate
obvious	ideal	situated
various	theory	situation

Building Transcription Skills

6 PUNCTUATION PRACTICE ● , if clause

An error sometimes made by the beginning transcriber is failing to make a complete sentence. In many cases the incomplete sentence is a dependent or subordinate introductory clause starting with a word such as *if, when,* or *as.* The clause is deceiving because it would be a complete sentence if it were not introduced by one of these words. This type of clause requires another clause to complete the thought.

The dependent or subordinate introductory clause often signals the coming of the main clause by means of a subordinate conjunction. The commonest subordinating conjunctions are *if, as,* and *when.* Other subordinating conjunctions include *though, although, whether, unless, because, since, while, where, after, whenever, until,* and *before.*

In this lesson you will consider only those clauses introduced by *if.* A subordinate clause introduced by *if* and followed by a main clause is separated from the main clause by a comma.

If you complete the lesson, *you may leave.*

If you would like to have one of our representatives call you, *please let us know.*

Each time a subordinate clause beginning with *if* occurs in the Reading and Writing Practice, it will be indicated thus in the shorthand: if (,)

7 Business Vocabulary Builder

forceful Having drive; effective.

morale The mental and emotional condition of an individual or of a group.

employment agencies Companies that find jobs for people or find people to fill jobs.

Reading and Writing Practice

8 Brief-Form Review Letter

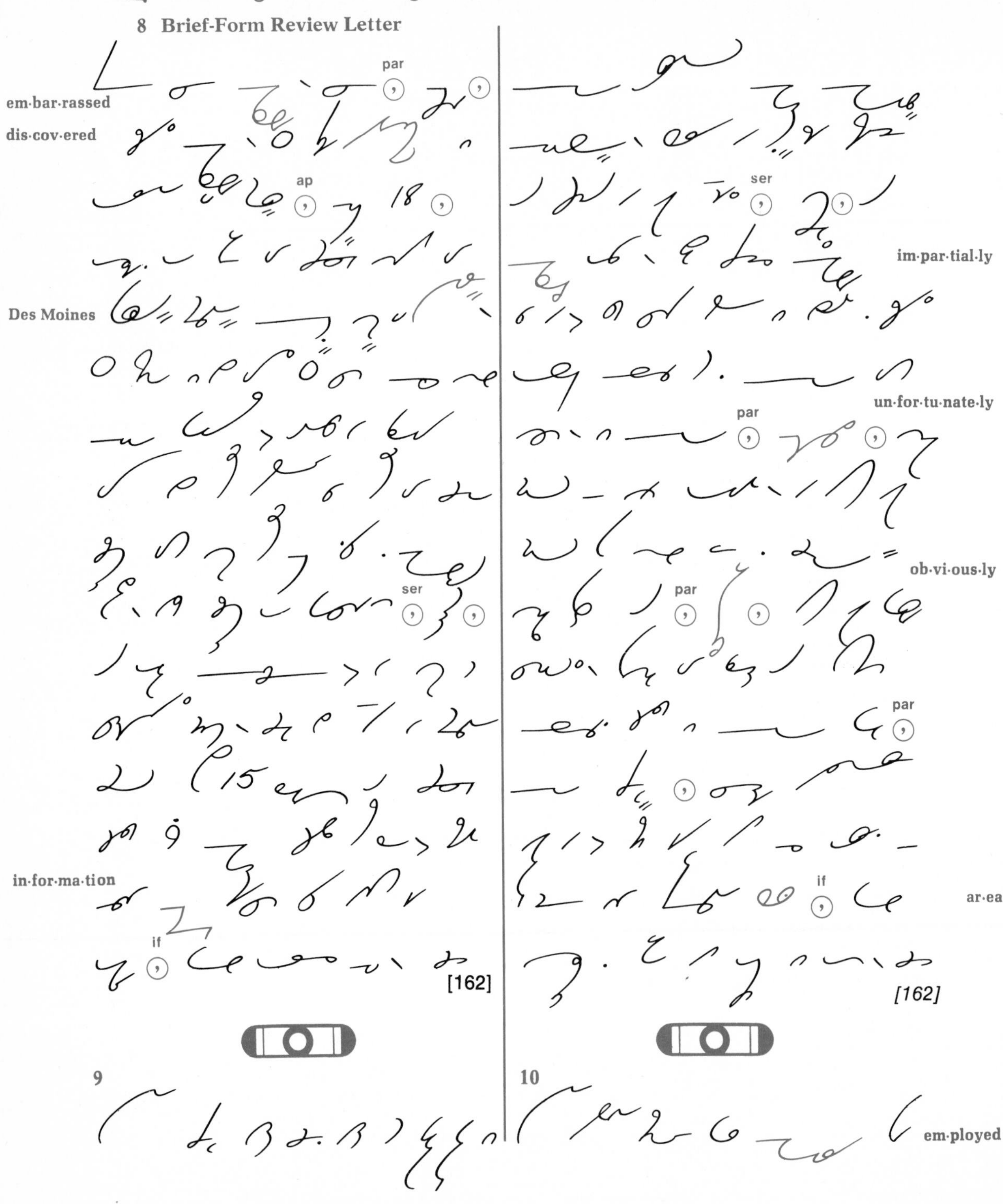

gov·ern·ment

ser

clas·si·fied

ap

per·son·nel

im·pact

ob·jec·tive

if

lead·ing

ap

[171]

11

if

div·i·dends

if

if

ser

par

[121]

12

ap

in·formed

15

25

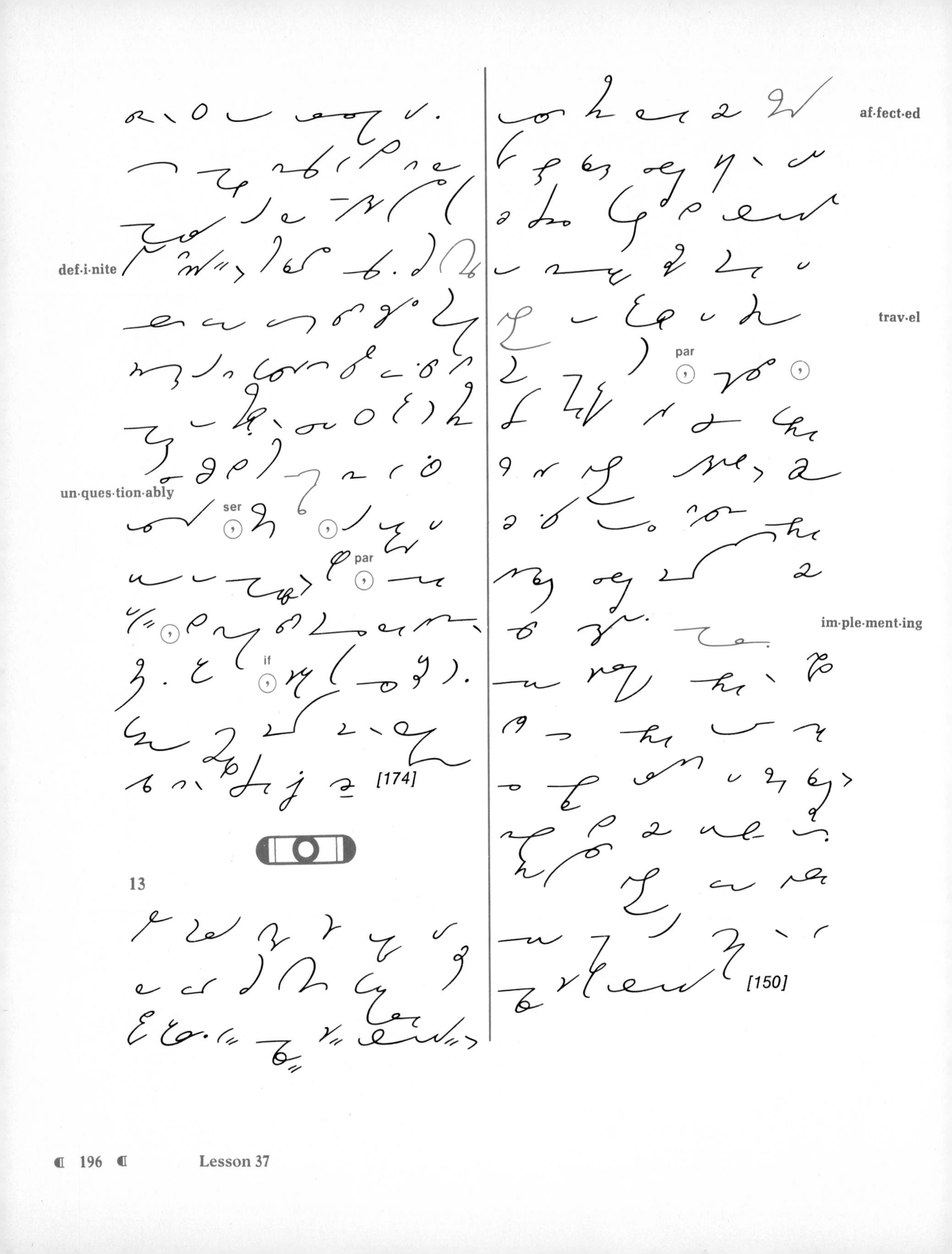

def·i·nite

un·ques·tion·ably

ser

par

if

[174]

13

af·fect·ed

trav·el

par

im·ple·ment·ing

[150]

Principles

1 **Word Ending -ship** The word ending *-ship* is represented by a disjoined *ish.*

Spell: f-r-e-end-ship, friendship

friendship membership scholarships
hardship ownership relationships

2 **Word Beginning Sub-** The word beginning *sub-* is represented by *s.*

Spell: sub-m-e-t, submit

submit subdivision suburban
subscribe substantiate sublease

3 **Word Ending -ulate** The word ending *-ulate* is represented by a disjoined *oo* hook.

Spell: r-e-gay-ulate, regulate

regulate formulates calculate
congratulate speculated calculator

4 **Word Ending -ulation** The word ending *-ulation* is represented by *oo-shun.*

Spell: r-e-gay-ulation, regulation

regulation population stipulations
accumulation insulation congratulations

5 Word Ending -rity The word ending *-rity* (and a preceding vowel) is represented by a disjoined *r*.

Spell: chay-rity, charity

charity	prosperity	authorities
majority	sincerity	securities
maturity	minority	integrity

Building Transcription Skills

6 PUNCTUATION PRACTICE ● , as clause

A subordinate clause introduced by *as* and followed by the main clause is separated from the main clause by a comma.

As you can see, *most of the work is finished.*

As you probably know, *Ms. Jane Ortega was made president of the company.*

Each time a subordinate clause beginning with *as* occurs in the Reading and Writing Practice, it will be indicated thus in the shorthand: as (,)

7 Business Vocabulary Builder

suburban Relating to the area on the outskirts of a city.

integrity Complete honesty.

everlasting Continuing indefinitely.

Reading and Writing Practice

8 Brief-Form Review Letter

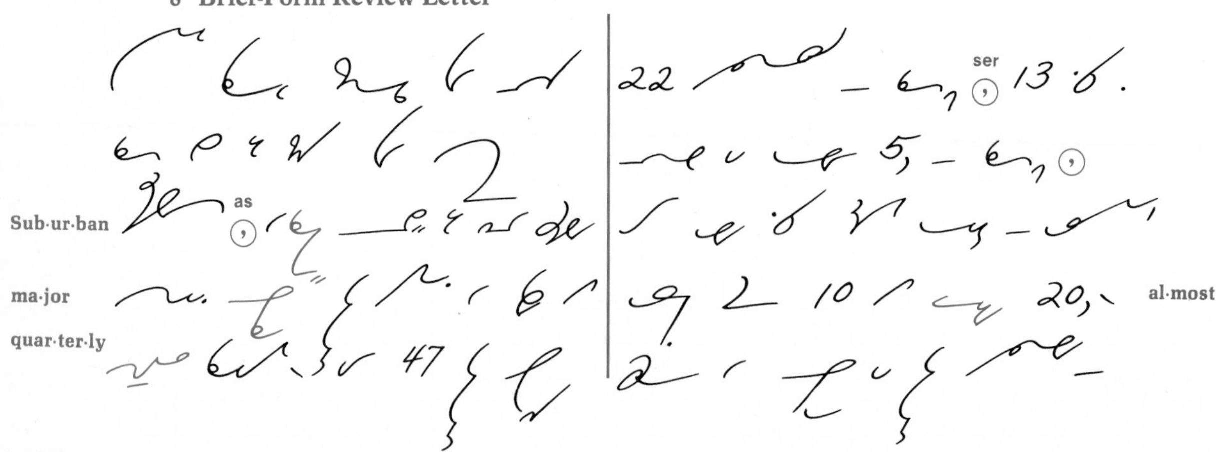

im·pres·sive

ex·ec·u·tive

if

in·tro·duc·to·ry

let·ter·head

[191]

9

ser

in·teg·ri·ty

ser

sign

as

amaz·ing·ly

[162]

10

pleas·ant

ac·cept·ed

par

con·grat·u·late

em·bossed

as

Chem·ist

ap

pe·ri·od·i·cal

ser

au·thor·i·ties

ev·er·last·ing

[158]

11

ma·jor·i·ty

if

as

raise

de·duc·tions

even·tu·al·ly

if

ap·prox·i·mate

dis·abled

in·for·ma·tion

par

[191]

Principles

1 Word Ending -lity The word ending *-lity* (and a preceding vowel) is represented by a disjoined *l*.

Spell: a-b-lity, ability

ability   locality   qualities

personality   reliability   responsibilities

2 Word Ending -lty The word ending *-lty* (and a preceding vowel) is also represented by a disjoined *l*.

Spell: f-a-k-ulty, faculty

faculty   loyalty   penalty

3 Word Ending -self The word ending *-self* is represented by *s*.

Spell: h-e-r-self, herself

herself   itself   myself

himself   yourself   oneself

4 Word Ending -selves The word ending *-selves* is represented by *ses*.

Spell: them-selves, themselves

themselves   ourselves   yourselves

Building Transcription Skills

5 PUNCTUATION PRACTICE ● , when clause

A subordinate clause introduced by *when* and followed by the main clause is separated from the main clause by a comma.

When I have an opportunity, *I will call him.*

When you finish the assignment, *raise your hand.*

Each time a subordinate clause beginning with *when* occurs in the Reading and Writing Practice, it will be indicated thus in the shorthand: when (,)

6 Business Vocabulary Builder

individuality Personality; a quality distinguishing one from another.

tonal A quality relating to sound, as in music.

compact *(adjective)* Closely drawn together or joined.

Reading and Writing Practice

7 Brief-Form Review Letter

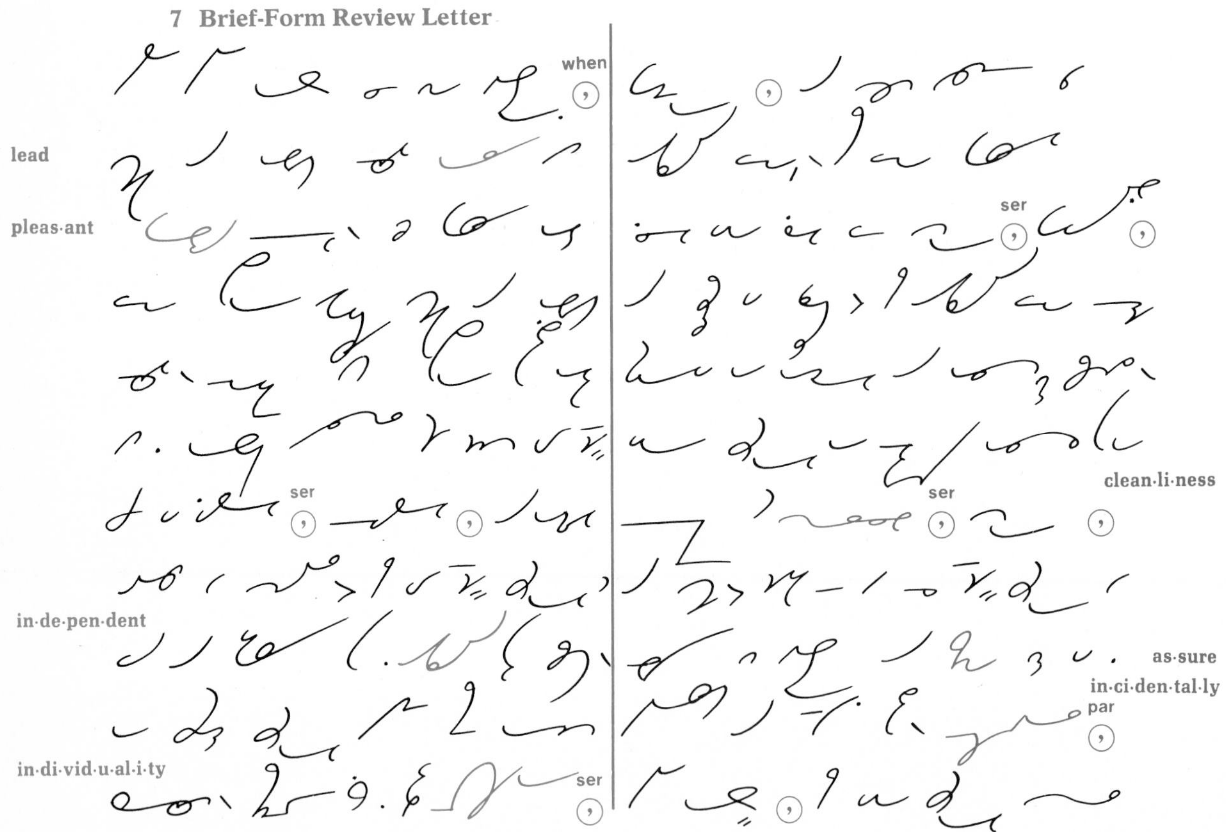

[217]

8

fi·del·i·ty

ser

sur·pris·ing·ly

ad·van·tage

par

re·ceive

when

ton·al

if

clar·i·ty

[188]

9

par

com·pact

when

al·most

scenes

sel·dom

de·scrip·tive

prob·a·bly

as

hes·i·tate

if

[161]

10

when

fac·ul·ty

an·nu·al

15 ser 16 17

par

suite

[134]

11

as

when

ap

if

ac·cess

par

as·pect

ser

[180]

12

ef·fi·cien·cy

its

dif·fi·cul·ties

ser

main·tain·ing

as

ap

if

when

re·ceive

par

me·di·um

[214]

Principles

1 **Abbreviated Words—in Families** Many long words may be abbreviated in shorthand by dropping the endings. This device is also used in longhand, as *Jan.* for *January*. The extent to which you use this device will depend on your familiarity with the words and with the subject matter of the dictation. When in doubt, write it out! The ending of a word is not dropped when a special shorthand word ending has been provided, such as *-lity,* in *ability.*

Notice how many of the words written with this abbreviating device fall naturally into families of similar endings.

-quent

consequent, consequence
consequently
subsequent
subsequently
eloquent, eloquence
frequent

-tribute

tribute
attribute
attributes
contribute
contributed
contribution
distribute
distributor
distribution

-quire

require
requirement
inquire
inquired
inquiries
acquire

-titute

substitute
substitution
institute
institution
constitute
constitution

-titude

aptitude gratitude latitude

-ology

psychology sociology apology

psychological sociological apologies

Building Transcription Skills

2 **PUNCTUATION PRACTICE ● , introductory**

A comma is used to separate a subordinate introductory clause from a following main clause. You have already studied the application of this rule to subordinate clauses introduced by *if, as,* and *when.* Here are examples of subordinate clauses introduced by other subordinating conjunctions.

Although the price is high, *I believe we should purchase the land.*

Before you leave, *please stop in to see me.*

Unless we hear from you, *we must cancel your subscription.*

While I am eager to finish the work, *I do not believe we should compromise its quality.*

A comma is also used after introductory words or phrases such as *furthermore, on the contrary,* and *for instance.*

Furthermore, the letter contained a typographical error.

On the contrary, you are to be commended for your effort.

For instance, the company was late with its last payment.

Each time a subordinate introductory word, phrase, or clause other than one beginning with *if, as,*or *when* occurs in the Reading and Writing Practice, it will be indicated thus in the shorthand: intro (,)

Note: If the subordinate clause or other introductory expression *follows* the main clause, the comma is usually not necessary.

I am enclosing an envelope for your convenience in sending me your answer.

3 **Business Vocabulary Builder**

aptitude A natural ability; talent.

gratitude Appreciation of benefits received.

enviable Highly desirable.

formative Developing; taking shape.

Reading and Writing Practice

4 Brief-Form Review Letter

ac·quire

for·eign

lan·guage

ex·pen·di·ture

en·roll

if

com·plet·ed

intro

con·grat·u·late

flu·ent·ly

[152]

5

intro

ap

as

de·vel·oped

psy·cho·log·i·cal·ly

intro

hours'

el·e·men·ta·ry

par

les·son

[138]

6

in·spi·ra·tion

ap

world's

en·vi·able

intro

par

fre·quent·ly

[134]

per·suade

par

though

as

ac·knowl·edge

ser

debt

intro

ser

opin·ions

[161]

7

morn·ing's

8

Neu·ro·log·i·cal

if

clerical

intro

as

process

capital

intro

intro

consequently

par

[163]

9

charities

intro

budgetary

intro

exhausted

[137]

Principles

1 Abbreviated Words—in Families (Continued)

-graph

photograph	stenographer	paragraph
photographic	autographed	paragraphed
photographically	typographical	telegraphing

2 Abbreviated Words—Not in Families The ending may be omitted from long words even though they do not fall into a family.

anniversary	significant, significance	reluctant, reluctance
memorandum	statistic	privilege
convenient, convenience	statistics	privileged
equivalent	statistical	privileges

3 Word Beginning Trans- The word beginning *trans-* is represented by a disjoined *t*.

Spell: trans-m-e-t, transmit

transmit	transport	translation
transact	transportation	transit
transaction	transfer	transistor

Building Transcription Skills

4 SIMILAR-WORDS DRILL • accept, except

accept To take.

Did you *accept* the offer?

except *(preposition)* Omitted; left out.

All the listed states, *except* one, border on the ocean.

5 Business Vocabulary Builder

alternative A choice.

pertinent Having direct bearing on the matter at hand; relevant.

autograph A person's handwritten signature.

Reading and Writing Practice

6 Brief-Form Review Letter

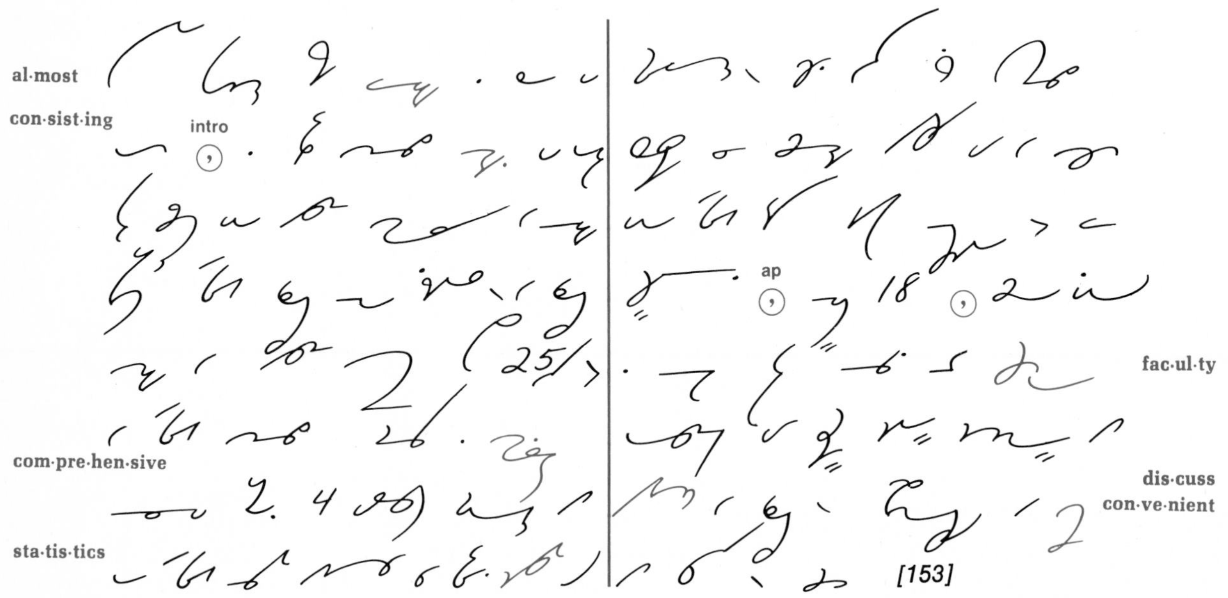

7

intro

ser

en·light·en·ing

per·formed

if

treat

intro

per·ti·nent

ser

rec·og·nized

as

ben·e·fit

[158]

8

ap

sig·nif·i·cant

re·veals

grat·i·tude

intro

gen·u·ine

par

when

if

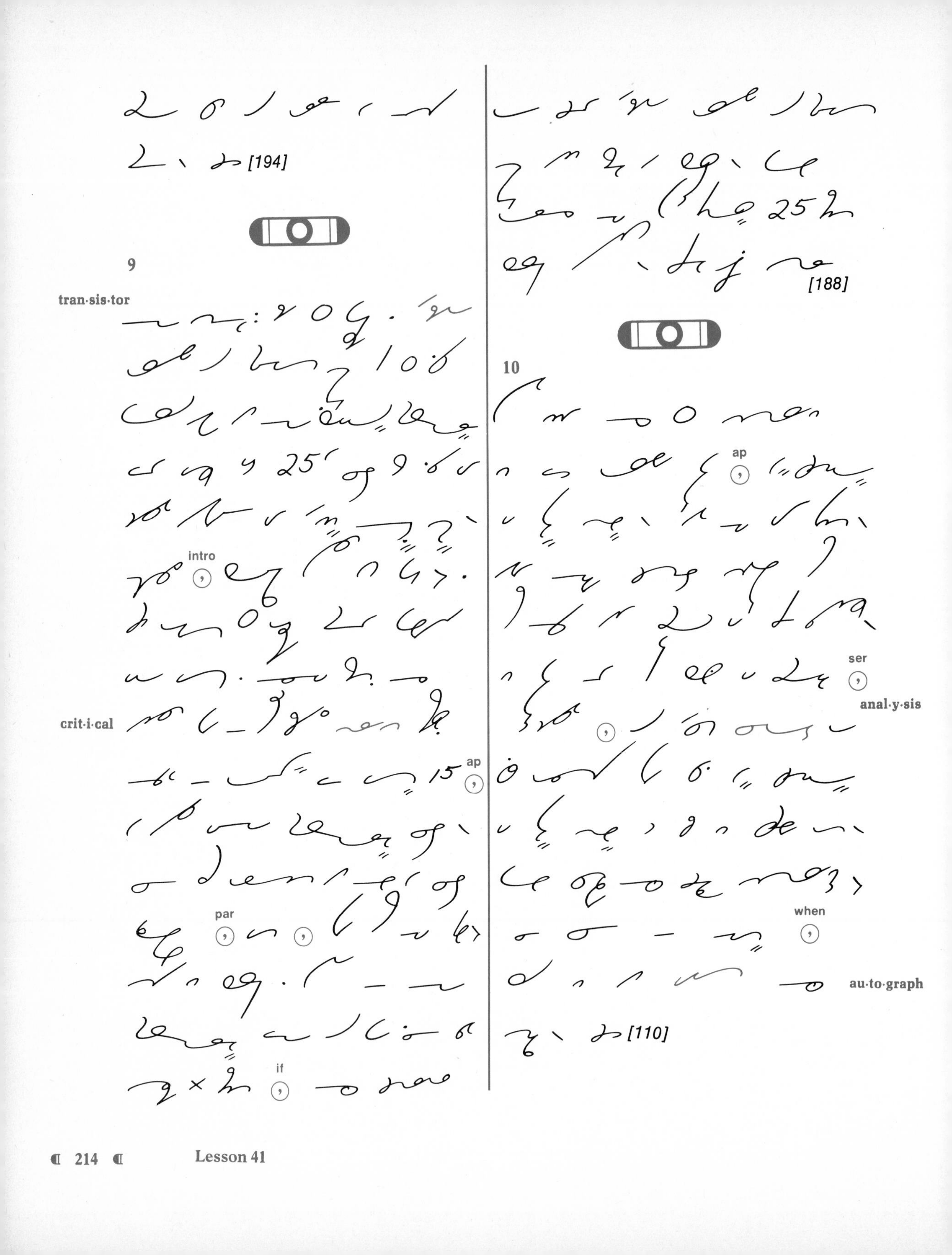

[194]

9

tran·sis·tor

intro

crit·i·cal

ap

par

if

[188]

10

ap

ser

anal·y·sis

when

au·to·graph

[110]

RECALL

There are no new shorthand devices for you to learn in Lesson 42. However, Lesson 42 does contain an Accuracy Practice, a review of word beginnings and endings you have studied thus far, and a Reading and Writing Practice.

Accuracy Practice

1 **My** **Lie** **Fight**

To write these combinations accurately:

☐ **a** Join the broken circle in the same way that you would join an **a** circle, but turn the **end** inside the circle.

☐ **b** Before turning the **end** of the circle inside, be sure that the stroke touches the stroke to which the **i** is joined.

☐ **c** Avoid making a point at the places indicated by arrows.

Practice Drill

My, night, sight, line, mile.

2 **Ow** **Oi**

To write these combinations accurately:

☐ **a** Keep the hooks deep and narrow.

☐ **b** Place the circles **outside** the hooks as indicated by the dotted lines.

Practice Drill

Out, now, doubt, scout, toy, soil, annoy.

3 **Ith** **Nt, Nd** **Mt, Md**

To write these combinations accurately:

- ☐ **a** Slant the strokes as indicated by the dotted lines.
- ☐ **b** Start these strokes to the right and upward.

Practice Drill

There are, and will, empty, health, lined, ashamed.

Compare:

Hint, heard; tamed, detailed.

4 **Recall Chart** There are 90 word beginnings and endings in the following chart. Can you read them in 5 minutes or less?

WORD BEGINNINGS AND ENDINGS

1						
2						
3						
4						

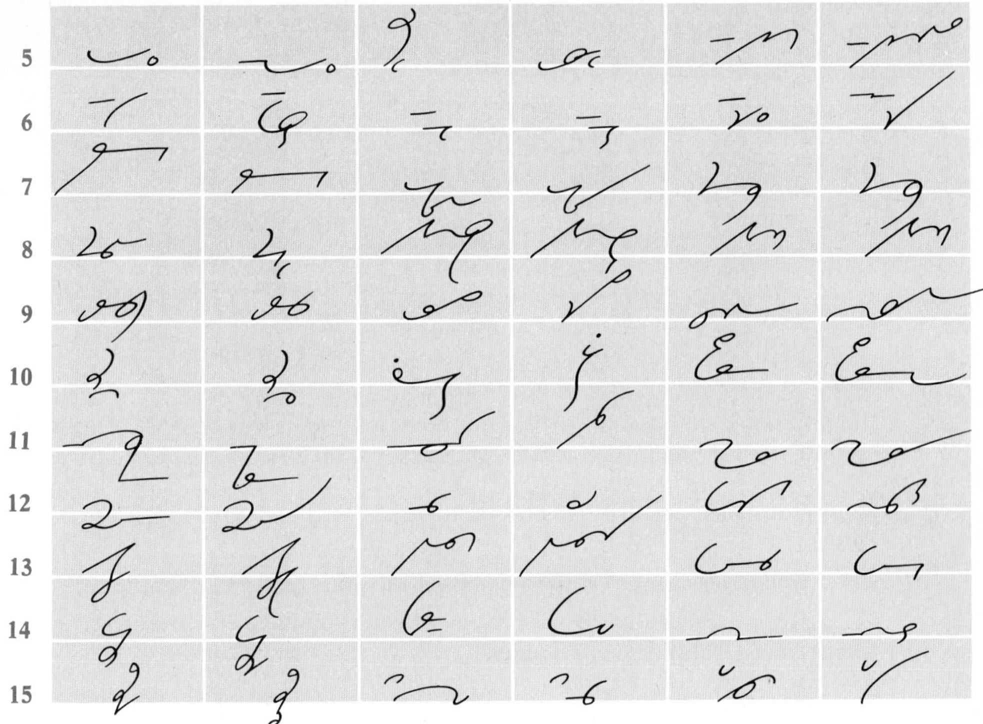

Building Transcription Skills

5 **Business Vocabulary Builder**

conversion The changing from one form to another.

complexity Difficulty; the state of being complex.

mechanized *(adjective)* Made automatic or routine; done by a machine.

Reading and Writing Practice

Reading Scoreboard Twelve lessons have gone by since you last measured your reading speed. You have, of course, continued to do each Reading and Writing Practice faithfully, and, consequently, your reading speed will reflect this faithfulness! The following table will help you measure your reading speed on the *first reading* of Lesson 42.

Lesson 42 contains 522 words

If you read Lesson 42 in	your reading rate is
15 minutes	**35 words a minute**
16 minutes	**32 words a minute**
17 minutes	**30 words a minute**
19 minutes	**28 words a minute**
21 minutes	**25 words a minute**
26 minutes	**20 words a minute**

If you can read Lesson 42 through the first time in less than 15 minutes, you are doing well. If you take considerably longer than 26 minutes, perhaps you should:

☐ **1** Pay closer attention in class while the shorthand devices are being presented to you.

☐ **2** Spend less time trying to decipher outlines that you cannot read.

☐ **3** Review, occasionally, all the brief forms you have studied by referring to the chart near the back of your text.

6 Data Processing

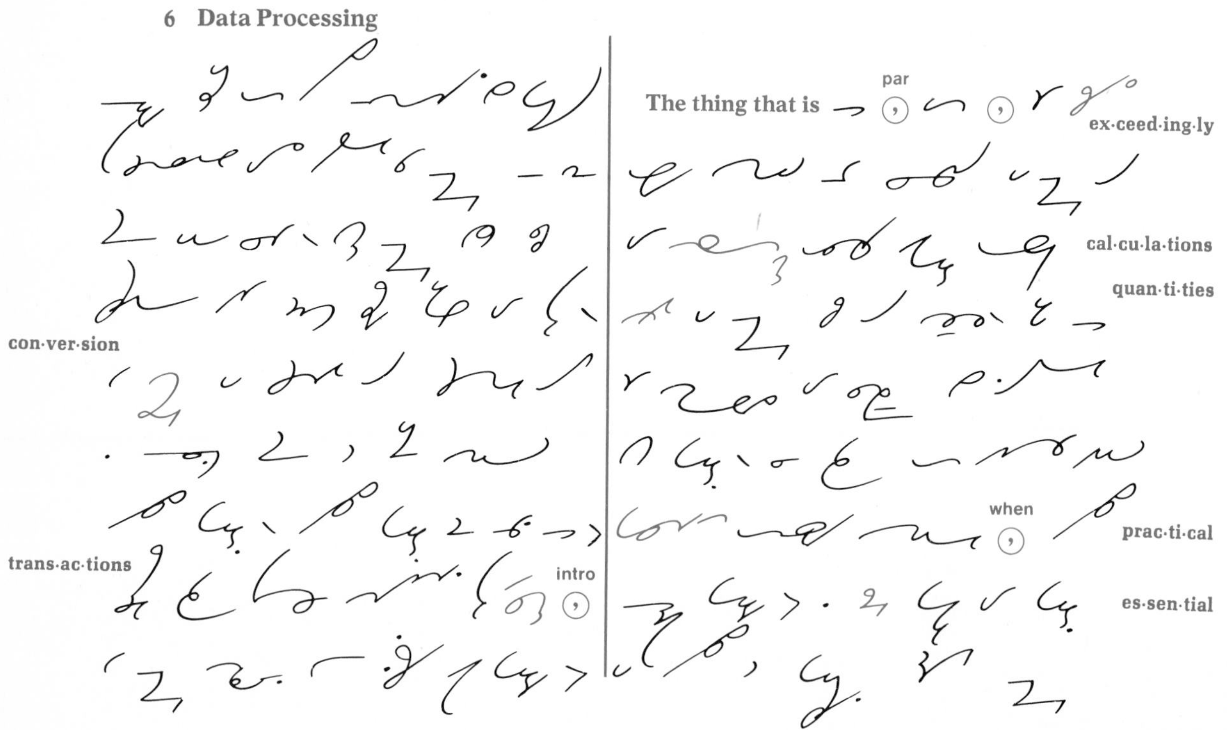

de·ci·sions ser

ini·ti·ate

if

ac·ces·si·ble

as

ser

elab·o·rate

[323]

7 Letters of Request

intro

ser

intro

ac·cu·rate

con·se·quent·ly

intro

intro

mech·a·nized

intro

lack

[199]

8 WHAT'S IN A NAME?

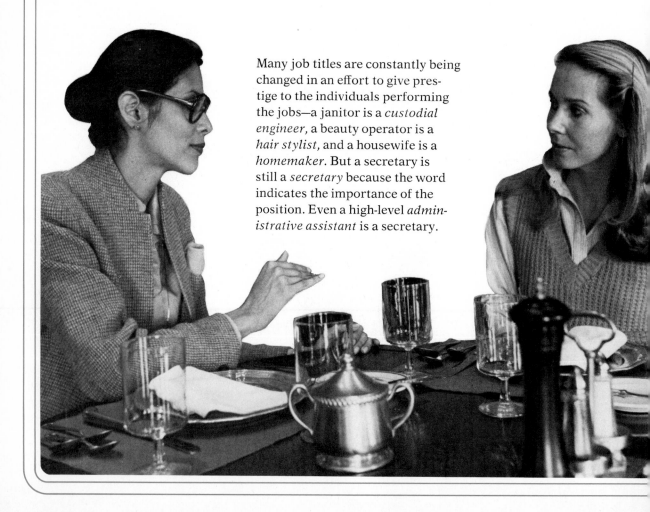

Many job titles are constantly being changed in an effort to give prestige to the individuals performing the jobs—a janitor is a *custodial engineer*, a beauty operator is a *hair stylist*, and a housewife is a *homemaker*. But a secretary is still a *secretary* because the word indicates the importance of the position. Even a high-level *administrative assistant* is a secretary.

Secretaries are close at hand when major executive decisions are made. Because of this, they gain status and prestige in the eyes of others. Moreover, secretaries gain a sense of self-value because they are needed, they make a valuable contribution to managerial performance, and they are involved in management decisions. Of course, with high status goes high pay, security, and pleasant surroundings.

Secretaries are indispensable. They handle all the routine items that executives usually aren't even aware of, and they take on special assignments to reduce the executive's work load. In a secretary's absence, it is SOP (standard operating procedure) for an executive to say, "My secretary, who's on vacation, worked on this project and will be able to help you next week."

Regardless of your exact title—secretary, executive secretary, administrative assistant—status is a built-in feature of the job.

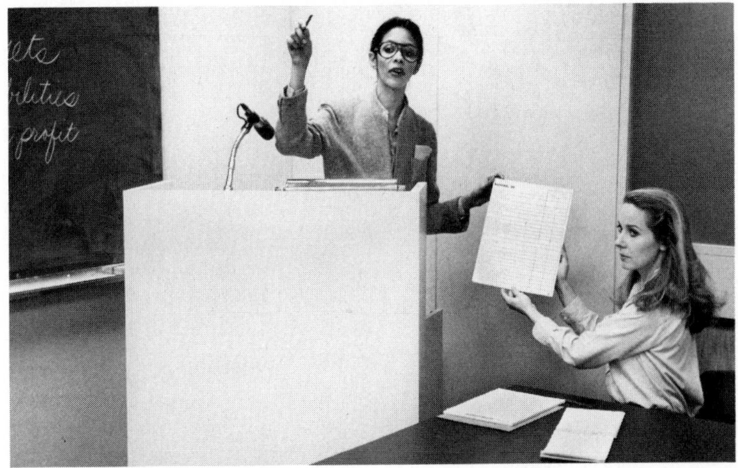

Principles

1 Word Beginning Mis- The word beginning *mis-* is represented by *m-s.*

Spell: mis-t-a-k, mistake

mistake misplaced misunderstand
misconception mislaid misunderstood
misprint misapprehension mystery

2 Word Beginning Super- The word beginning *super-* is represented by a disjoined right *s.*

Spell: super-v-ī-s, supervise

supervise superintendent superior
supervisor superhuman superb
supervision superimpose supersede

3 U Represented by OO The *oo* hook may be used after *n* and *m* to represent the sound of *u,* as in *music.*

Spell: m-oo-s-e-k, music

music musical municipal
mutual communicate continue
manuscript monument discontinue

Building Transcription Skills

4 PUNCTUATION PRACTICE ● , conjunction

A comma is used to separate two independent clauses that are joined by one of the following conjunctions: *and, but, or, for, nor.*

An independent clause (sometimes called a main or a principal clause) is one that has a subject and a predicate and that could stand alone as a complete sentence.

We have nine students in the organization, but *only six of them can attend the meeting.*

The first independent clause is:

We have nine students in the organization.

And the second independent clause is:

Only six of them can attend the meeting.

Both clauses could stand as separate sentences, with a period after each. Because the thoughts of the two clauses are closely related, however, the clauses were joined to form one sentence. Because the two independent clauses are connected by the conjunction *but,* a comma is used between them and is placed before the conjunction.

Each time this use of the comma occurs in the Reading and Writing Practice, it will be indicated thus in the shorthand: conj (,)

5 Business Vocabulary Builder

misconceptions Wrong impressions; misunderstandings.

commuter One who travels back and forth regularly, as between a suburb and a city.

rejected Refused to accept.

role An assigned or assumed function.

Reading and Writing Practice

6 Brief-Form Review Letter

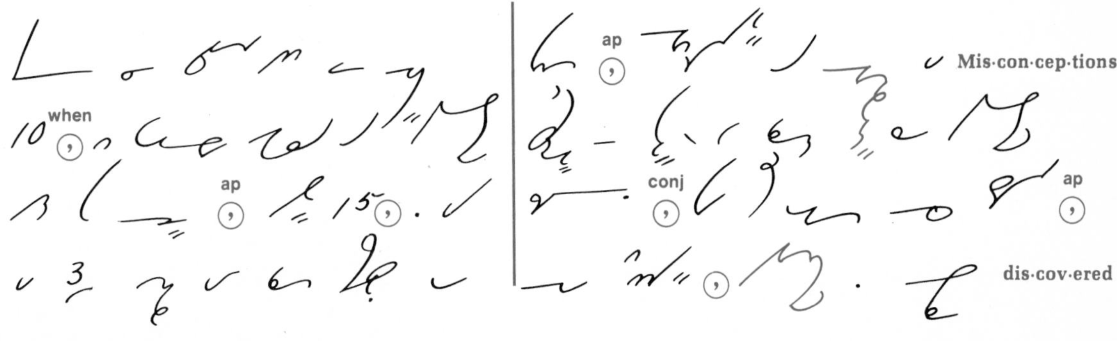

mis·spelled

mis·take

oc·curred

conj

photo·to·graph·ic

intro

intro

[165]

7

ex·cel·lent

equiv·a·lent

conj

col·lege

de·scribed

if

555-1026

su·perb

en·roll

ser

re·turn

en·closed

pro·vid·ed

[195]

8

Mu·nic·i·pal

sub·mit·ted

sup·port

su·pe·ri·or

con·firmed

[190]

9

per·son·nel

role

ben·e·fi·cial

su·per·vi·so·ry

val·u·able

con·tin·ue

if

555-8164

par

[181]

10

mis·ap·pre·hen·sions

ser

en·thu·si·asm

555-9263

[123]

11

con·grat·u·la·to·ry

as

conj

[106]

Principles

1 Word Beginning Self- The word beginning *self-* is represented by a disjoined left *s.*

Spell: self-m-a-d, self-made

self-made self-addressed selfish

self-control self-improvement selfishness

self-reliance self-explanatory unselfishly

2 Word Beginning Circum- The word beginning *circum-* is also represented by a disjoined left *s.*

Spell: circum-s-ten-s, circumstance

circumstance circumstances circumstantial

3 Word Ending -ification The word ending *-ification* is represented by a disjoined *f.*

Spell: r-a-t-ification, ratification

ratification notification modifications

classification gratification qualifications

justification identification specifications

Building Transcription Skills

4 PUNCTUATION PRACTICE ● , and omitted

When two or more consecutive adjectives modify the same noun, they are separated by commas.

Enclosed is a stamped, self-addressed *envelope.*

However, the comma is not used if the first adjective modifies the combined idea of the second adjective plus the noun.

The suit is made of beautiful blue *material.*

Note: You can quickly determine whether to insert a comma between two consecutive adjectives by mentally placing *and* between them. If the sentence makes good sense with *and* inserted between the adjectives, then the comma is used.

For example, the first sentence would make good sense if it read:

Enclosed is a stamped and *self-addressed envelope.*

Each time this use of the comma occurs in the Reading and Writing Practice, it will be indicated thus in the shorthand: and o (,)

5 Business Vocabulary Builder

motivate Provide a need or desire for a person to act.

rigid Strictly observed; inflexible.

controller A financial officer of a company.

Reading and Writing Practice

6 Brief-Form Review Letter

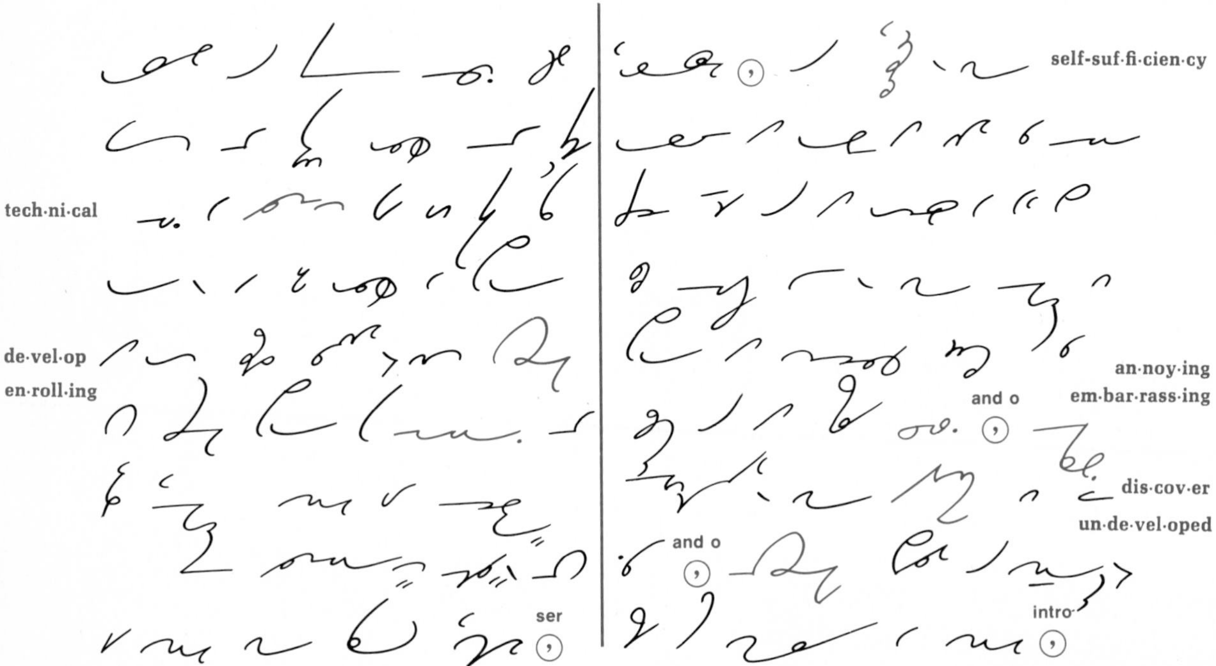

intro

cir·cum·stances

[197]

7

intro

self-em·ploy·ment

if

al·most

when

par

pen·al·ty

with·draw·al

par

sen·si·ble

and o

[173]

8

out·stand·ing

conj

and o

ab·so·lute·ly

intro

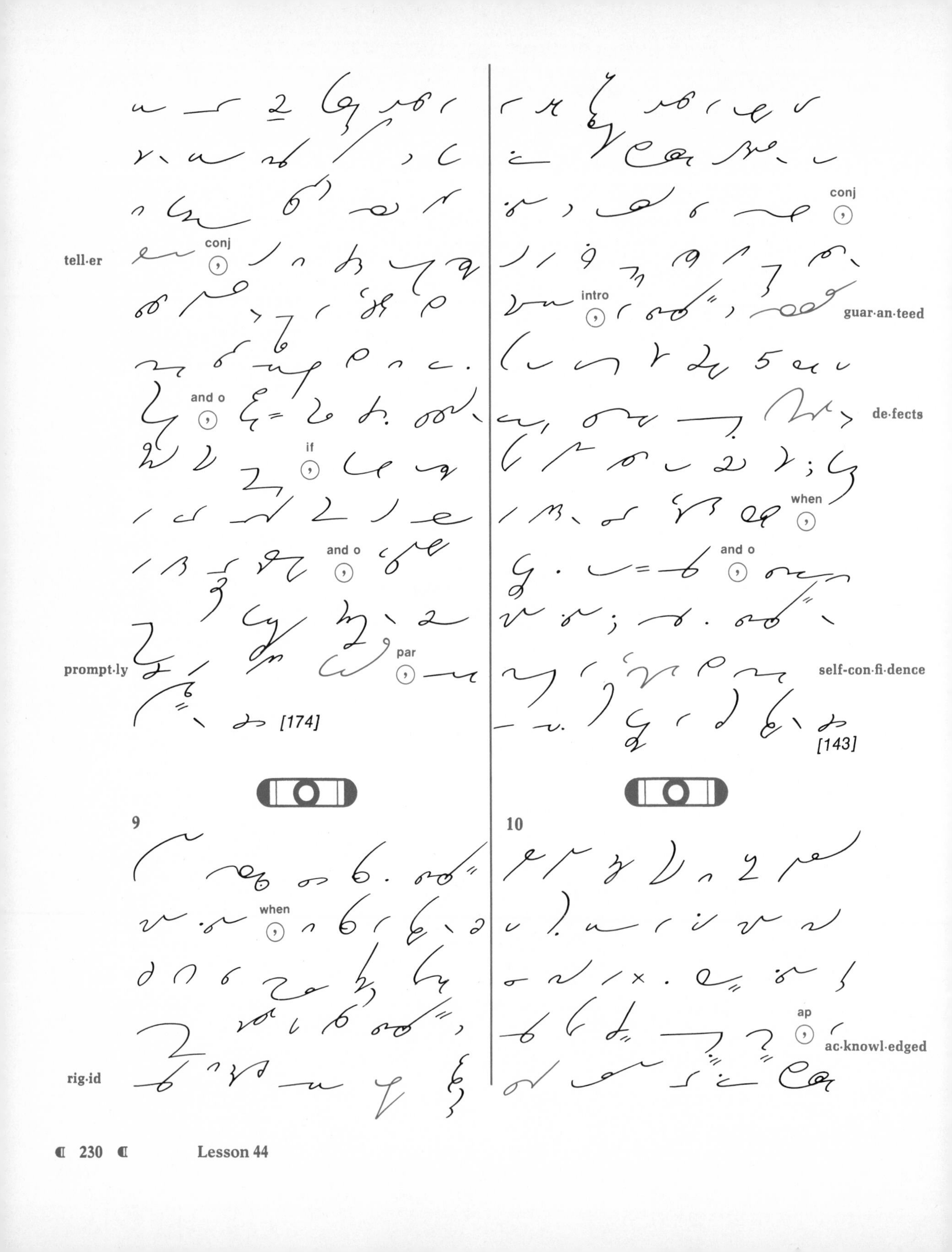

conj

tell·er

and o

if

and o

par

prompt·ly

[174]

conj

intro

guar·an·teed

de·fects

when

and o

self-con·fi·dence

[143]

9

when

rig·id

10

ap

ac·knowl·edged

self-ex·plan·a·to·ry

if

and o

par

[135]

11

ap

re·gard·ing

li·brary

3104

18

as

mi·nor

550

intro

item·ized

con·trol·ler

and o

[164]

Principles

1 Word Ending -hood The word ending *-hood* is represented by a disjoined *d.*

Spell: n-a-b-r-hood, neighborhood

neighborhood	boyhood	likelihood
childhood	girlhood	parenthood

2 Word Ending -ward The word ending *-ward* is also represented by a disjoined *d.*

Spell: o-n-ward, onward

onward	outward	rewarding
backward	upward	forward
afterward	inward	forwarded

3 Ul *Ul* is represented by *oo* when it precedes a forward or upward stroke.

Spell: re-s-ul-t, result

result	consultant	cultured
consult	ultimately	culminate
insult	multitude	simultaneous

4 Quantities and Amounts Here are a few more helpful abbreviations for quantities and amounts.

600		$5,000,000,000		several hundred	
$600		a dollar		5 pounds	
$8,000,000		a million		8 feet	

◉ *Observe that the* n *for* hundred *is written* under *the figure as a positive distinction from* million, *in which the* m *is written* beside *the figure.*

Building Transcription Skills

5 SPELLING FAMILIES ● silent e dropped before -ing

An effective device to improve your ability to spell is to study words in related groups, or spelling families, in which all the words contain a common spelling problem.

To get the most benefit from these spelling families, practice them in this way:

☐ **1** Spell each word aloud, pausing slightly after each syllable.

☐ **2** Write the word once in longhand, spelling it aloud as you write it.

Words in Which Silent E Is Dropped Before -ing

chal-leng-ing	**mak-ing**	**sav-ing**
hav-ing	**man-u-fac-tur-ing**	**stim-u-lat-ing**
hous-ing	**pre-par-ing**	**su-per-vis-ing**
in-creas-ing	**re-ceiv-ing**	**typ-ing**

You will find a number of the words in this spelling family used in the Reading and Writing Practice of this lesson.

6 Business Vocabulary Builder

anthology A collection of literary pieces or passages.

alleviate Ease.

superficial Shallow; concerned only with the obvious.

Reading and Writing Practice

7 Brief-Form Review Letter

ap

15

su·per·vis·ing

de·vel·op·ment

An·thol·o·gy

mem·o·ran·dum

ac·qui·si·tion

15 as

5

45

and o

[100]

intro

al·le·vi·ate

par

mi·nor

su·per·fi·cial

par

ser

8

rough·ly

deemed

conj

mak·ing

ecol·o·gy

[198]

9

par

intro

ap

ser

prob·a·bly

as

rec·og·nized

and o

mul·ti·tude

intro

serv·ing

par

if

con·ve·nient

[174]

10

gov·ern·ment

ser

42

neigh·bor·hoods

in·di·cated

75,

par

ex·traor·di·nary

when

ul·ti·mate·ly

par

[184]

11

as

ap

intro

pe·ri·od

if

intro

guar·an·tee

ex·ceed

[181]

Principles

1 **Word Ending -gram** The word ending *-gram* is represented by a disjoined *gay*.

Spell: t-e-l-gram, telegram

telegram	monogram	programs
diagram	monogrammed	programmer

2 **Word Beginning Electric** The word beginning *electric-* (and the word *electric*) is represented by a disjoined *el*.

Spell: electric-l, electrical

electric	electrically	electric wire
electrical	electric typewriter	electric motor

3 **Word Beginning Electr-** The word beginning *electr-* is also represented by a disjoined *el*.

Spell: electro-n-e-k, electronic

electronic	electrician	electricity

4 **Compounds** Most compound words are formed simply by joining the outlines for the words that make up the compound. In some words, however, it is desirable to modify the outline for one of the words in order to obtain an easier joining.

anyhow	someone	within
anywhere	worthwhile	withstand
thereupon	however*	notwithstanding

*The dot may be omitted in *however*.

5 **Intersection** Intersection, or the writing of one shorthand character through another, is sometimes useful for special phrases. This principle may be used when constant repetition of certain combinations of words in your dictation makes it clearly worthwhile to form special outlines for them.

a.m.		vice versa	
p.m.		Chamber of Commerce	

Building Transcription Skills

6 **SIMILAR-WORDS DRILL • it's, its**

it's Contraction for *it is*.

It's not necessary to bring all your books to class.

its Possessive form of *it*.

You will be pleased with *its* efficiency.

7 **Business Vocabulary Builder**

grapevine An informal person-to-person means of passing information.

via By means of; by way of.

subsidiaries Companies wholly controlled by other companies.

plausible Appearing worthy of belief.

Reading and Writing Practice

8 **Brief-Form Review Letter**

conj

grape·vine

its sub·sid·iar·ies

intro

intro

ad·van·tage

when

[157]

9

intro

our·selves

in·stall·ing ef·fi·cient

and o

help·ful

char·ac·ter·is·tic

intro

as·signed

it's

ser

intro

ac·cu·ra·cy

160

intro

as

great

[244]

10

intro

4

par

like·li·hood

ul·ti·mate·ly 48 50

8

and o

prime

me·di·um 10

and o

par

when

if

[178]

11

via

ap

15

mis·spelled

oc·curred

ac·cept

and o

conj

[148]

12

it's

plau·si·ble

intro

ap

intro

sin·cer·i·ty

intro

conj

intro

intro

par

ap

[150]

Principles

1 **Geographical Expressions and Names** In geographical expressions and proper names, the ending *-burg* is represented by *b*; the ending *-ville*, by *v*; the ending *-ington*, by a disjoined *ten* blend; the ending *-ingham*, by a disjoined *m*.

-burg

Spell: h-a-r-e-s-burg, Harrisburg

Harrisburg Pittsburgh Hamburg

-ville

Spell: n-a-ish-ville, Nashville

Nashville Jacksonville Evansville

-ington

Spell: oo-o-ish-ington, Washington

Washington Wilmington Harrington

-ingham

Spell: f-r-a-m-ingham, Framingham

Framingham Buckingham Cunningham

Building Transcription Skills

2 **GRAMMAR CHECKUP**

Most business executives have a good command of the English language; some rarely make an error in grammar. There are times, though, when even the best dictators will inadvertently use a plural verb with a singular noun or use the objective case when they should use the nominative. They usually know better, but in concentrating intently on expressing a thought or idea, they occasionally suffer a grammatical lapse.

It will be your job as a secretary to catch these occasional errors in grammar and to correct them when you transcribe.

From time to time in the lessons ahead, you will be given an opportunity to brush up on some of the rules of grammar that are frequently violated.

GRAMMAR CHECKUP • subject and verb

A verb must agree with its subject in number.

Our president is *on vacation.*

The receipts are *being processed now.*

The inclusion of a phrase such as *in addition to, as well as,* or *along with* after the subject does not affect the number of the verb. If the subject is singular, use a singular verb; if the subject is plural, use a plural verb.

Our president, *as well as the treasurer,* is *on vacation.*

The receipts, *along with the invoice,* are *being processed now.*

3 Business Vocabulary Builder

unsurpassed Cannot be exceeded or outdone.

stabilize To hold steady.

overwhelmingly Overcome by force of numbers; crushingly.

Reading and Writing Practice

4 Brief-Form Review Letter

com·mer·cial

when

quan·ti·ties

if

if

re·ceive

un·sur·passed

intro

and o

[148]

5

if

brak·ing

icy

if

prac·ti·cal

de·vel·op·ment

sta·bi·lize

ser

240

if

max·i·mum

ef·fi·cien·cy

ser

and o

if

when

intro

[208]

6

as

intro

great

in·sig·nif·i·cant

par

par

par

con·sult

ap

neigh·bor·hood

[144]

7

intro

intro

frayed

par

if

and o

par

[170]

8

over·whelm·ing·ly

Con·se·quent·ly

re·plen·ish

as

intro

and o

conj

par

col·umns

[127]

9

if

for·ward

par

ser

when

ap

au·tho·riz·ing

conj

[137]

RECALL

In Lesson 47 you studied the last of the new shorthand devices of Gregg Shorthand. In this lesson you will find an Accuracy Practice, a Recall Chart that reviews word-building principles of Gregg Shorthand, and a Reading and Writing Practice.

Accuracy Practice

1 **Def**

To write this stroke accurately:

☐ **a** Make it large, almost the full height of your notebook line.

☐ **b** Make it narrow.

☐ **c** Start and finish the stroke on the same level of writing, as indicated by the dotted line.

Practice Drill

Divide, definite, defeat, devote, differ, endeavor.

2 **Ith** **Ten** **Tem**

To write these strokes accurately:

☐ **a** Slant the strokes as indicated by the dotted lines.

☐ b Make the **beginning** of the curves deep.

☐ c Make the **tem** large, the **ith** small, and the **ten** about half the size of the **tem**.

Practice Drill

In the, in time, tender, teeth, detain, medium.

3 **Recall Chart** This chart contains illustrations of word-building and phrasing principles of Gregg Shorthand.

WORDS

1

2

3

4

5

6

7

8

9

10

11

12

13

14

PHRASES, AMOUNTS, QUANTITIES

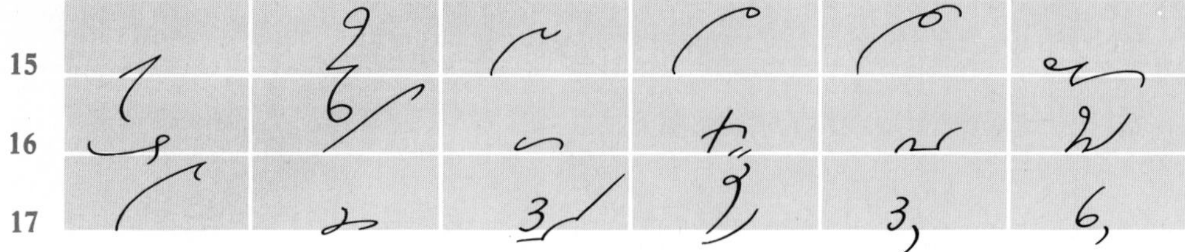

Building Transcription Skills

4 Business Vocabulary Builder

attainment Achievement; accomplishment.
composure Self-possession; calmness.
clarify Make clear or plain.
adverse Hostile; unfavorable.

Reading and Writing Practice

5 The Secretary Writes Letters

ir·re·spon·si·ble
in·dif·fer·ent
ul·ti·mate·ly
its

Good business

mo·nop·o·ly
com·pose
at·tain·ment

rou·tine

and o

suc·cess·ful

if

and o

com·pli·cat·ed

If your

if

com·po·sure

clar·i·fy

par

if

quite
worth·while
self-as·sur·ance

as

conj

intro

di·min·ish

tri·umph

ser

when

def·i·nite·ly

[404]

6 Human Relations

conj

de·stroyed
mis·take

ser

and o

ad·verse

intro

par

ex·ert

and o

[120]

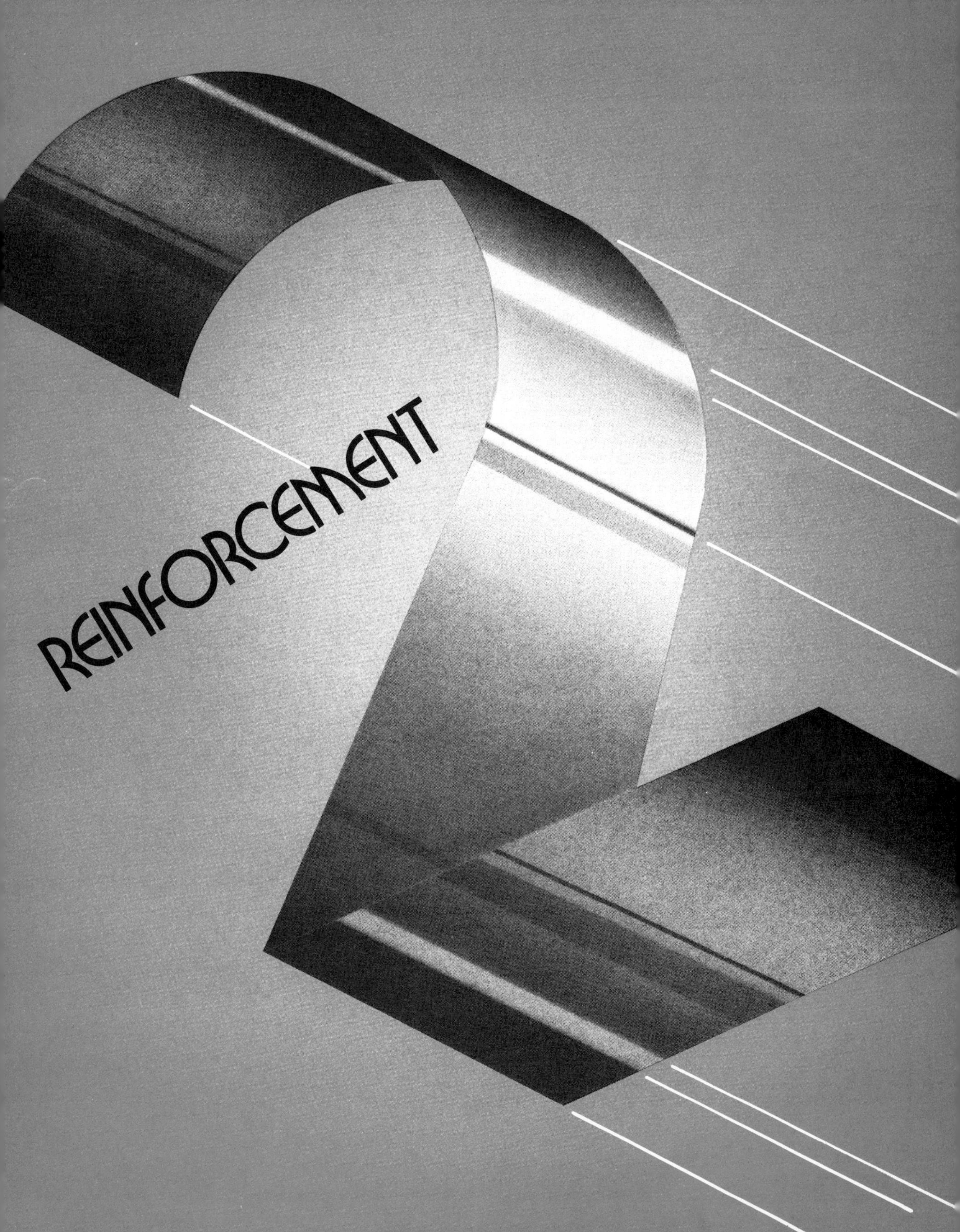
REINFORCEMENT

THE IDEAL SECRETARY

The list of desirable traits in an employee is endless—intelligence, dependability, honesty, cooperativeness, and so on. For the ideal secretary, however, there are four very important qualifications that are needed for success on the job.

Good Communication Skills

Because it is probably the secretary's main function, this qualification is of primary importance. It is the secretary's responsibility to convey the employer's instructions and messages through written and verbal communications. The secretary is expected to produce written communications that are correct in fact, in grammar, in form, and in style without explicit instructions to do so. Through verbal contacts with the various people involved in the employer's work, the secretary's tone of voice and facial expressions say just as much, if not more, than the words spoken. The secretary must always be on the alert in order to handle all communications successfully.

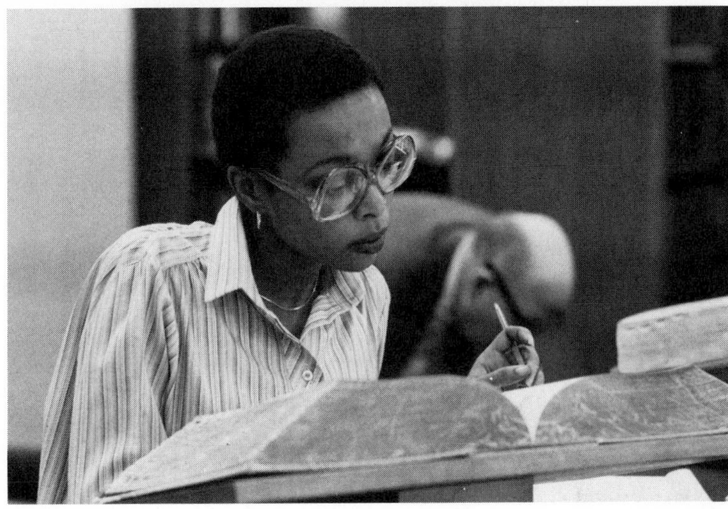

Excellent Stenographic Skills

Most commonly thought of in terms of dictation and transcription speeds, excellent stenographic skills go hand in hand with written communications skills. The more knowledgeable you are about what is needed for accurate and well-prepared letters and reports, the faster your transcription speed will be. Of course, good typing speed—at least 60 words a minute—is an important factor.

As for taking dictation, the secretary is expected to be able to keep up with the dictator and not say "You're going too fast for me." A dictation speed of at least 100 words a minute will usually prevent this from happening.

Poise

Poise is often thought of as the state of being calm, cool, and collected no matter what's going on around you. But poise is also knowing how to cope with any situation. A poised person does not get flustered by irate customers, persistent salespeople, disgruntled co-workers, or people who have been inadvertently "stood up" by an employer. Poise consists of tact, self-confidence, maturity, and, once again, good communication skills.

Good Grooming

Good grooming is an admirable quality in anyone. It is a "must" for secretaries because they are a reflection of their employers and their companies. Cleanliness, neatness, and a well-rested appearance project a favorable image. Proper attire is of the utmost importance; extremes in dress and hair style are to be avoided. *Good taste* is the catchword.

Lesson 49 provides a review of the shorthand principles you studied in Chapter 1.

1 BRIEF FORMS, DERIVATIVES, AND PHRASES

1 Am, in-not, it-at, a-an, will-well, are-hour-our, have, Mr., I.
2 Willing, wills, ours, increase, invite, indeed.
3 But, with, of, Mrs., you-your, can, that, the, is-his.
4 I will, I will not, in that, in the, with the, of the, I am, I have.

Reading Practice

2

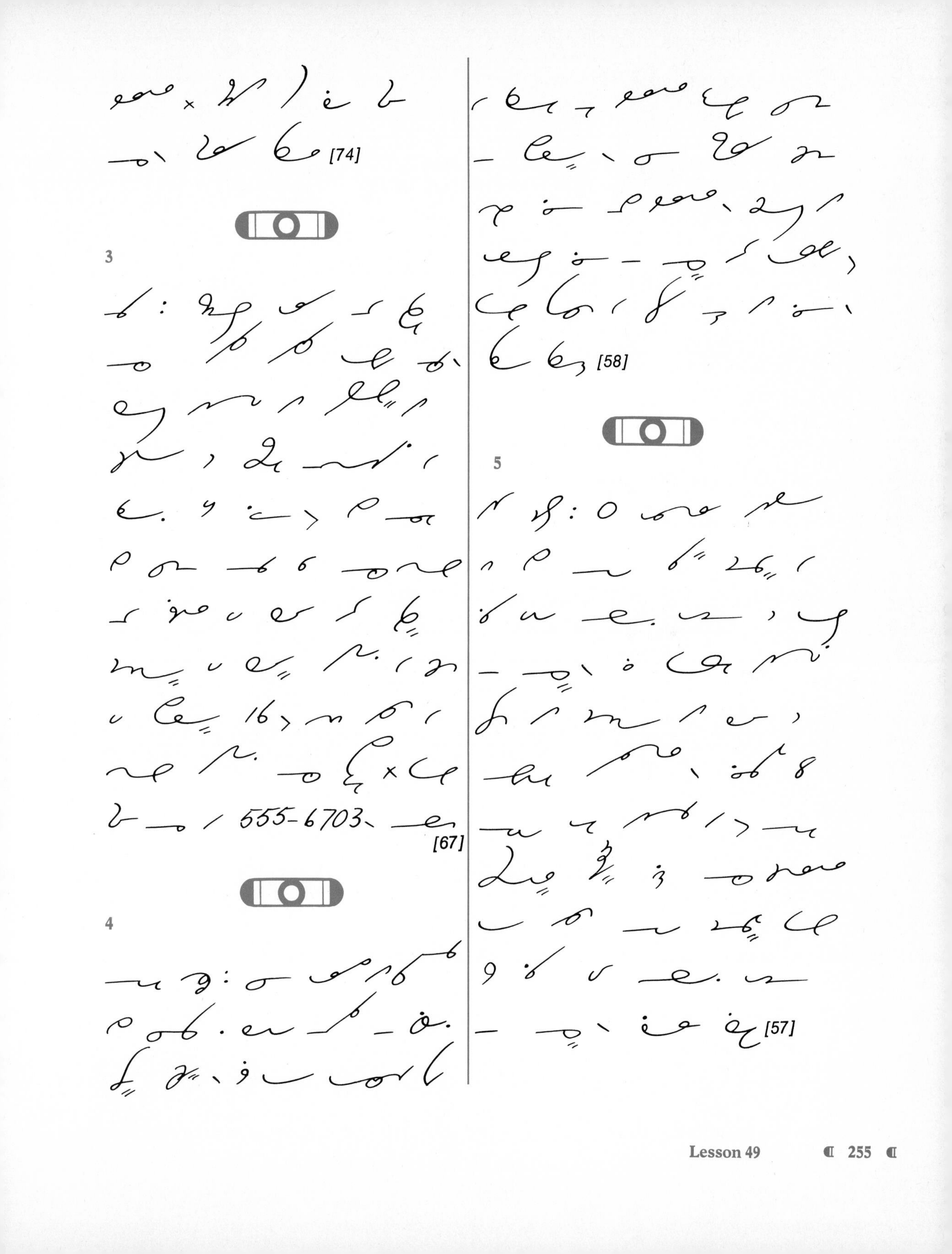

[74]

3

555-6703

[67]

4

[58]

5

[57]

6

[50]

[46]

7

8

[68]

9

10

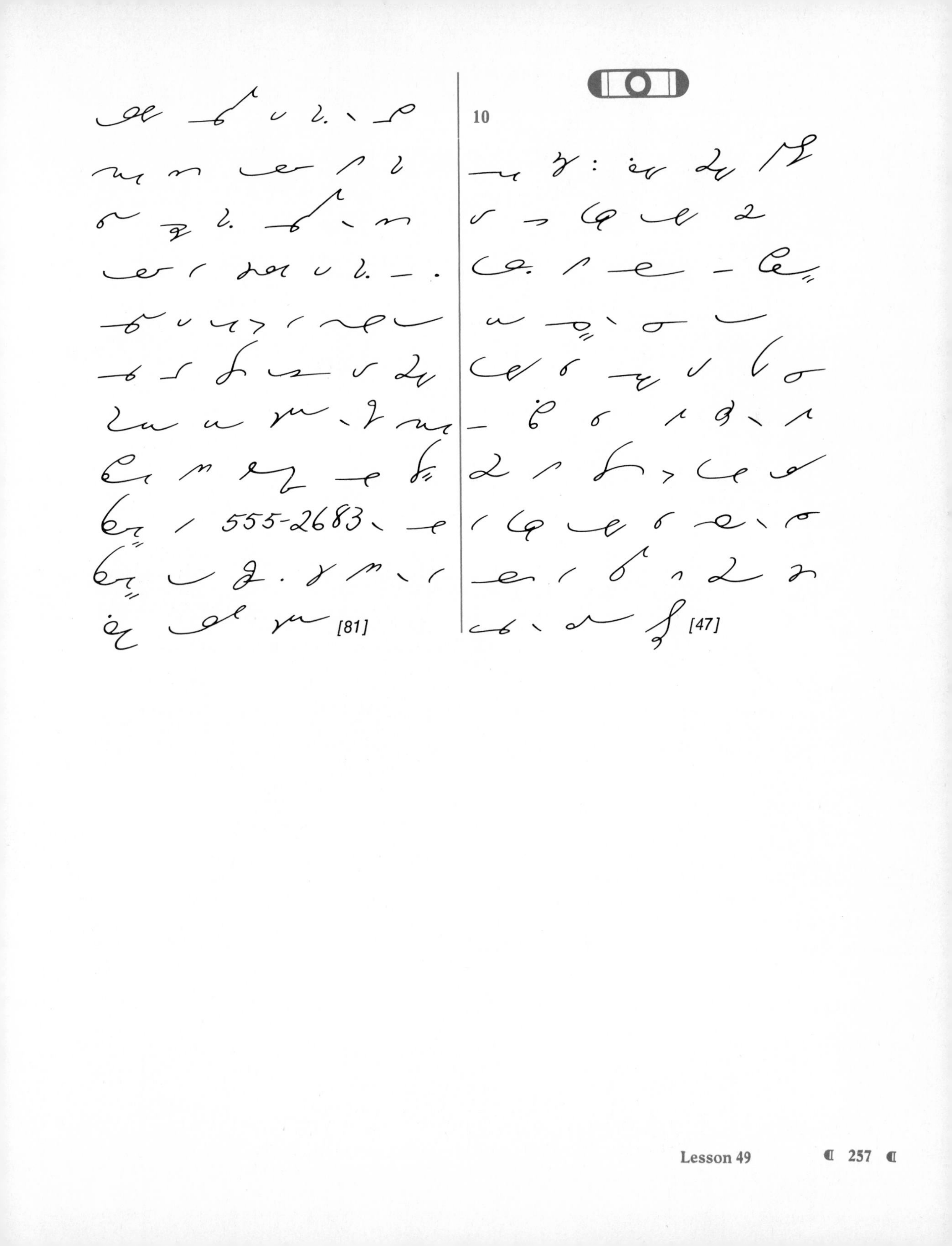

555-2683

[81]

10

[47]

The practice material in Lesson 50 concentrates on the principles you studied in Chapter 2.

1 BRIEF FORMS, DERIVATIVES, AND PHRASES

1 Be-by, begin, became, beneath, for, before, would, there (their), therefore.
2 This, good, goods, they, which, them, and, when.
3 From, should, could, send, sending, were, after, street.
4 I would, for the, this is, they are, to them, from the, I have been, I have not been able.

Reading and Writing Practice

2

[112]

[90]

3

[111]

4

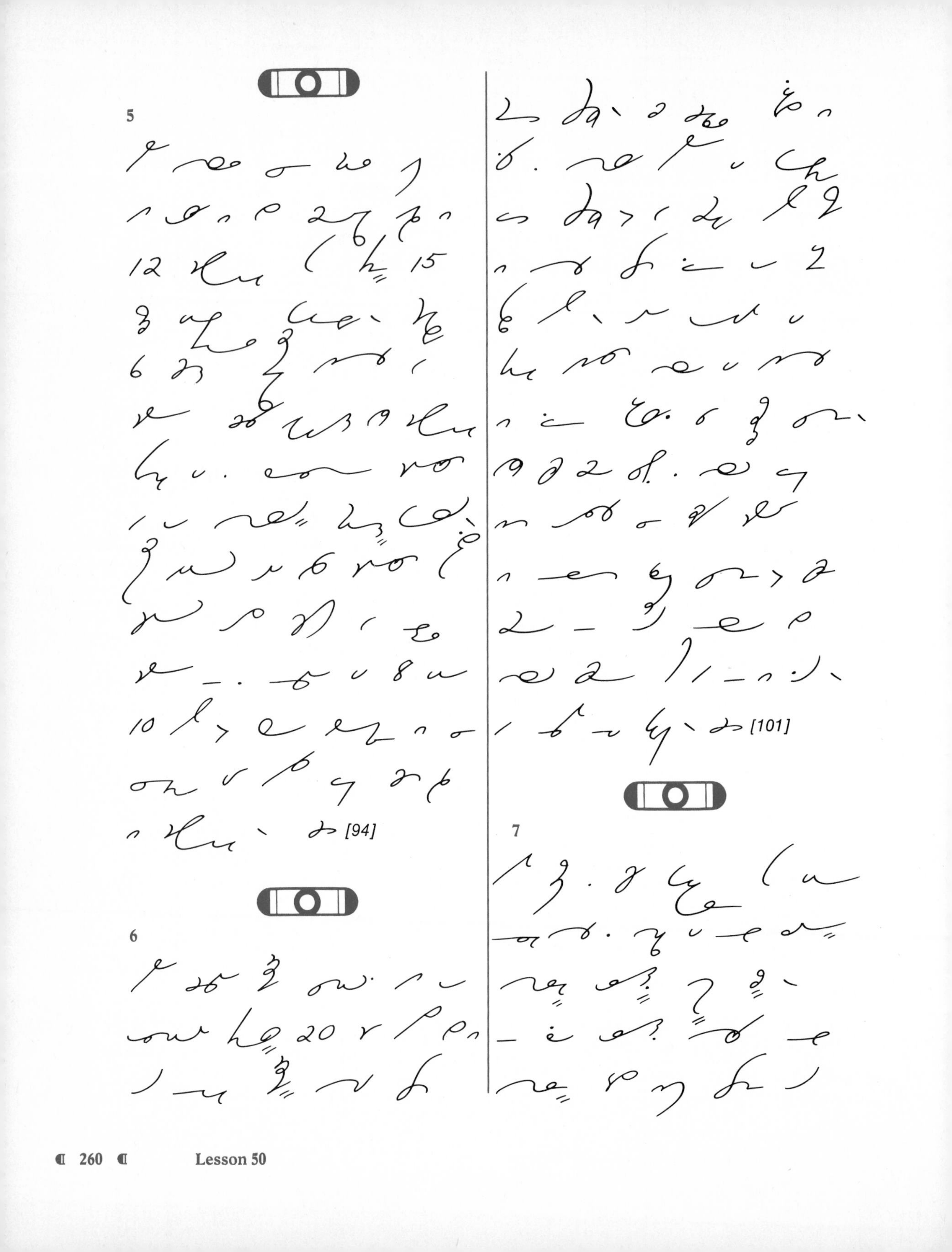

5

[94]

6

[101]

7

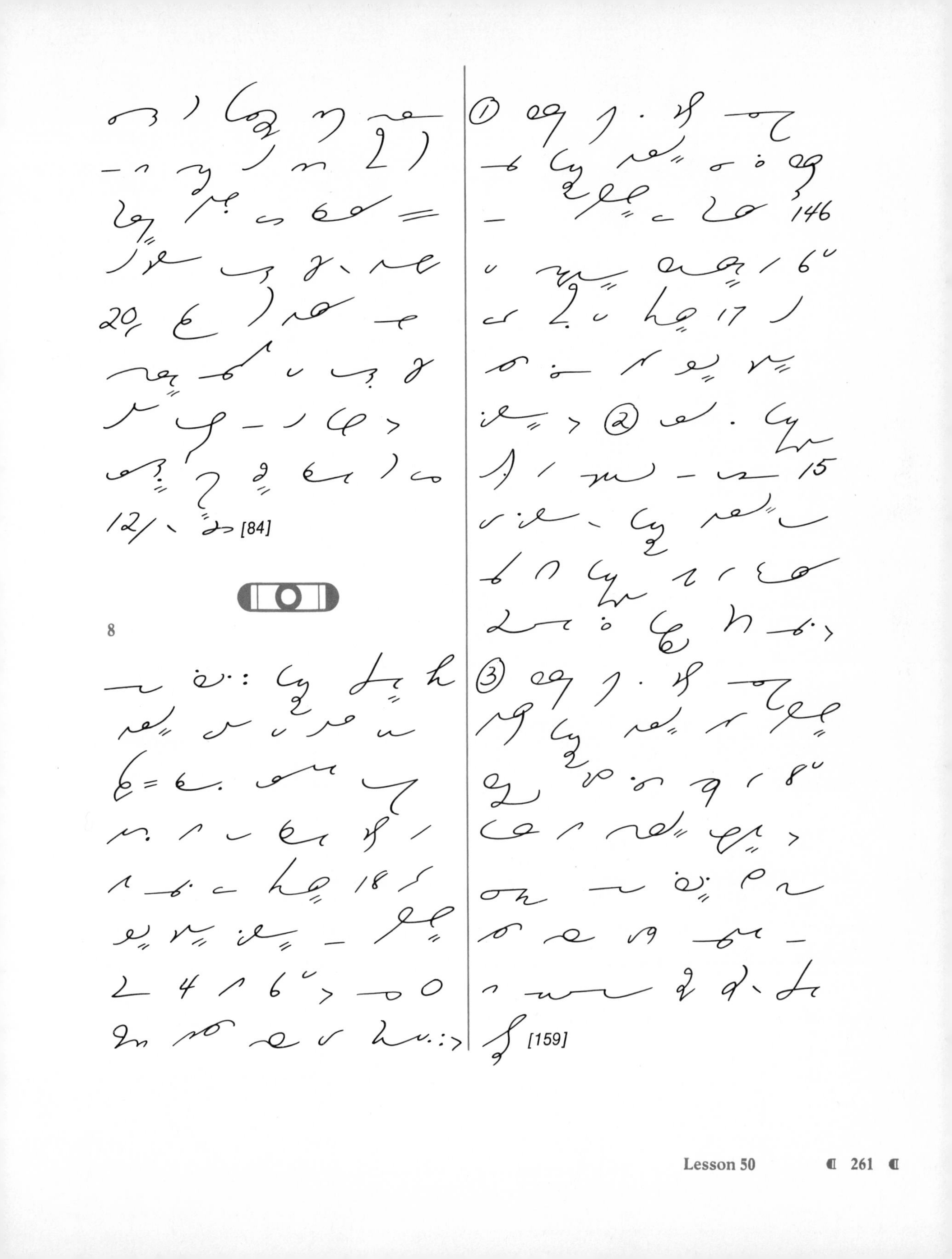

[84]

8

[159]

This lesson reviews the principles you studied in Chapter 3.

1 BRIEF FORMS, DERIVATIVES, AND PHRASES

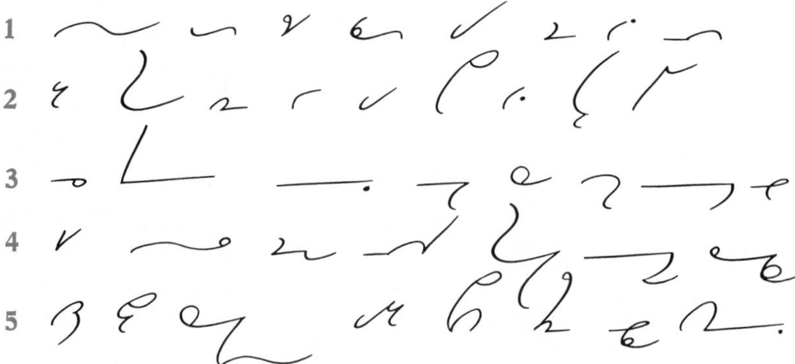

1 Glad, work, yesterday, circular, order, soon, thank, enclose.

2 Was, value, one (won), than, what, about, thing-think, business, doctor.

3 Any, gentlemen, morning, important-importance, where, company, manufacture, next.

4 Short, gladly, sooner, enclosed, valuable, manufacturer, elsewhere.

5 Thank you for, I was, I will be glad, what was, about this, everyone, next year, this morning.

Building Transcription Skills

2 Business Vocabulary Builder

earnestly With serious intent; gravely.

urgently Insistently; calling for immediate action.

semester A school term, usually 18 weeks.

3

1970

[174]

4

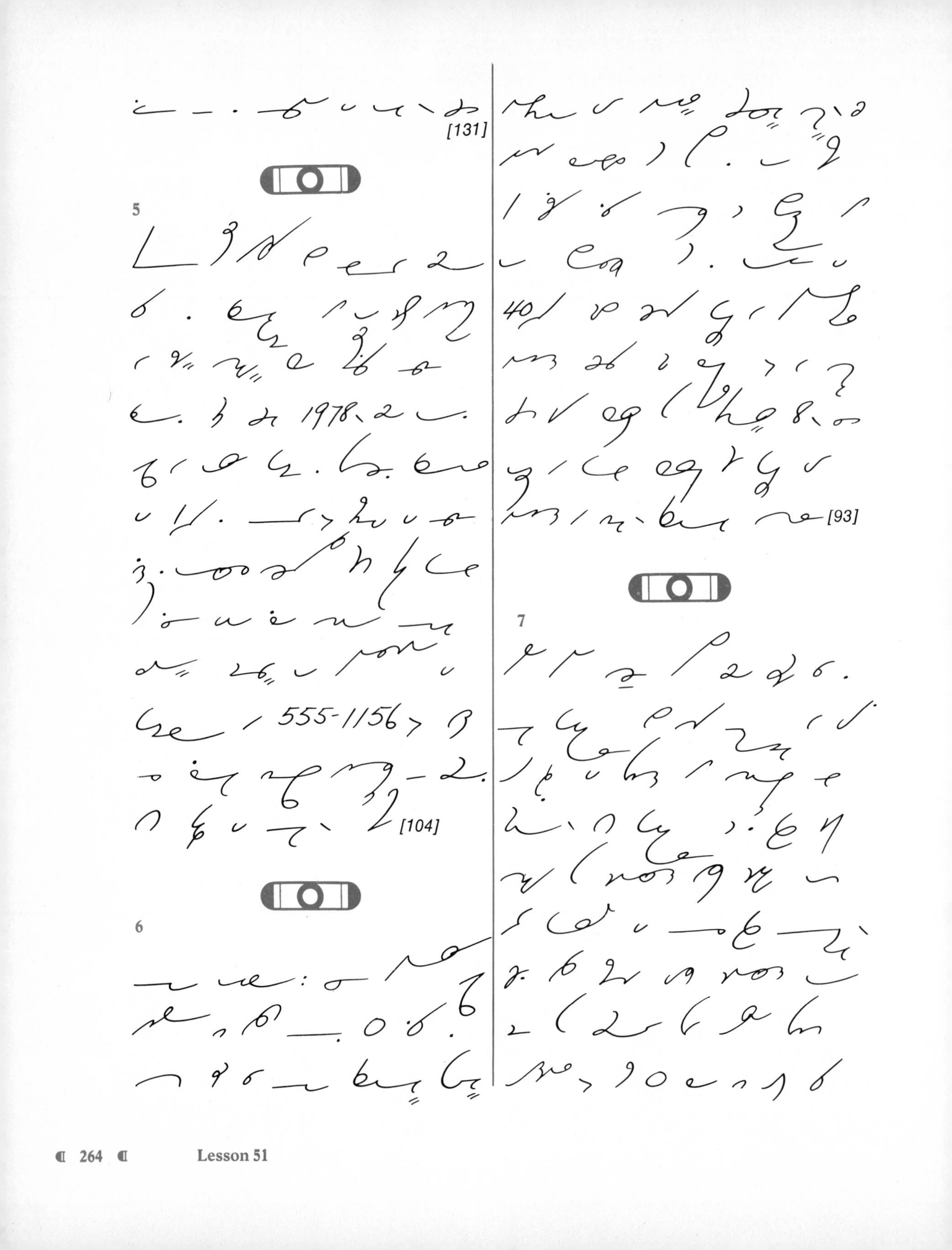

[131]

5

[104]

6

[93]

7

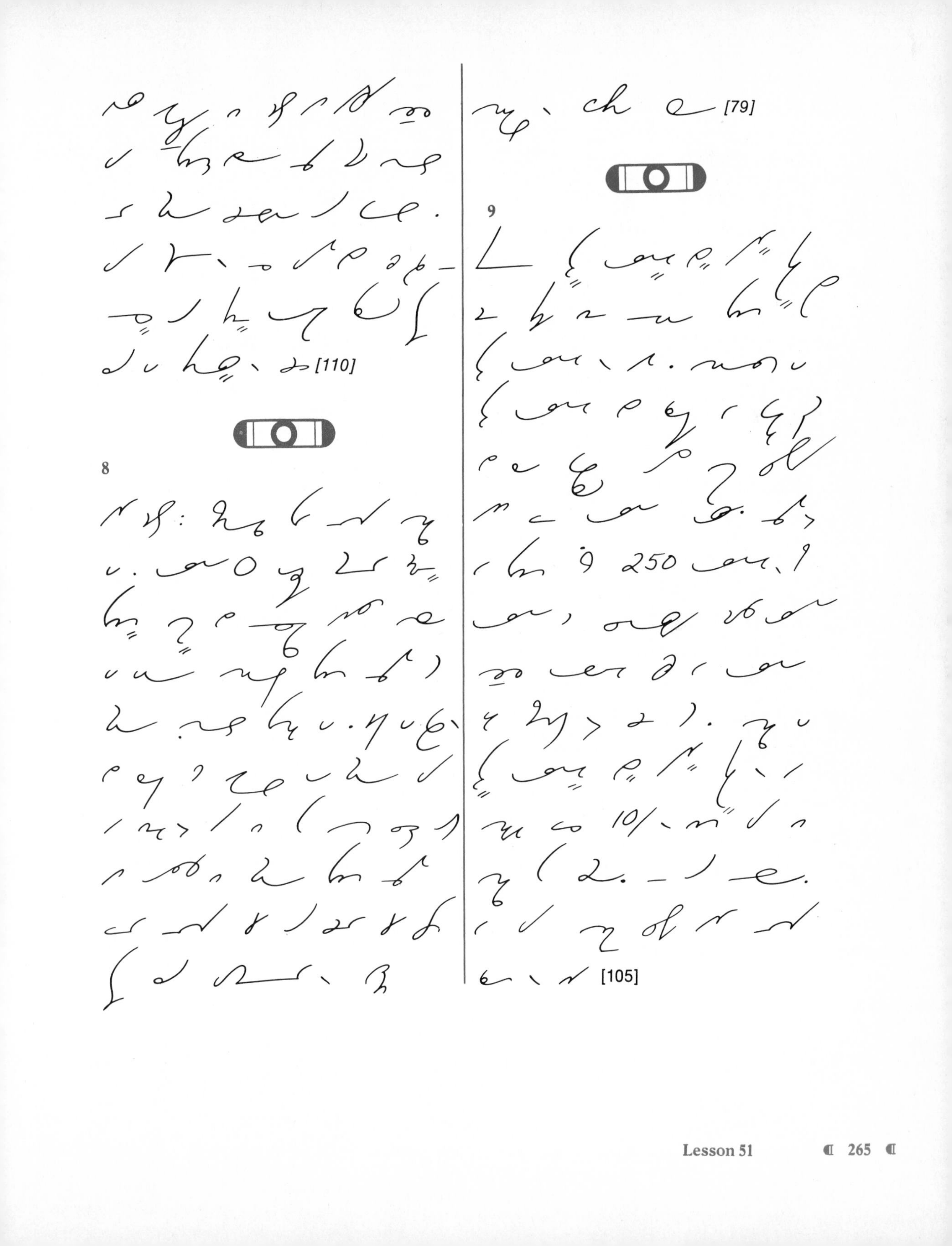

[110]

8

[79]

9

250

10/

[105]

This lesson concentrates on the principles presented in Chapter 4.

1 BRIEF FORMS, DERIVATIVES, AND PHRASES

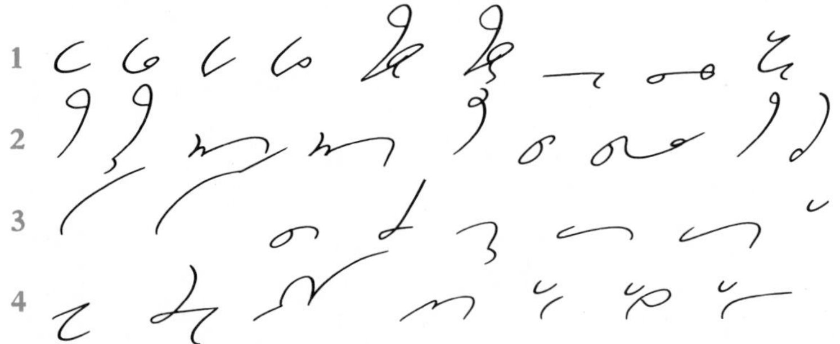

1 Present, presently, part, partly, advertise, advertises, Ms., immediately, opportunities.

2 Advantage, advantages, suggest, suggestion, several, out, outlet, ever-every, very.

3 Time, timed, acknowledge, general, questions, organize, organization, over.

4 To present, very important, at this time, to question, over the, over that, over them.

Building Transcription Skills

2 SPELLING FAMILIES • silent e dropped before -ment

Most words ending in *e* retain the *e* before the ending *-ment*.

ad-ver-tise-ment	**ar-range-ment**	**man-age-ment**
amuse-ment	**en-cour-age-ment**	**re-quire-ment**
an-nounce-ment	**en-gage-ment**	**state-ment**
but		
ac-knowl-edg-ment	**judg-ment**	**ar-gu-ment**

3 Business Vocabulary Builder	**not up to par** Not up to a usual standard of excellence. **potential** *(adjective)* Possible but not yet realized. **name-dropper** One who casually mentions the name of a well-known person in order to impress the listener.

Reading and Writing Practice

4

ad·ver·tise·ment

Dai·ly

great

[130]

5

re·ceived

wheth·er

ac·knowl·edg·ment

re·al·ly

[119]

6

Cal·en·dar

in·valu·able

ap·point·ments

bot·tom

[130]

7

ar·gu·ments

po·ten·tial

omit·ted

dem·on·stra·tion

[109]

8

dif·fer·ent

its

38 [133]

9

brochure

nephew

decisively

proud

[73]

10

inflation

beat

models

10

22

spinets

uprights

10

22 [123]

This lesson reviews the principles you studied in Chapter 5.

1 BRIEF FORMS, DERIVATIVES, AND PHRASES

1 Difficult, envelope, progress, satisfy-satisfactory, state, request, success, under, wish.

2 Particular, probable, regular, speak, subject, regard, newspaper, opinion, idea.

3 Responsible, worth, public, publish-publication, ordinary, experience, usual, world, recognize.

4 Recognition, probably, extraordinary, to progress, to speak, to publish, under the, under that.

Building Transcription Skills

2 Business Vocabulary Builder

mart A market; place where things are bought and sold.

in arrears Behind.

poultry Hens, roosters, turkeys, geese, etc.

Reading and Writing Practice

3

de·duc·tions

en·ti·tled

5

10

rec·og·nized

sat·is·fac·to·ri·ly

15

[172]

4

Award

15

rec·og·ni·tion

1976

di·rec·tor

oc·ca·sion

10

[209]

5

ex·tend

wel·come

[139]

un·spoiled

6

350/

ar·rears

in·stall·ment

ar·range·ments

[138]

7

re·al·ize

poul·try

gro·cer·ies

min·i·mum

[110]

SHORTHAND NOTEBOOK CHECKLIST

Your shorthand notebook is an important tool of your trade.

■ **1** Use a notebook with a spiral binding so that the pages always lie flat.

■ **2** Write on the front cover your name and the first and last dates on which you use the notebook.

■ **3** Place a rubber band around the used portion of your notebook so that it opens automatically to the first blank page.

■ **4** Date the first page of each day's dictation at the bottom of the page for quick and convenient reference.

■ **5** Check before class to see that there are sufficient pages remaining in your notebook for the day's dictation and, if not, supply yourself with a second notebook so that you will not run out of paper in the middle of dictation.

The practice material in Lesson 54 provides an intensive review of the principles you studied in Chapter 6.

1 BRIEF FORMS, DERIVATIVES, AND PHRASES

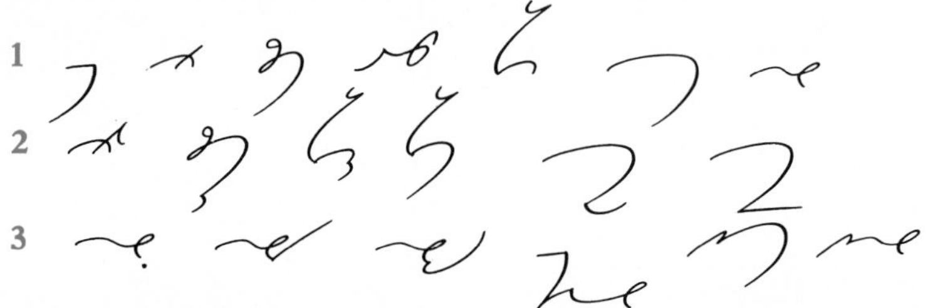

1 Never, quantity, executive, throughout, object, govern, correspond-correspondence.
2 Quantities, executives, objects, objective, governor, government.
3 Corresponding, corresponded, correspondent, nevertheless, to govern, to correspond.

Building Transcription Skills

2 SIMILAR-WORDS DRILL • their, there, they're

their Possessive form of *they*.

All students should bring *their* texts.

there In or at that place.

We went *there* on vacation.

they're Contraction for *they are*.

They're not here now.

3 **resourcefulness** The ability to meet and handle situations.
Business Vocabulary Builder
excess *(adjective)* More than usual or necessary.
conceivable Imaginable; possible.

Reading and Writing Practice

4

dis·ap·point·ed

ca·pac·i·ty

par

de·scribed

ap

tech·ni·cal

ini·tia·tive

re·source·ful·ness

ser

par

char·ac·ter

[154]

5

butch·ers

their

theirs

ex·cess
quan·ti·ties

ser

trimmed

par

[154]

par

par

par

re·ceive

de·scribed

[143]

6

there

con·ceiv·able

7

re·ceived

ap

ap

their

com·pe·tent

[152]

8

an·tic·i·pat·ing

par

they're

speak

[138]

In Lesson 55 you will review intensively the shorthand principles you studied in Chapter 7.

1 **BRIEF FORM DERIVATIVES AND PHRASES**

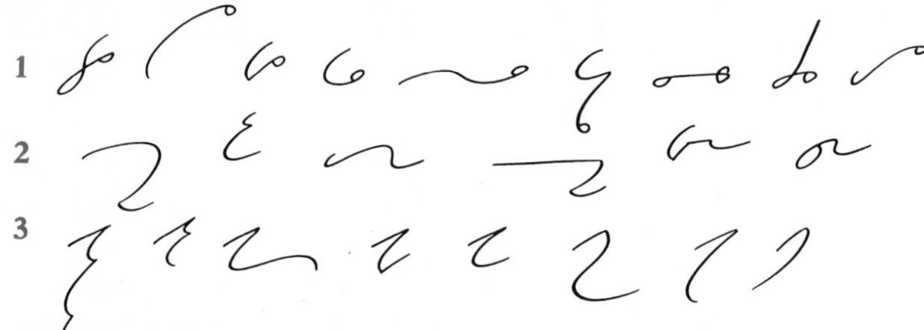

1 Particularly, timely, partly, presently, gladly, probably, immediately, generally, ordinarily.

2 Governor, speaker, organizer, manufacturer, partner, outer.

3 To publish, to speak, to progress, to part, to present, to value, to be, to have.

Building Transcription Skills

2 **GRAMMAR CHECKUP • the infinitive**

The infinitive is the form of the verb introduced by *to—to see, to be, to have, to do.*

Careful writers try to avoid "splitting" an infinitive, that is, inserting a word or phrase between *to* and the following verb.

no

To properly do *the job, you need to work slowly.*

yes

To do *the job* properly, *you need to work slowly.*

no

We were asked to carefully prepare *the paper.*

yes

We were asked to prepare *the paper* carefully.

3 Business Vocabulary Builder

expand Grow larger.
scores Indefinitely large numbers.
equivalent Equal in importance or value.

Reading and Writing Practice

4

re·ceived

par

intro

sub·mit·ted

[137]

5

ap

pros·per·i·ty

pho·to·graph·ic

when

dreamed

ex·pand

gen·u·ine·ly

ser

loy·al·ty

fur·ther

[151]

6

ac·cept

psy·cho·log·i·cal
so·cio·log·i·cal

ap

en·roll

if

res·i·den·cy

as

cat·a·log

di·plo·ma
its

when

fur·ther

if

par

[159]

7

gov·ern·ment

re·sponse

par

ser

intro

intro

ads

com·pe·tent

when

par

col·umns

[160]

8

7

intro

5

ef·fi·cient cor·re·spon·dents

in·qui·ries

48

if

421

de·scribes

[149]

This practice material in Lesson 56 concentrates on the principles you studied in Chapter 8.

1 BRIEF FORMS, DERIVATIVES, AND PHRASES

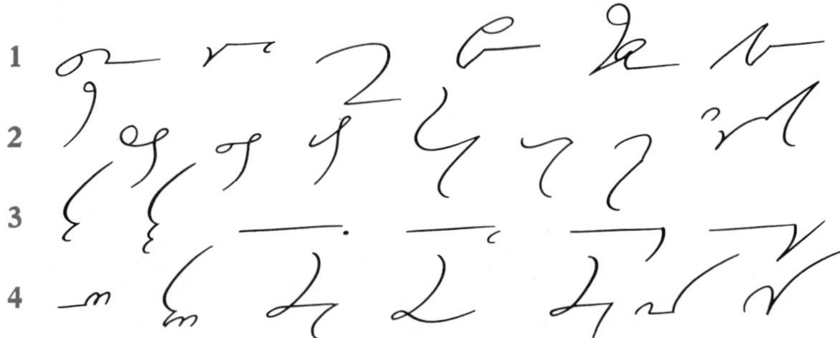

1 Acknowledgment, statements, government, apartment, advertisement, department.

2 Ever, wherever, whenever, whatever, valuable, workable, questionable, understandable.

3 Business, businesses, morning, mornings, manufacture, manufactured.

4 In the world, business world, very important, very well, very much, one time, this time.

Building Transcription Skills

2 COMMON PREFIXES

Many words in the English language contain common prefixes. An understanding of the meanings of these prefixes will often give you a clue to the meaning of an unfamiliar word.

Perhaps you never heard of the word *superfluous*. However, if you know that *super* means *more than*, you will probably be able to figure out that *superfluous* means *more than enough*.

In each "Common Prefixes" exercise you will be given a common prefix, its meaning, and a list of words in which the prefix is used.

Read each definition carefully; then study the illustrations that follow. A number of the illustrations are used in the Reading and Writing Practice.

COMMON PREFIXES • super-

super- over; more than

supervise To oversee.

supervisor One who oversees.

superior Over in rank; higher.

superfluous More than enough.

---

3 Business Vocabulary Builder

masterpiece A work done with great skill.

digits Numbers.

alterations Changes.

misgivings Doubts; fears.

Reading and Writing Practice

4

Elec·tron·ics

ef·fi·cient

ser

mas·ter·piece

busy

when

intro

con·fer·ence

con·sul·ta·tion

if

and o

self-ad·dressed

intro

if

[166]

5

as·sis·tant intro ap

di·a·gram

ser

dis·cuss

ser

ap 15

3 × 16

sat·is·fac·to·ry if

[147]

6

trans·mit·ted

spec·i·fi·ca·tions

conj

sub·stan·tial

par

ap

intro

re·ceive

[137]

7

gov·ern·ing
mu·nic·i·pal

ser

intro

ex·pe·ri·enced

and o

intro

par

fur·ther·more

de·ci·sions

if

[170]

mis·take

8

as

mis·giv·ings

intro

conj

in·qui·ries

cur·tail

intro

ten·der

intro

par

intro

[139]

9

au·dited

su·perb

ap

or·der·ly

heart

conj

[167]

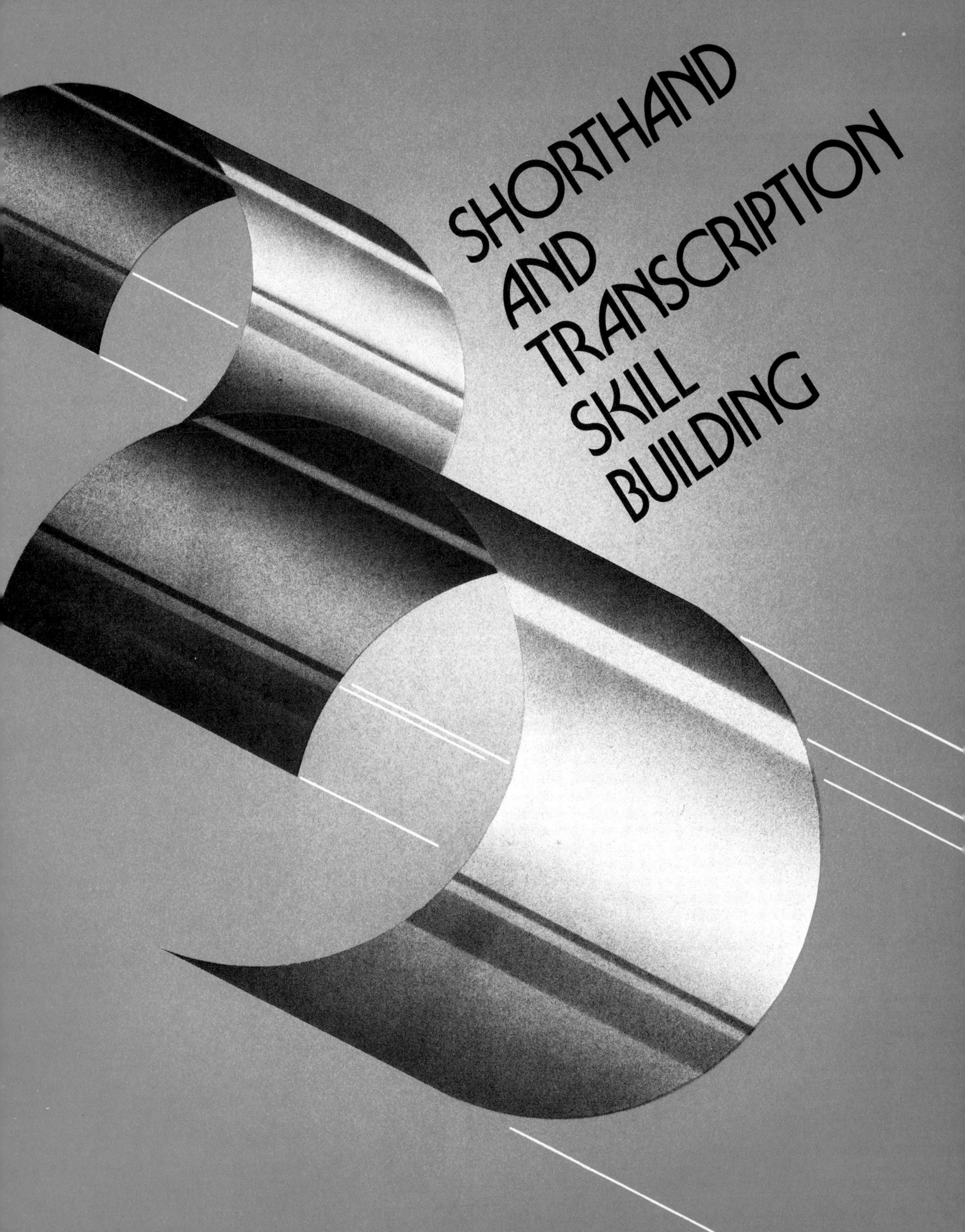
SHORTHAND
AND
TRANSCRIPTION
SKILL
BUILDING

10 ONWARD AND UPWARD

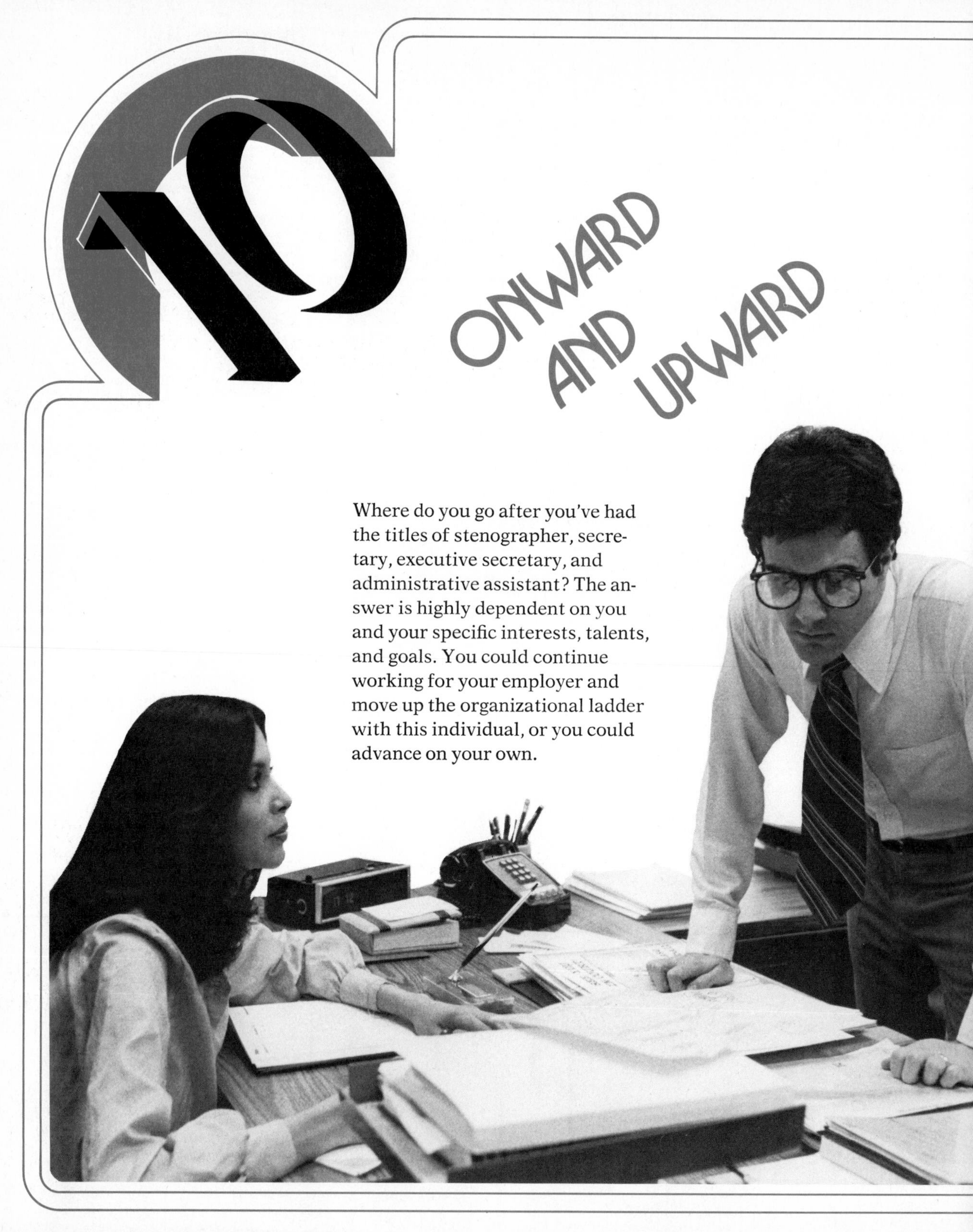

Where do you go after you've had the titles of stenographer, secretary, executive secretary, and administrative assistant? The answer is highly dependent on you and your specific interests, talents, and goals. You could continue working for your employer and move up the organizational ladder with this individual, or you could advance on your own.

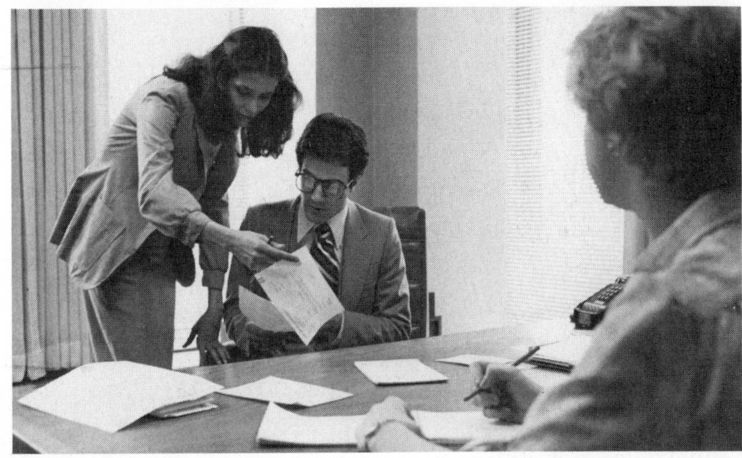

If you want to advance beyond the administrative assistant level, you might become a supervisor, office manager, assistant department manager, or department manager. In many instances, if an administrative assistant has the necessary qualifications, it happens that this person succeeds the executive because, next to the executive, no one knows the job better.

No matter which route you take, the more you help your boss, the more you will be helping yourself.

If you advance with your employer, you will probably attain a higher rank (commanding a higher salary and greater prestige) but still retain the title of administrative assistant. In effect, administrative assistants are executives because they generally have the privileges of making a number of decisions on their own and of supervising other secretaries and office employees. How far your boss advances depends a great deal on you. The more you do to help run an effective, efficient office, the better the chances for advancement for both of you.

The letters in Lesson 57 contain the brief forms or brief-form derivatives of Gregg Shorthand. Because you have seen and written the brief forms of Gregg Shorthand many, many times, you should be able to read the letters in this lesson in record time!

Building Transcription Skills

1 SPELLING FAMILIES ● -tion, -sion

Words Ending in -tion

ap-pli-ca-tion	**in-for-ma-tion**	**ques-tion**
cir-cu-la-tion	**or-ga-ni-za-tion**	**sat-is-fac-tion**
con-tri-bu-tion	**pro-tec-tion**	**se-lec-tion**

Words Ending in -sion

con-clu-sion	**oc-ca-sion**	**pro-fes-sion**
de-ci-sion	**per-mis-sion**	**ses-sion**

2 Business Vocabulary Builder

mature *(verb)* Become due or payable.
vandals Those who willfully destroy or damage property.
trespassers Those who enter another's property unlawfully.

Reading and Writing Practice

3

ques·tion

par

conj

ex·ec·u·tives'

ex·traor·di·nary

op·por·tu·ni·ty

conj

[196]

4

un·usu·al·ly

if

an·swers

re·ceive

par

conj

se·lec·tion

un·fa·mil·iar

eas·i·ly

ser

intro

some·time

achieve

ul·ti·mate

def·i·nite

par

di·vi·sion

[184]

5

re·ceived

per·son·nel

ap

suc·cess·ful
cor·re·spon·dent

as

and o

or·ga·ni·za·tion

char·ac·ter·is·tic

when

ac·knowl·edge

oc·ca·sion

ocean
voy·age

intro

when

[212]

6

cor·re·spon·dence

ap

as

bi·month·ly

self-ad·dressed

and o

de·ci·sion

[113]

7

intro

intro

roll·ing

7:30

9:30

intro

[138]

8 **Transcription Quiz** In Lessons 31 through 56 you have been learning to apply nine rules for the correct use of the comma. In Lessons 57 through 69 you will have an opportunity to test your mastery of these rules through a Transcription Quiz—a letter in which no commas are indicated in the shorthand. It will be your job, as you copy the letter in shorthand in your notebook, to insert the commas in the proper places and to give the reasons why the commas are used. The shorthand in your notebook should resemble the following example:

if ap

At the head of each Transcription Quiz you will find the number and types of commas you should supply.

The correct punctuation of the following letter calls for 4 commas—1 comma *and* omitted, 2 commas series, 1 comma parenthetical.

[94]

Lesson 58 provides you with an opportunity to increase your skill in writing the frequently used phrases of Gregg Shorthand. The following letters are packed with phrases. Several illustrations of the phrasing principles of Gregg Shorthand appear in the letters.

Building Transcription Skills

1 GRAMMAR CHECKUP ● sentence structure

Parallel ideas should be expressed in parallel form.

no

The class was interesting, informative, and of value *to all of us.*

yes

The class was interesting, informative, and valuable *to all of us.*

no

As soon as we verify your credit, your account will be opened and we will send your order.

yes

As soon as we verify your credit, your account will be opened and your order will be sent.

It is especially important to keep parallel all ideas in a tabulation.

no

The main duties were:

1. *Typing letters*
2. *Answering the telephone*
3. To take *dictation*

yes

The main duties were:

1. *Typing letters*
2. *Answering the telephone*
3. Taking *dictation*

2	**rotate** To alternate in a series.
Business Vocabulary Builder	**dedicated** *(adjective)* Committed to a cause, ideal, or purpose.
	expeditiously Promptly and efficiently.

Reading and Writing Practice

3

as

and o

ap

ex·cel·lent

conj

re·pairs

par

urge

mis·take

par

ex·pen·sive

if

and o

[149]

4

lem·on

neigh·bor·hood

fla·vors

fa·vor·ite

intro

10

ap·pre·ci·a·tion
thought·ful·ness

cou·pon

intro

gal·lon

par

[127]

5

intro

10

ac·com·plish

and o

com·pe·tent

ser

ef·fi·cient

friend·li·est

par

if

re·ceive

when

[145]

6

intro

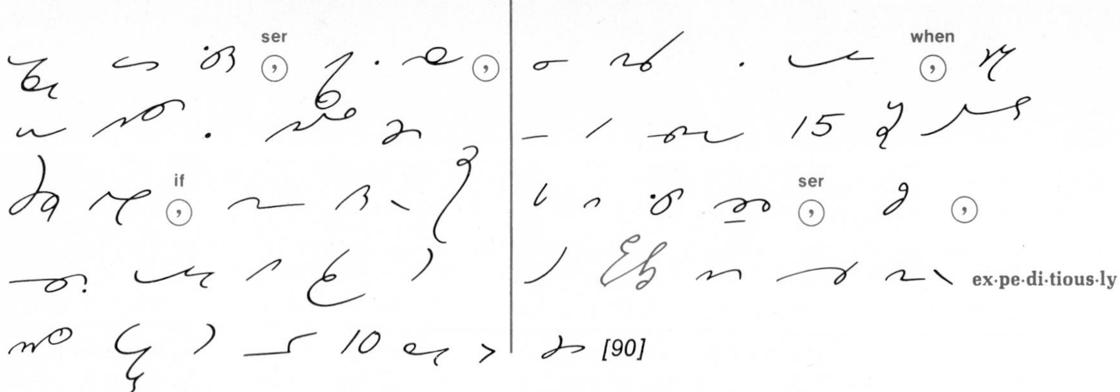

7 Transcription Quiz To punctuate the following letter correctly, you must supply 6 commas—1 comma *as* clause, 1 comma apposition, 1 comma introductory, 1 comma conjunction, 2 commas parenthetical.

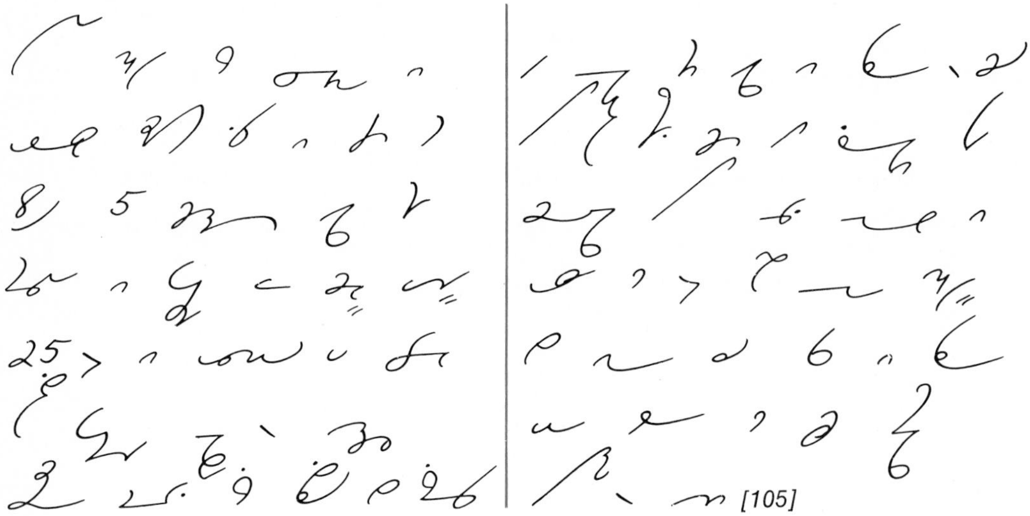

[105]

PERSONAL-USE CHECKLIST

Put your shorthand knowledge to work for you by:

■ 1 Writing all your assignments in shorthand.

■ 2 Making drafts of term papers and reports in shorthand.

■ 3 Corresponding with friends in shorthand.

■ 4 Making notes to yourself on things to do, people to see, and appointments to keep in shorthand.

The letters in Lesson 59 give you an opportunity to review the joined word beginnings of Gregg Shorthand.

Building Transcription Skills

1 SPELLING FAMILIES ● -able, -ible

Words Ending in -able

avail-able	**con-sid-er-able**	**un-for-get-ta-ble**
ca-pa-ble	**re-li-able**	**un-pre-dict-able**
com-fort-able	**suit-able**	**un-rea-son-able**

Words Ending in -ible

ad-mis-si-ble	**im-pos-si-ble**	**leg-i-ble**
de-duct-ible	**in-cred-i-ble**	**re-spon-si-ble**
flex-i-ble	**in-de-fen-si-ble**	**sen-si-ble**

2 Business Vocabulary Builder

unpredictable Not capable of being foretold.
perpetually Continuing forever; everlasting.
interior designer One who plans and supervises the design or construction of rooms and their furnishings.
median *(adjective)* Being in the middle.

Reading and Writing Practice

3

al·most

ex·plo·ra·tion

un·pre·dict·able

intro

in·de·fen·si·ble

mis·take

sen·si·ble

Con·se·quent·ly

intro

per·pet·u·al·ly

un·tapped

fur·ther

if

sources

ap

de·scrip·tive

[199]

4

intro

dis·tinct

im·per·son·al

intro

intro

when

rep·re·sen·ta·tive

browse
dis·ap·pears
re·ap·pears

if

de·cid·ed

if

421

en·joy·able

and o

[154]

5

de·sign·er

par

ef·fi·cient

me·di·an

20

rea·son·able

4

60

intro

14

[162]

6

intro

and o

re·li·able

en·roll·ment

intro

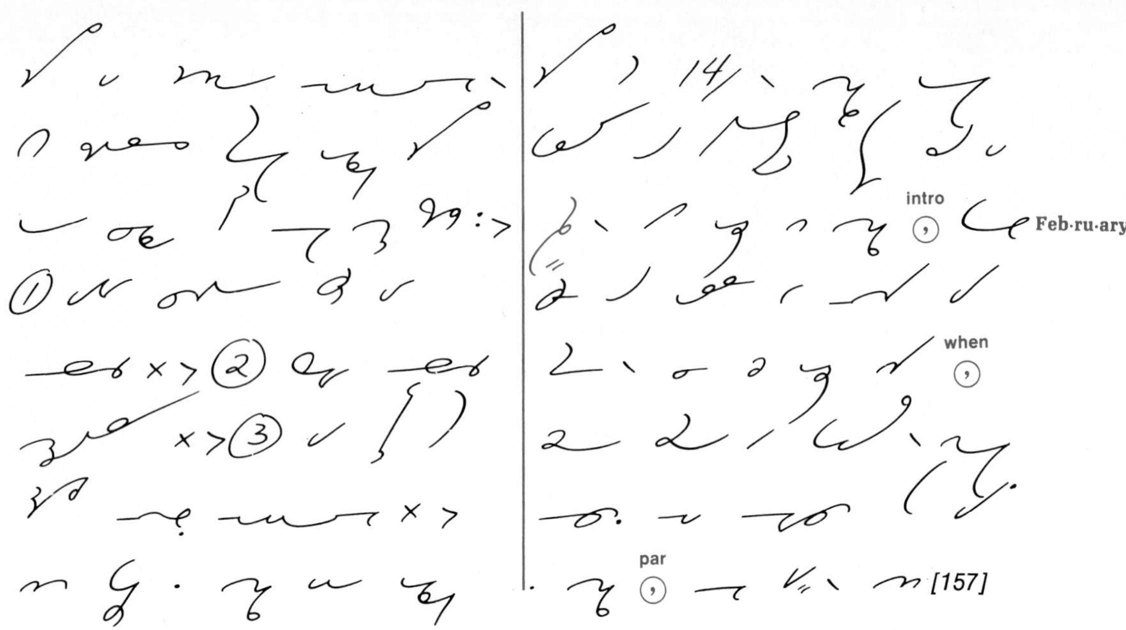

7 Transcription Quiz The correct punctuation of the following letter calls for 6 commas—1 comma *as* clause, 2 commas series, 1 comma *and* omitted, 1 comma parenthetical, 1 comma *if* clause.

[173]

Lesson 60 gives special attention to the joined word endings of Gregg Shorthand. The letters in the Reading and Writing Practice contain many illustrations of the joined word endings.

Building Transcription Skills

1 COMMON PREFIXES ● pre-

pre- before; beforehand; in advance

- **preliminary** Before the main business or action.
- **predict** To tell beforehand; forecast.
- **precaution** Care taken in advance.
- **preventive** Acting ahead of; to ward off.
- **preview** An advance showing or viewing.

---

2 Business Vocabulary Builder

- **credit line** The previously approved amount of a loan.
- **nominal** Small; in name only.
- **curtail** To cut off; shorten.
- **implement** *(verb)* To carry out.

Reading and Writing Practice

3

per·mis·sion

ap

man·u·al

re·ferred

clear

bot·tom

intro

pre·cau·tion

sew·age

conj

nom·i·nal

pol·lu·tion
pre·ven·tion

if

ac·cept·able

[165]

when

[131]

4

5

and o

world's

as

over·due conj

grate·ful

par

here·af·ter

[87]

6

cur·tailed

conj

pe·ti·tioned

re·lief

im·ple·ment

intro

conj

par

Be·gin·ning

dis·counts

amaze

[146]

7 Transcription Quiz The correct punctuation of the following letter calls for 7 commas—1 comma introductory, 2 commas series, 2 commas apposition, 1 comma *and* omitted, 1 comma *if* clause.

As you copy the Transcription Quiz in your notebook, be sure to insert the necessary commas at the proper points and to indicate the reason for the punctuation.

[150]

Disjoined word beginnings are given intensive treatment in Lesson 61. The letters in the Reading and Writing Practice contain many illustrations of the disjoined word beginnings of Gregg Shorthand.

Building Transcription Skills

1 GRAMMAR CHECKUP ● comparisons

The comparative degree of an adjective or adverb is used when reference is made to two objects; the superlative degree is used when reference is made to more than two objects.

comparative

Of the two students, Lee is the taller.

Which clerk is more efficient, Jane or Bill?

Mildred is the better qualified of the two pupils.

superlative

Of the three students, Lee is the tallest.

Which clerk is most efficient, Jane, Bill, or Kay?

Mildred is the best qualified of the three pupils.

2 Business Vocabulary Builder

interpreter A person who translates for people speaking different languages.

creamery A place where butter and cheese are made or where milk and cream are prepared or sold.

transforms Changes in character or condition.

Reading and Writing Practice

3

in·ter·pret·er

re·ferred

em·ploy

self-re·li·ant

ser

ef·fi·cient

di·vi·sion

for·eign

intro

intro

if

[150]

4

when

re·ceive

ar·ti·cles

and o

prac·ti·cal

as

cir·cu·la·tion

intro

intro

in·tro·duc·to·ry

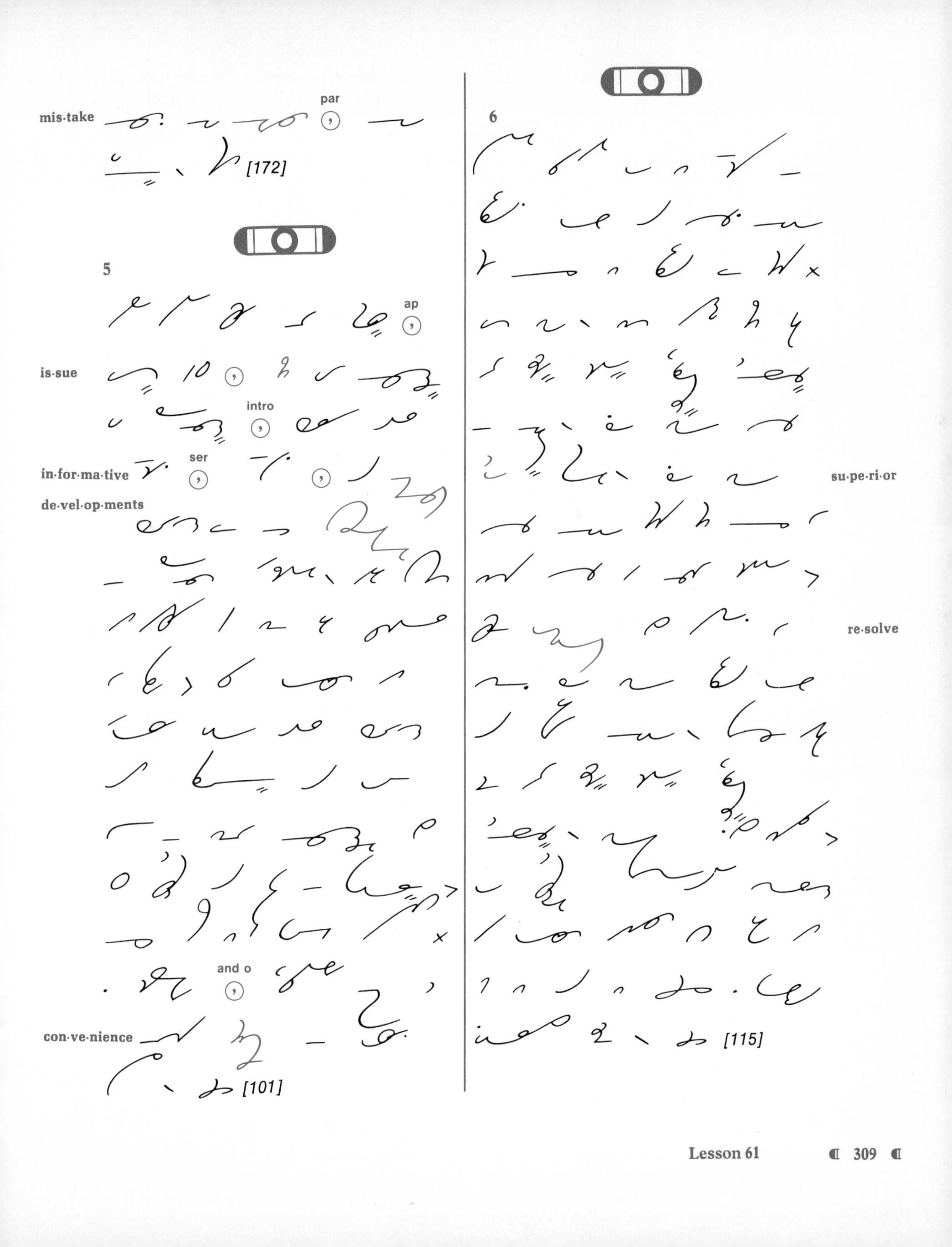

mis·take

par

[172]

5

ap

is·sue

intro

in·for·ma·tive

ser

de·vel·op·ments

and o

con·ve·nience

[101]

6

su·pe·ri·or

re·solve

[115]

7 Transcription Quiz To punctuate the following letter correctly, you must supply 7 commas—2 commas series, 2 commas *when* clause, 2 commas parenthetical, 1 comma introductory.

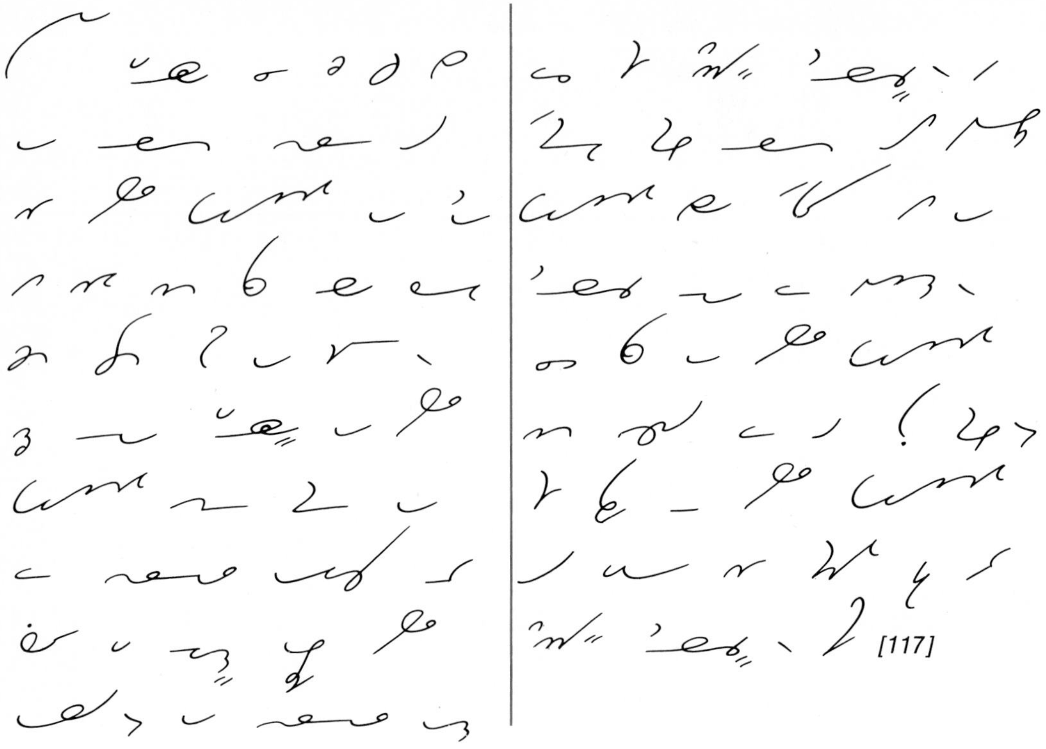

[117]

BRIEF-FORM CHECKLIST

Are you making good use of the brief-form chart that appears near the back of your textbook? Remember, the brief forms represent many of the most frequently used words in the language. The better you know them, the more rapid progress you will make in developing your shorthand speed.

Be sure to:

■ 1 Spend a few minutes reading from the chart each day.

■ 2 Time yourself and try to cut a few seconds off your reading time with each reading.

■ 3 Read the brief forms in a different order each time—from left to right, from right to left, from top to bottom, from bottom to top.

In this lesson you will brush up on the disjoined word endings of Gregg Shorthand. The disjoined word endings are used a number of times in the Reading and Writing Practice.

Building Transcription Skills

1 SIMILAR-WORDS DRILL ● county, country

county A political subdivision of a state.

Miami is in Dade *County*.

country A nation.

Our *country* produces a great deal of aluminum.

2 Business Vocabulary Builder

salient Standing out prominently.

seminar An advanced or graduate course featuring informality and discussion.

eligibility Qualification to be chosen.

Reading and Writing Practice

3

intro

ve·hi·cle

neigh·bor·hood

prac·ti·cal

intro

amaz·ing·ly

if

qual·i·fi·ca·tions

when

sa·lient

[134]

4

wel·come

in·tro·duc·to·ry

intro

and o

as

re·ceive

5

5

vol·umes

ex·ceed·ing·ly

5/

28

par

stim·u·lat·ing

[123]

5

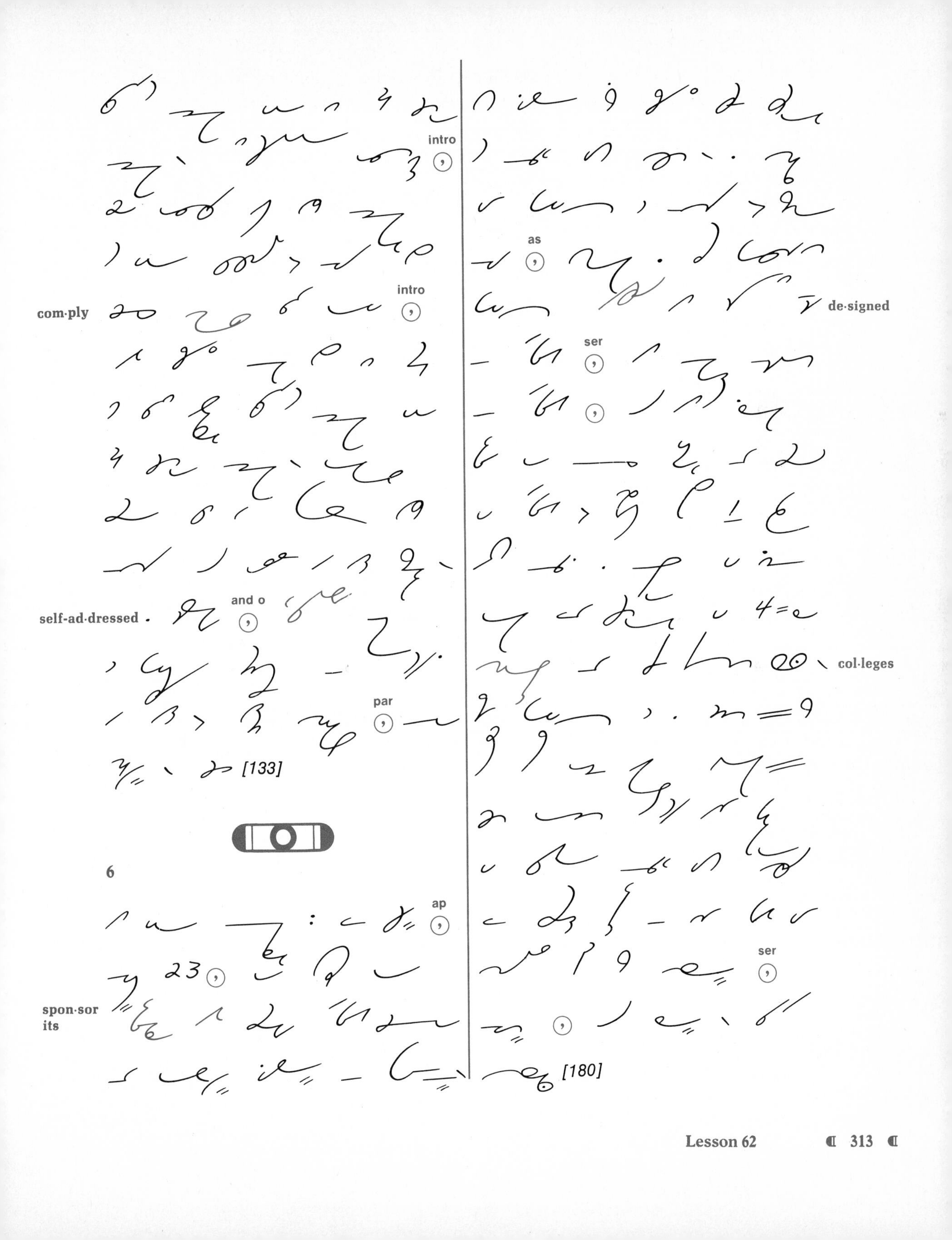

intro

comply

intro

self-addressed

and o

par

[133]

6

ap

sponsor its

as

designed

ser

colleges

ser

[180]

7 Transcription Quiz The following letter requires 6 commas—1 comma *as* clause, 3 commas apposition, 1 comma conjunction, 1 comma *if* clause.

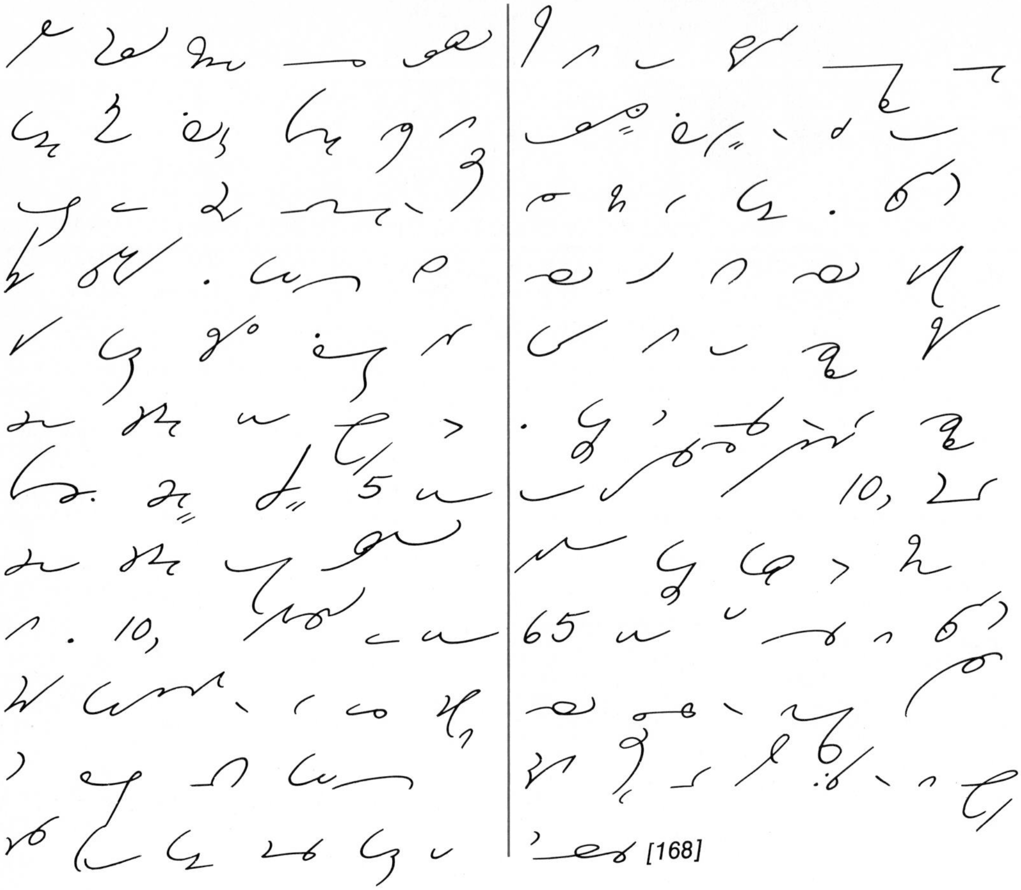

One of the major reasons why Gregg Shorthand can be written so rapidly and fluently is its blends—single strokes that represent two or more sounds. In the Reading and Writing Practice of this lesson, you will find many words and phrases that employ these blends.

Building Transcription Skills

1 COMMON PREFIXES ● pro-

pro- In many words in the English language, *pro-* means *before, ahead,* or *forward.*

progress A moving ahead; a going forward.

produce To bring forward; to make.

proceed To go ahead.

program A plan for the future.

promote To move ahead.

2 Business Vocabulary Builder

appropriate *(adjective)* Especially suitable or fitting.

ingredients Things that are parts of compounds or mixtures.

dunning Making persistent demands upon.

Reading and Writing Practice

3

an·nu·al

Guide

conj

ap·pear

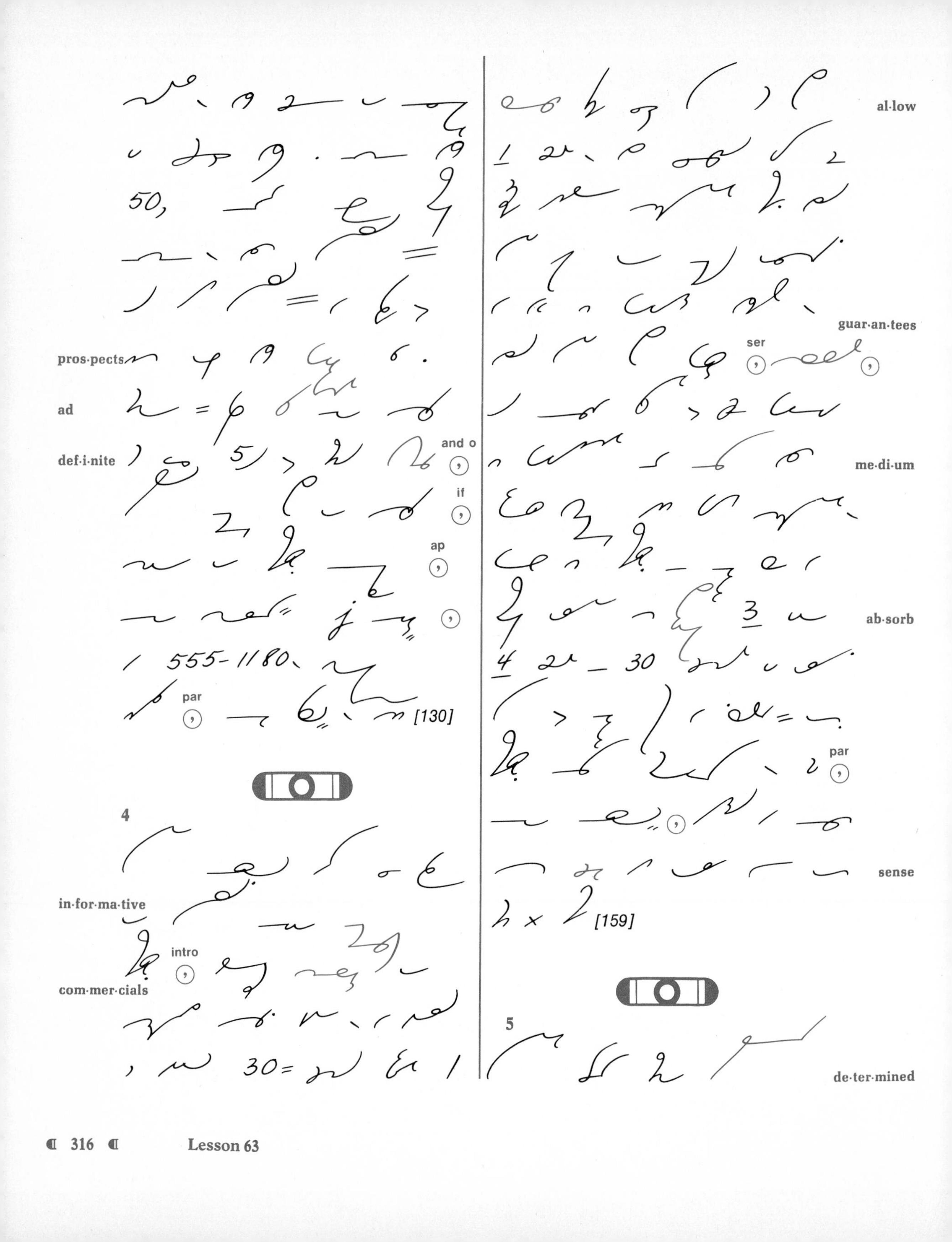

50,

pros·pects

ad

def·i·nite 5 and o

if

ap

555-1180

par [130]

4

in·for·ma·tive

intro

com·mer·cials

30

al·low

1

guar·an·tees

ser

me·di·um

3 ab·sorb

4 30

par

sense

[159]

5

de·ter·mined

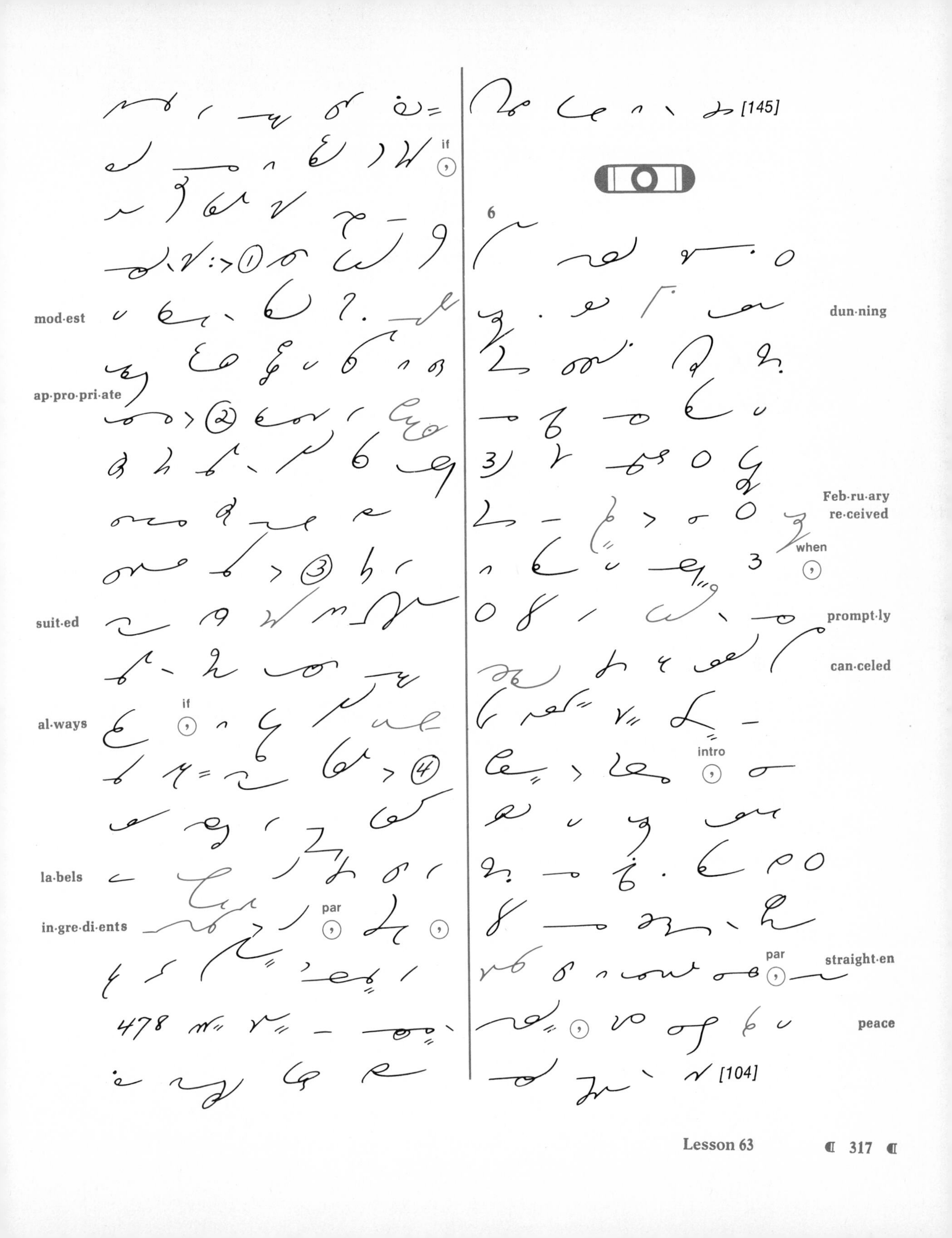

[illegible] [145]

6

[illegible]

mod·est

ap·pro·pri·ate

suit·ed

al·ways

la·bels

in·gre·di·ents

dun·ning

Feb·ru·ary

re·ceived

prompt·ly

can·celed

straight·en

peace

[illegible] [104]

7 Transcription Quiz The following letter requires 6 commas in order to be punctuated correctly—1 comma *as* clause, 1 comma apposition, 2 commas series, 1 comma introductory, 1 comma *if* clause.

Remember to indicate each comma in your shorthand notes and to give the reason for its use.

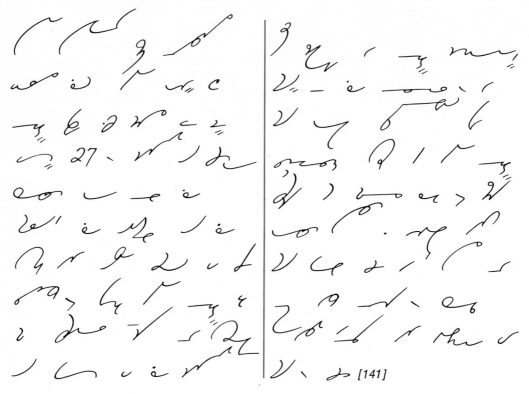

[141]

As you learned during the early stages of your study of Gregg Shorthand, unnecessary vowels are omitted in some words to help you gain fluency in writing without sacrificing legibility. In the Reading and Writing Practice of this lesson, there are many illustrations of words from which unnecessary vowels are omitted.

Building Transcription Skills

1 **SPELLING FAMILIES ● -ious, -eous**

Words Ending in -ious

con-scious	**gra-cious**	**pre-vi-ous**
de-li-cious	**in-ge-nious**	**se-ri-ous**
de-vi-ous	**ju-di-cious**	**te-dious**
en-vi-ous	**ob-vi-ous**	**var-i-ous**

Words Ending in -eous

ad-van-ta-geous	**er-ro-ne-ous**	**si-mul-ta-neous**
cour-te-ous	**mis-cel-la-neous**	**spon-ta-ne-ous**

2 **Business Vocabulary Builder**

emissions Substances discharged into the air, such as smoke and gasoline fumes.

continuously Without interruption.

miscellaneous Consisting of many different things or members.

Reading and Writing Practice

3

intro

raise

sub·scrip·tion

intro

ad·van·ta·geous

par

re·new·al

re·mit·tance

[125]

4

uti·liz·ing

dis·cov·ered
ob·vi·ous

when

intro

and o

emis·sions

intro

par

if

[124]

5

Wel·come

gen·u·ine

prompt·ly

ser

cour·te·ous·ly

1960 conj

rec·og·nized

its

ser

conj

par

[130]

6

handy

car's

26

mis·cel·la·neous

com·pli·men·ta·ry

par

if

re·quest·ing

at·ten·dant

[148]

7 Transcription Quiz For you to supply: 5 commas—2 commas apposition, 1 comma *as* clause, 1 comma introductory, 1 comma parenthetical.

30

40% 240%

[103]

TRANSCRIPTION CHECKLIST

To get the full benefit from the spelling and punctuation helps in the Reading and Writing Practice, be sure to:

■ 1 Circle the punctuation marks in your notes as you copy each Reading and Writing Practice.

■ 2 Note the reason for the use of each punctuation mark to be sure that you understand why it was used.

■ 3 Spell aloud at least once the spelling words given in the margin of the shorthand.

When you take dictation on a job, you will have to write many numbers. Because of the extreme importance of accuracy in transcribing numbers, you should take special care in writing numbers in your shorthand notes. The letters in the Reading and Writing Practice of this lesson will help you to review the devices of Gregg Shorthand used for expressing numbers and quantities.

Building Transcription Skills

1 SIMILAR-WORDS DRILL ● ad, add

ad Short for *advertisement.*

Did you see the *ad* in the newspaper?

add To make an addition; to include.

Please *add* my name to your list of subscribers.

---

2 Business Vocabulary Builder

newsprint A relatively inexpensive paper made from wood pulp and used mostly for newspapers.

opulent Wealthy; rich.

plaque *(pronounced plăk)* An inscribed tablet presented and displayed to note a special event.

Reading and Writing Practice

3

cli·ents

ap ,

ads

care·ful·ly

and o

intro

al·most

in·qui·ries

po·ten·tial

intro

your·self

par

mis·take

[178]

4

im·pres·sive

news·print

intro

add

ser

and o

var·ied

if

af·flu·ent

au·di·ence

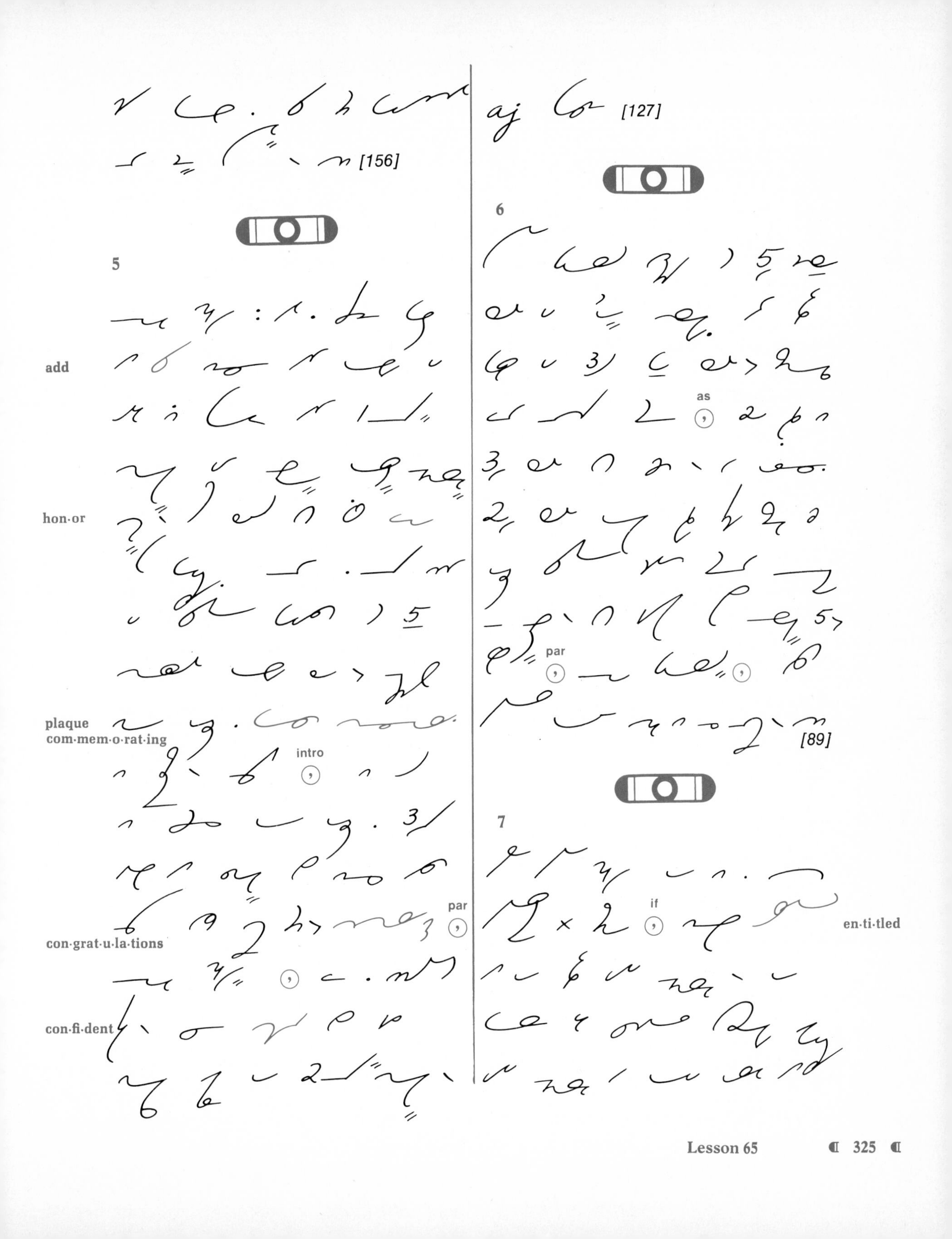

[156]

5

add

hon·or

plaque

com·mem·o·rat·ing

intro

par

con·grat·u·la·tions

con·fi·dent

[127]

6

as

par

[89]

7

if

en·ti·tled

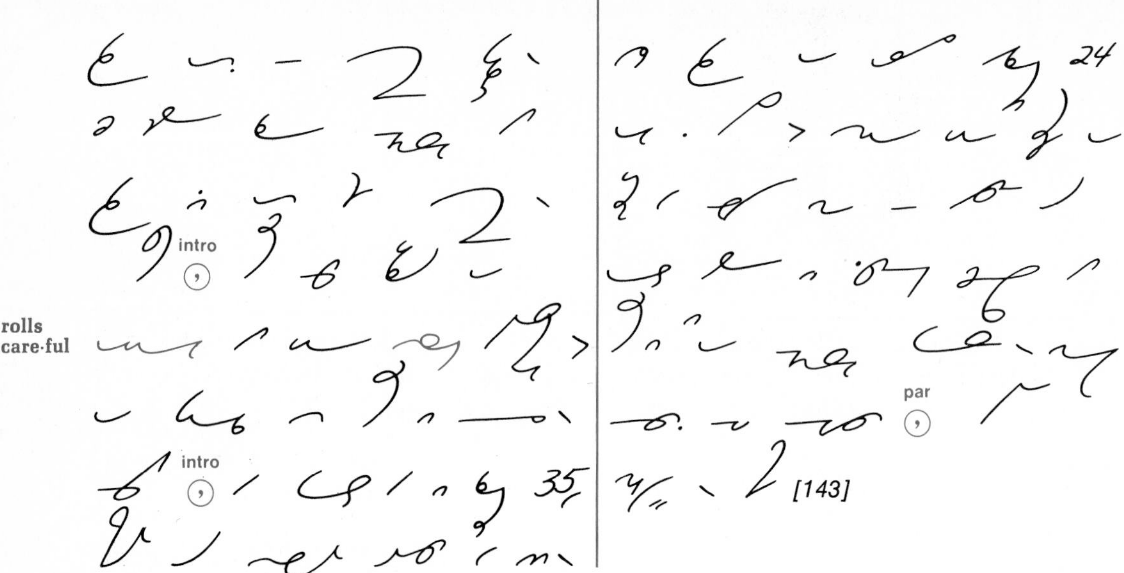

8 Transcription Quiz For you to supply: 4 commas—2 commas series, 1 comma introductory, 1 comma parenthetical.

15
[128]

This lesson provides another opportunity for you to test your knowledge of the brief forms of Gregg Shorthand. The Reading and Writing Practice contains the brief forms or brief-form derivatives of Gregg Shorthand.

Building Transcription Skills

1 **COMMON PREFIXES ● un-**

un- not

undisputed Not disputed; accepted without argument.

unsatisfactory Not satisfactory; not acceptable.

uncommon Not common; rare.

uncertain Not sure; indefinite.

unsolicited Not asked for; voluntary.

2 **Business Vocabulary Builder**

franchise The right to vote.

exhausted Used up; entirely consumed.

mystified Perplexed; bewildered.

Reading and Writing Practice

3

intro

suc·cess·ful·ly

launched

un·dis·put·ed

ser

cor·re·spon·dents

conj

un·doubt·ed·ly

great

re·spon·si·bly

ser

Com·pa·ny's

if

[167]

4

cel·e·brate

intro

and o

ex·traor·din·ary

to·ken

par

[125]

5

ap

ex·er·cise

ap

[173]

6

polls

intro

conj

ex·haust·ed

when

can·di·dates

ser

ap

as

if

fran·chise

[140]

7 Transcription Quiz For you to supply: 4 commas—1 comma introductory, 1 comma conjunction, 2 commas parenthetical.

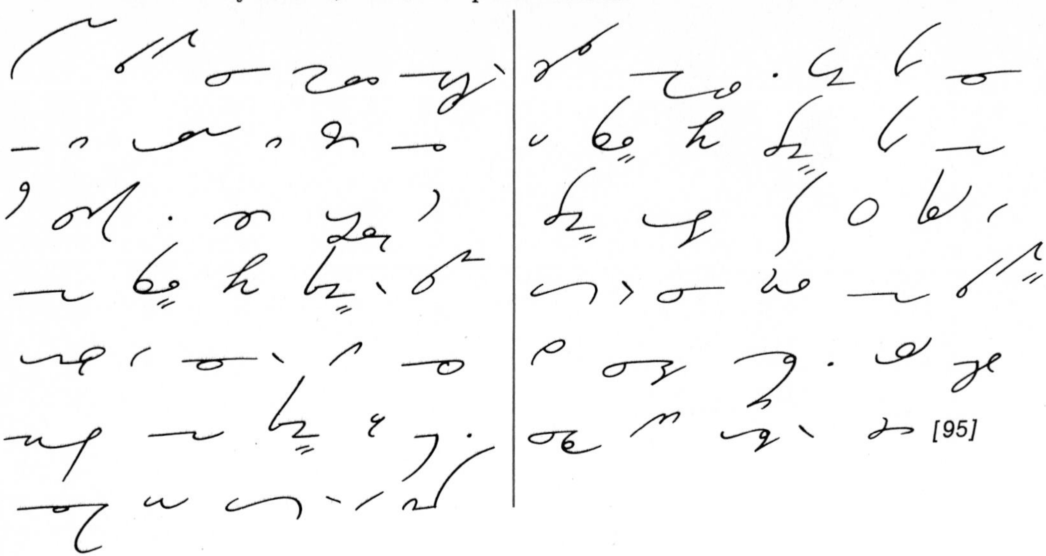

DICTATION CHECKLIST

When you take dictation, be sure to:

■ 1 Make every effort to keep up with the dictator.

■ 2 Refer to your textbook whenever you are in doubt about any outline.

■ 3 Insert periods and question marks in your shorthand notes.

■ 4 Make a real effort to observe good proportion as you write.

■ 5 Write down the first column of your notebook and then down the second column.

You have another opportunity in Lesson 67 to develop your phrasing skill. The letters in the Reading and Writing Practice contain a number of illustrations of the phrasing principles of Gregg Shorthand.

Building Transcription Skills

1 **GRAMMAR CHECKUP ● verbs—with "one of"**

□ **1** In most cases, the expression *one of* takes a singular verb, which agrees with the subject *one.*

One *of the* workers *on the staff* is *out of the office.*

One *of our* computers is *out of order.*

□ **2** When *one of* is part of an expression such as *one of those who* or *one of the things that,* the verb following is usually plural, to agree with the plural object of the preposition *of.*

Mark is one of those *who* drive *to work.*

We solved one of the problems *that* have been *causing us difficulty.*

2 Business Vocabulary Builder

merger A joining; a union.

confront To face.

renovating Improving by cleaning, repairing, or rebuilding.

Reading and Writing Practice

3

pop·u·lar

(216) 555-8106

ser

intro

prompt

help·ful

cus·tom·ers

intro

min·i·mum

par

[140]

4

ap

ap

par

re·serve

merg·er

dis·cussed

par

when

def·i·nite

[97]

5

conj

cus·tom·er's

good·will

par

as

and o

self-ad·dressed

[96]

6

conj

ren·o·vat·ing

if

as

busy

[118]

7

ap

rep·re·sen·ta·tive

as

shipped

conj

ap

re·ceive

par

[93]

8 Transcription Quiz For you to supply: 6 commas—3 commas *if* clause, 1 comma introductory, 1 comma *when* clause, 1 comma parenthetical.

[125]

SPELLING AND PUNCTUATION CHECKLIST

Be careful to punctuate and spell correctly when you:

- 1 Write your compositions in English.
- 2 Prepare papers for other classes.
- 3 Correspond with friends.

Lesson 68 contains a general review of the major principles of Gregg Shorthand.

Building Transcription Skills

1 **SIMILAR-WORDS DRILL ● loss, lose, loose**

loss *(noun)* That which one is deprived of.

We suffered a major financial *loss.*

lose *(verb)* To be deprived of.

Did you *lose* the contract?

loose Unattached; not fastened.

The screw in the table is *loose.*

2 Business Vocabulary Builder

versatile Having many uses or applications.

delinquent *(noun)* One who is behind in payments.

retraction An act of taking back.

pharmacists Druggists.

Reading and Writing Practice

3

au·to·mat·i·cal·ly

if

loss

theft

ser

ex·ceed·ing·ly

world's suc·cess·ful

and o

if

lose

[120]

4

ver·sa·tile

conj

mys·te·ri·ous

fu·els

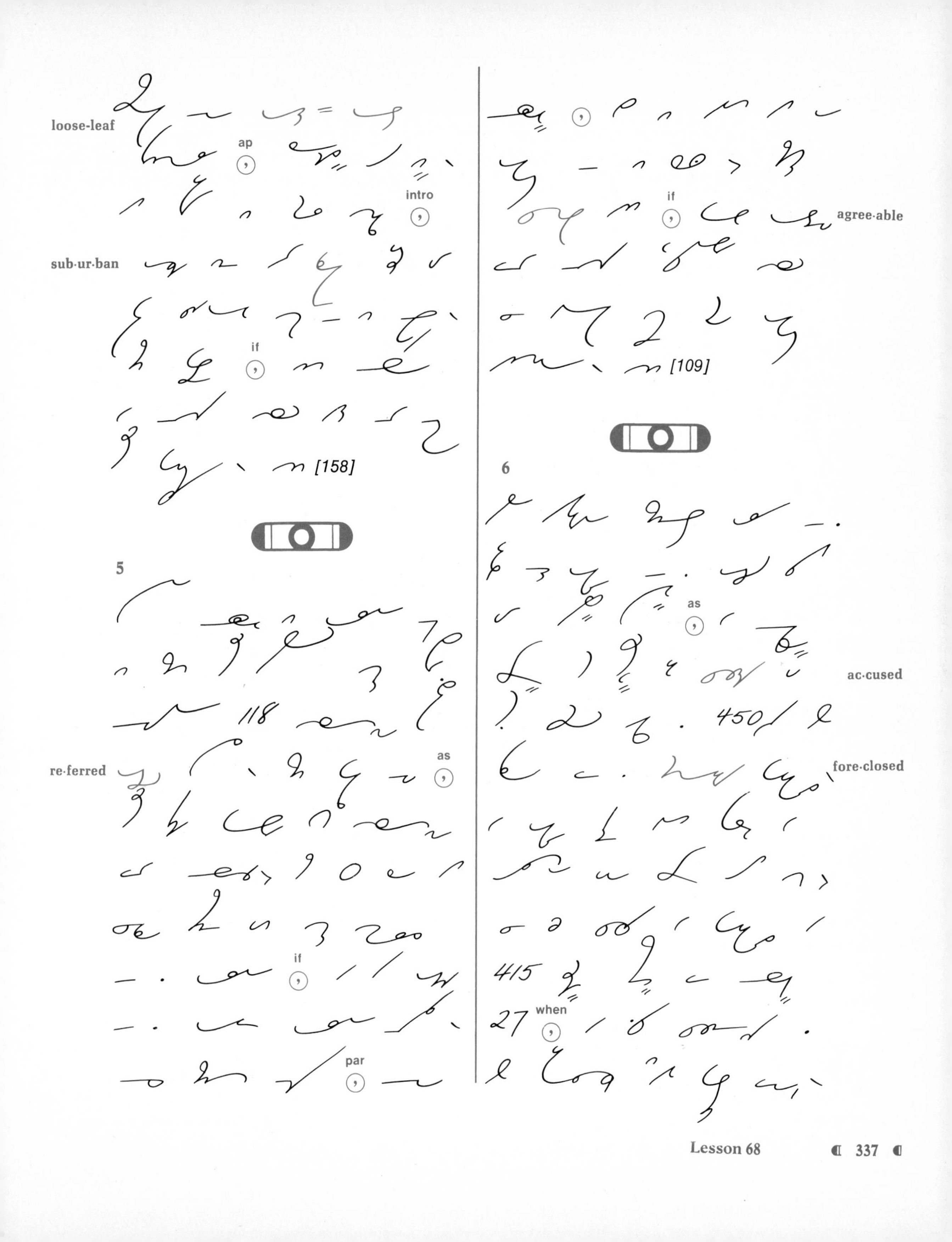

loose-leaf

ap

intro

sub·ur·ban

if

[158]

5

118

re·ferred

as

if

par

if

agree·able

[109]

6

as

ac·cused

450

fore·closed

415

27

when

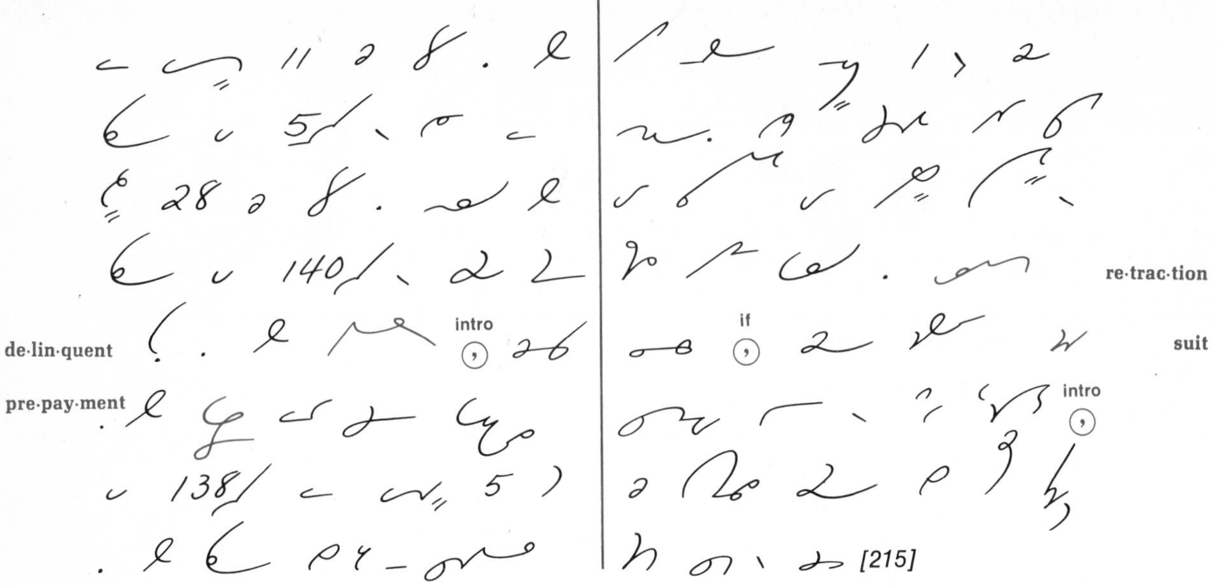

7 Transcription Quiz For you to supply: 7 commas—3 commas introductory, 2 commas parenthetical, 2 commas series.

[115]

Lesson 69, like Lesson 68, contains a general review of the major principles of Gregg Shorthand.

Building Transcription Skills

1 COMMON PREFIXES ● trans-

trans- across; over; from one place to another.

transcontinental Across a continent.

transfer Convey from one person or place to another.

transport Carry from one place to another.

transmit Hand over from one person to another.

2 Business Vocabulary Builder

pitfalls Hidden or not easily recognized dangers or difficulties.

confirmations New assurances of the validity of something.

linked Joined to.

Reading and Writing Practice

3

sweep·er

conj

ap

slipped

conj

su·ing

conj

pit·falls

180

intro

par

555-

ar·range 9236

par

ob·li·ga·tion

[179]

4

ser

rent·al

when

com·plet·ed

res·er·va·tions

and o

ef·fi·cient

linked

[124]

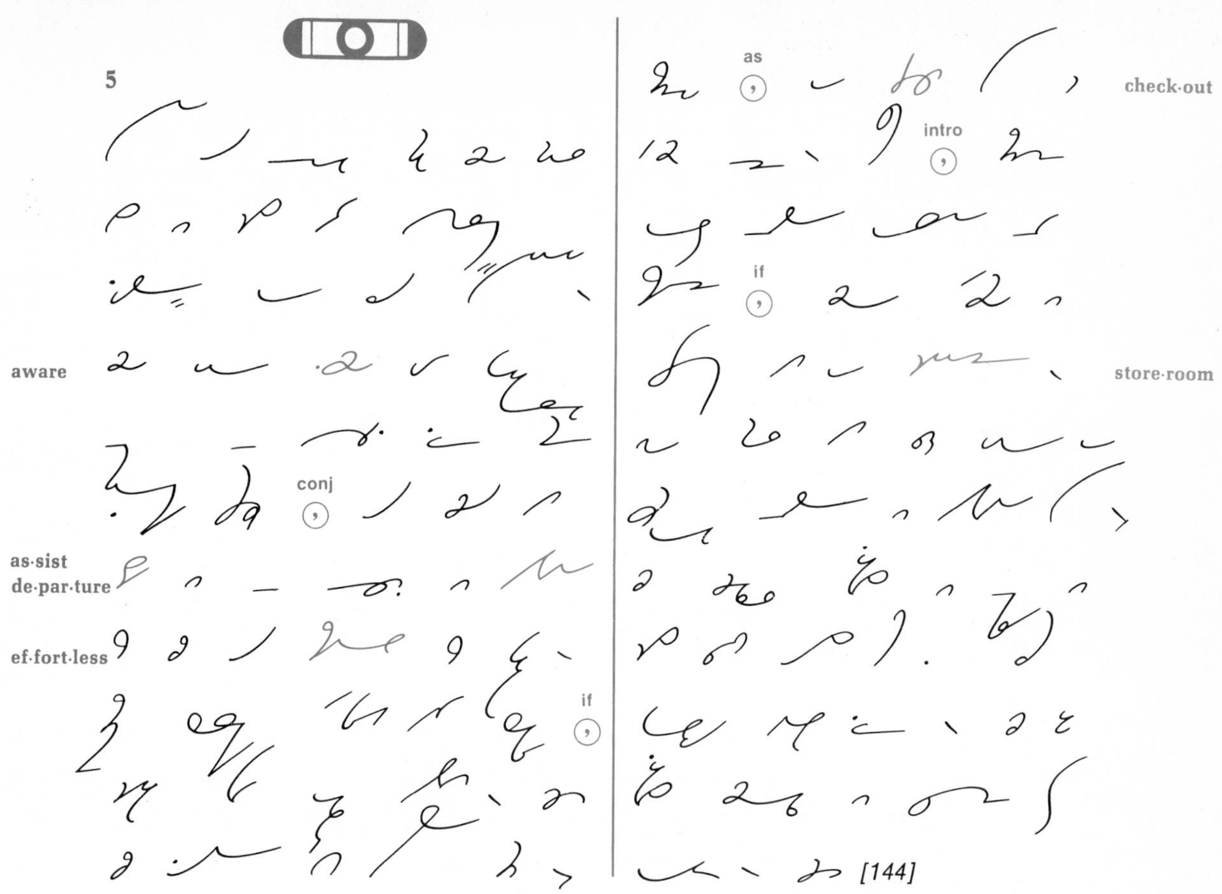

6 Transcription Quiz For you to supply: 4 commas—2 commas conjunction, 1 comma introductory, 1 comma *if* clause.

50,

[81]

You will find the article in Lesson 70 interesting and enlightening.

Building Transcription Skills

1 SPELLING FAMILIES ● -er, -or, -ar

Be very careful when transcribing words ending in the sound of *er*; the ending may be spelled *-er, -or,* or *-ar*. When in doubt, look the word up!

Words Ending in -er

con-sum-er	**of-fer**	**set-tler**
cus-tom-er	**read-er**	**sweat-er**
man-ag-er	**re-tail-er**	**sub-scrib-er**

Words Ending in -or

col-or	**gov-er-nor**	**pro-fes-sor**
dic-ta-tor	**hu-mor**	**sen-a-tor**
fac-tor	**ma-jor**	**su-per-vi-sor**

Words Ending in -ar

cel-lar	**gram-mar**	**reg-u-lar**
col-lar	**par-tic-u-lar**	**sug-ar**

2 Business Vocabulary Builder

basically Fundamentally.
site The place, scene, or point of something.
era The period of existence of something.

Reading and Writing Practice

Reading Scoreboard Now that you are on the last lesson, you are no doubt very much interested in your final shorthand reading rate. If you have followed the practice suggestions you received early in the course, your shorthand reading rate at this time should be a source of pride to you.

To get a real picture of how much your shorthand reading rate has increased with practice, compare it with your reading rate in Lesson 18, the first time you measured it.

LESSON 70 CONTAINS 318 WORDS

If you read Lesson 70 in	your reading rate is
8 minutes	**38 words a minute**
9 minutes	**35 words a minute**
10 minutes	**33 words a minute**
11 minutes	**30 words a minute**
13 minutes	**25 words a minute**
14 minutes	**23 words a minute**

3 The Retail Store

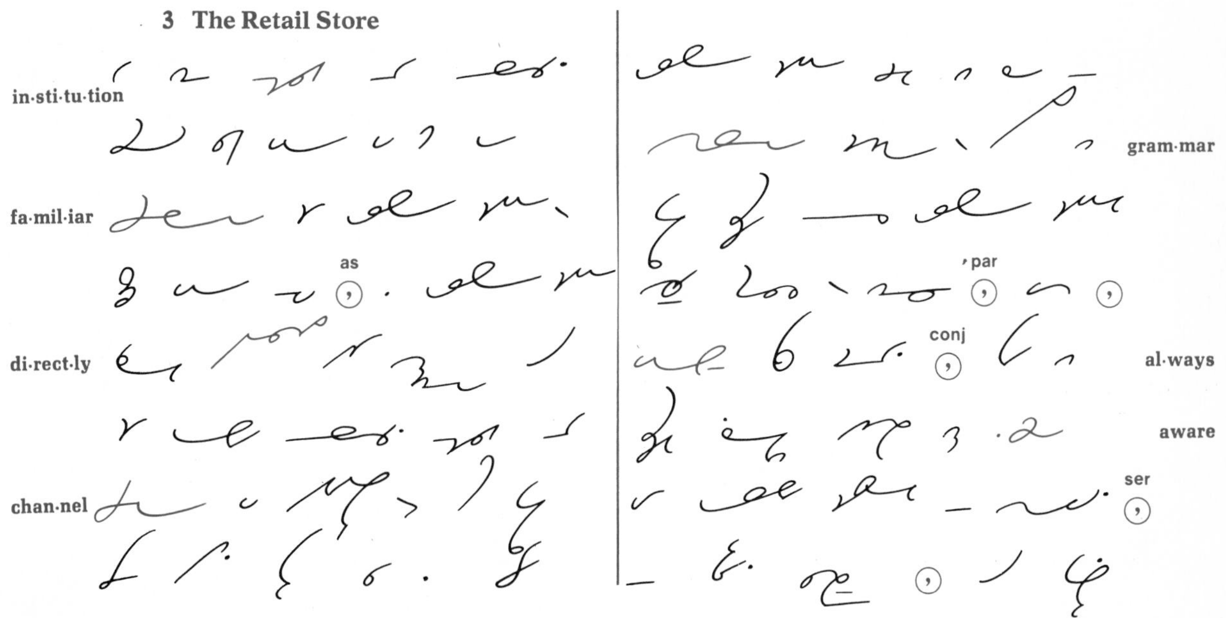

Retailing Is Important

for·est

ocean

ser

intro

fac·to·ry

re·tail·er

ser

co·lors

and o

com·pet·i·tive

Early Trading

trad·ing

intro

uten·sils

intro

set·tlers

site

intro

opened

conj

era

[318]

APPENDIX

States

The abbreviations in parentheses are those recommended by the Postal Service.

Alabama [AL]

Alaska [AK]

Arizona [AZ]

Arkansas [AR]

California [CA]

Colorado [CO]

Connecticut [CT]

Delaware [DE]

Florida [FL]

Georgia [GA]

Hawaii [HI]

Idaho [ID]

Illinois [IL]

Indiana [IN]

Iowa [IA]

Kansas [KS]

Kentucky [KY]

Louisiana [LA]

Maine [ME]

Maryland [MD]

Massachusetts [MA]

Michigan [MI]

Minnesota [MN]

Mississippi [MS]

Missouri [MO]

Montana [MT]

Nebraska [NE]

Nevada [NV]

New Hampshire [NH]

New Jersey [NJ]

New Mexico [NM]

New York [NY]

North Carolina [NC]

North Dakota [ND]

Ohio [OH]

Oklahoma [OK]

Oregon [OR]

Pennsylvania [PA]

Rhode Island [RI]

South Carolina [SC]

South Dakota [SD]

Tennessee [TN]

Texas [TX]

Utah [UT]

Vermont [VT]

Virginia [VA]

Washington [WA]

West Virginia [WV]

Wisconsin [WI]

Wyoming [WY]

Selected Cities of the United States

Akron
Albany
Anchorage
Atlanta
Baltimore
Baton Rouge
Birmingham
Boston
Bridgeport
Buffalo
Cambridge
Camden
Charleston
Charlotte
Chattanooga
Cheyenne
Chicago
Cincinnati
Cleveland
Columbia
Columbus
Dallas

Dayton
Denver
Des Moines
Detroit
El Paso
Fairbanks
Fargo
Fort Worth
Grand Rapids
Hartford
Honolulu
Houston
Indianapolis
Jacksonville
Jersey City
Kansas City
Knoxville
Laramie
Las Vegas
Lincoln
Little Rock
Los Angeles

Louisville
Memphis
Miami
Milwaukee
Minneapolis
Montpelier
Nashville
Newark
New Orleans
New York
Norfolk
Oakland
Oklahoma City
Omaha
Philadelphia
Phoenix
Pittsburgh
Portland
Providence
Richmond
Rochester
Sacramento

St. Louis	*Shreveport*	*Toledo*
St. Paul	*Spokane*	*Trenton*
Salt Lake City	*Springfield*	*Tucson*
San Antonio	*Syracuse*	*Tulsa*
San Diego	*Tacoma*	*Washington*
San Francisco	*Tallahassee*	*Wichita*
Seattle	*Tampa*	*Wilmington*

Common Geographical Abbreviations

America	*England*	*Canada*
American	*English*	*Canadian*
United States	*Great Britain*	*Puerto Rico*

The Metric System

If you take dictation in which there are many occurrences of metric measurements, you will have frequent use for the abbreviated forms given below. It is not wise to attempt to learn these forms until you know you will have use for them.

The metric system was devised by France and adopted there by law in 1799. Since that time its use has become almost universal except in Great Britain and the United States. It is rapidly coming into use in those two countries and, therefore, it is possible that you will need these special outlines. If the terms occur only infrequently in your dictation, it is better to write them in full.

The following abbreviations will be useful to those who must frequently take metric measurements in dictation.

		meter	liter	gram
kilo-	1,000			
hekto-	100			
deka-	10			

		meter	liter	gram
deci-	1/10			
centi-	1/100			
milli-	1/1,000			
micro-	1/1,000,000			
nano-	1/1,000,000,000			

ADDITIONAL METRIC MEASUREMENTS

Celsius	*kilowatt*	*microsecond*
centigrade	*kilowatt-hour*	*milliampere*
cubic centimeter	*megabit*	*millibar*
kilobit	*megahertz*	*millifarad*
kilocalorie	*megaton*	*millihenry*
kilocycle	*megawatt*	*millimicrosecond*
kilohertz	*megohm*	*millivolt*
kiloton	*micromicron*	*milliwatt*
kilovolt	*micron*	*nanosecond*

Index of Gregg Shorthand

In order to facilitate finding, this Index has been divided into six main sections—Alphabetic Characters, Brief Forms, General, Phrasing, Word Beginnings, Word Endings.

The first figure refers to the lesson; the second refers to the page.

ALPHABETIC CHARACTERS

BRIEF FORMS

GENERAL

PHRASING

WORD BEGINNINGS

WORD ENDINGS

INDEX OF BRIEF FORMS

The first figure refers to the lesson; the second figure to the page.

INDEX OF BUILDING TRANSCRIPTION SKILLS

The first figure refers to the lesson; the second figure to the page.

COMMON PREFIXES

GRAMMAR CHECKUP

PUNCTUATION PRACTICE—COMMAS

SIMILAR WORDS

SPELLING FAMILIES

Brief Forms of Gregg Shorthand

IN ORDER OF PRESENTATION

A	B	C	D	E	F	G
3						
		5				
				8		
						11
	13					
			15			
					17	
						19
					21	
				23		
			25			
					27	
29						
		31